ENERGIES OF THE SPIRIT
Trinitarian Models in
Eastern Orthodox and Western Theology

American Academy of Religion
Academy Series

edited by
Barbara A. Holdrege

Number 96

ENERGIES OF THE SPIRIT
Trinitarian Models in
Eastern Orthodox and Western Theology
by
Duncan Reid

Duncan Reid

ENERGIES OF THE SPIRIT
Trinitarian Models in Eastern Orthodox and Western Theology

Scholars Press
Atlanta, Georgia

ENERGIES OF THE SPIRIT
Trinitarian Models in Eastern Orthodox and Western Theology

by
Duncan Reid

© 1997
The American Academy of Religion

Library of Congress Cataloging in Publication Data
Reid, Duncan.
    Energies of the spirit : trinitarian models in Eastern Orthodox and Western theology / Duncan Reid.
        p.   cm. — (American Academy of Religion academy series ; no. 96)
    Originally presented as the author's thesis (doctoral)—Universität Tübingen, 1992 under the title: Die Lehre von den ungeschaffenen Energien : Ihre Bedeutung für die ökumenische Theologie.
    Includes bibliographical references and index.
    ISBN 0-7885-0344-8 (cloth : alk. paper). — ISBN 0-7885-0345-6 (pbk. : alk. paper)
    1. Trinity—History of doctrines. 2. Orthodox Eastern Church—Doctrines. I. Title II. Series.
BT109.R45 1997
231'.044—dc21   97-5574
                                  CIP

Printed in the United States of America
on acid-free paper

For Fiona

Contents

Acknowledgements ix
Abbreviations xi
A Note on Language xii
Foreword xiii

Introduction 1

1: Background to the Divergence between
   the Identity Principle and the Doctrine of Energies 7
2: The Two Positions in Twentieth-Century Theology 27
3: Comparison of the Two Approaches 55
4: Critical Questions about the Doctrine of the Trinity 67
5: Critical Questions about the Doctrine of Creation 93
6: Critical Questions about the Doctrine of Grace 113
7: Different Concerns and Common Intentions
   in the Two Approaches 121

Bibliography 135
Index 147

Acknowledgements

This work is an edited version of a dissertation in German, entitled "Die Lehre von den ungeschaffenen Energien: Ihre Bedeutung für die ökumenische Theologie," which was accepted in 1992 by the Evangelisch-Theologische Fakultät of the University of Tübingen in the Federal Republic of Germany.

A great many people have helped this work come to its present stage—too many, in fact, to name. Even so, there are people to whom I would like to express my particular gratitude. Prof. Jürgen Moltmann acted as my supervisor and guided my reading and thinking throughout the project. He also kindly agreed to write the preface for this published version. Prof. Luise Abramowski, with whom I consulted on several occasions during the "hunting and gathering" stage of the project, acted as referee and offered me very valuable advice on possible revisions after my final examination. The idea of writing on the doctrine of the uncreated energies first arose in a conversation with Prof. Dietrich Ritschl, who also took an ongoing interest in the progress of the work. Dr. Rowan Williams kindly made parts of his unpublished dissertation available to me. I am also much indebted to the hospitality of the Ostkirchliches Institut in Würzburg, which I visited several times to collect material. The English text was typed by Mrs. Alison Cedarblad, and Mrs. Barbara Dalton helped in its formating for publication.

The work could not have been brought to completion without the financial support of the Australian Research Theology Foundation, the Council of St. Barnabas College, Adelaide, and above all, the trustees of the Sir George Turner Fellowship (Trinity College, Melbourne), which allowed me a stay in Tübingen from 1983 to 1986. My parents, Pat and Craig Reid, and my parents-in-law, Heather and Jim Horne, offered both encouragement and at times financial support, especially during the writing stage of the project.

Finally, I would like to express my deep gratitude for their support, forbearance, and love to those who accompanied me most closely during this work: my wife Fiona, who has never lost confidence in the value of this project, and our children, Isaac, Nathanael, and Hannah.

Duncan Reid
Adelaide, Epiphany 1996

ABBREVIATIONS

CD	K. Barth, *Church Dogmatics*, vols. 1–5. Edinburgh: T. & T. Clark, 1936ff.
CW	G. V. Florovsky, *Collected Works*, vols. 1–4. Belmont: Nordland, 1972–76.
ECQ	*Eastern Churches Quarterly*
ECR	*Eastern Churches Review*
EvTh	*Evangelische Theologie*
FreiburgZPhTh	*Freiburger Zeitschrift für Philosophie und Theologie*
FranzS	*Franziskanische Studien*
GMP	A. H. Armstrong (ed.), *The Cambridge History of Later Greek and Early Medieval Philosophy*. Cambridge: Cambridge University Press, 1970.
GregPa	Γρηγοριος ο Παλαμας
GrOrthThR	*The Greek Orthodox Theological Review*
IKZ	*Internationale Kirchliche Zeitschrift*
Investigations	K. Rahner, *Theological Investigations*, vols. 1–21. London: Darton, Longman and Todd, 1961ff.
JÖBG	*Jahrbuch der Österreichischen Byzantinischen Gesellschaft*
KD	K. Barth, *Die Kirchliche Dogmatik*, vols. 1–4. Zürich: EVZ-Verlag, 1932–67.
KerDo	*Kerygma und Dogma*
Messager	*Messager de l'exarchat du patriarche Russe en Europe occidentale*
NZSysTh	*Neue Zeitschrift für Systematische Theologie und Religionsphilosophie*
MThZ	*Münchner Theologische Zeitschrift*
Myst. Sal.	J. Feiner and M. Löhrer (eds), *Mysterium Salutis: Grundriß Heilsgeschichtlicher Dogmatik*, vol. 2. Einsiedeln: Benziger Verlag, 1967.
NPNF	*A Select Library of Nicene and Post-Nicene Fathers of the Christian Church*
OrientChrPer	*Orientalia Christiana Periodica*
OstkirchSt	*Ostkirchliche Studien*
Schriften	K. Rahner, *Schriften zur Theologie*, vols. 1–16. Einsiedeln: Benziger Verlag, 1954ff.
ScotJTh	*Scottish Journal of Theology*
StTh	*Studia Theologica: Scandinavian Journal of Theology*

StVladSQ	St. Vladimir's Seminary Quarterly
StVladThQ	St. Vladimir's Theological Quarterly
TDNT	G. Kittel (ed.), *Theological Dictionary of the New Testament*. Grand Rapids: Eerdmans, 1968ff.
Theol(A)	Θεολογια (Athens)
ThLit	*Theologische Literaturzeitung: Monatschrift für das gesamte Gebiet der Theologie und Religionswissenschaft*
ThPh	*Theologie und Philosophie*
ThZ	*Theologische Zeitschrift*
TU	*Studia Patristica (Texte und Untersuchungen)*
ZKG	*Zeitschrift für Kirchengeschichte*
ZThK	*Zeitschrift für Katholische Theologie*
ZZ	*Zwischen den Zeiten*

A Note on Language

I have tried as far as possible to avoid gender-specific language for God, except when directly quoting other writers. I have, however, retained the traditional names and pronouns for the trinitarian persons. The reason for this is not that I consider these traditional names unproblematic, but because the argumentation here is at times already quite complex without adding the further complication of unfamiliar namings of the trinitarian persons. Direct quotes from German and Russian texts have, wherever possible, been taken from the standard translations cited in the accompanying footnotes. Where the footnote refers directly to the German or Russian original, the translation is my own.

Foreword

After early, exciting levels of agreement, ecumenical dialogues between western and Orthodox theologians have stuck fast on deep-seated differences. We began with "Ecumenical Reflections on the Filioque Controversy" (Lukas Vischer [ed.], *Spirit of God, Spirit of Christ* [London: SPCK; Geneva: WCC, 1980]) and discovered that in the course of the centuries very different understandings of the trinity have come to be bound up with both the defense and the rejection of the *filioque* clause in the Nicene Creed. The *filioque* is not simply about the question of the procession of the Holy Spirit from the Father alone or from the Son as well, but about the total understanding of the triune God, and about corresponding differences in the teachings about creation and salvation.

In this significant work, Duncan Reid, an Australian theologian educated in Melbourne and Tübingen, takes us a considerable step forward. He compares the "filioquist" conceptions of the trinity in Karl Barth and Karl Rahner on the one hand with the "monopatristic" conceptions in G. V. Florovsky and V. N. Lossky. Modern western teachings on the trinity think in terms of the movement "from God to the world," in a trinity of mission. In Barth it is the movement of the "self-revelation of God"; in Rahner the same movement of the "self-communication of God." In this undivided movement, God's being is revealed in God's works, and God's eternal essence in God's revelation. The author characterizes this conception as the "identity principle." The Orthodox teachings on the trinity, by contrast, are developed from the movement of doxology "from the world to God." Here the theologian as worshiper is conscious of the difference between the experienced revelation and the eternal essence of God, or between the experienced salvation and the eternal holiness of God. The author speaks here with justification of a "difference principle." Once we are clear about these different tendencies in thinking, it immediately becomes evident why the western position sees the economic and immanent trinity in close correspondence, while the eastern position does not. It is the difference between "descriptive" and "doxological" speech about God, where one refers to "God in relation to us" and the other to "God in Godself." From the doxological perspective, God is always greater than what is revealed of God to us human beings. It is understandable from this perspective that we cannot, as Florovsky says, speak with Barth of a total "self-revelation" of God.

The "aeonic" energies constitute that which in Orthodox teaching mediates between the eternal being of God and God's revelation. The author has made the Palamite doctrine of the "uncreated energies" the major theme of his work, and has sought to bring this theme into the ecumenical dialogue. He discusses it, aptly in my opinion, in relation to the doctrine of the energies of the Holy Spirit and discovers thereby the deeper dimensions of the doctrine of charisms, which till now has barely been noticed by western theologians.

Duncan Reid's work displays throughout a high degree of clarity and a deep understanding of a way of thinking unfamiliar to western theology. His judgements are always measured, and serve the interests of ecumenical fellowship in theology. I myself agree with his findings, and have expressed similar positions in *Spirit of Life: An Universal Affirmation* (London, 1992), p. 289ff., and "Die trinitarische Personalität des Geistes" in *Persoana si Communune: Princos de Cinstere: Gedenkbuch für Dimitru Staniloae, 1903–1993* (Sibiu, 1993), pp. 435–68.

It is not sufficient for ecumenical fellowship to restrict itself to the practical fields of common action for service. It also needs to address itself to a common theological understanding. Duncan Reid's work offers us new hope for an ecumenical theology in which we no longer mutually struggle against one another, but rather mutually support one another's growth in the knowledge of God.

Jürgen Moltmann
Tübingen, Christmas 1995

INTRODUCTION

Each then of the affirmations about God should be thought of as signifying not what He is in essence, but either something that it is impossible to make plain, or some relation to some of those things which are contrasts or some of those things that follow the nature, or an energy.[1]

With these words John of Damascus gives expression to the idea of God's incomprehensibility, the essential inaccessibility of God to human inquiry. This basic idea, already found in the Cappadocians, reaches its fullest and clearest expression some six hundred years later in the work of Gregory Palamas. The distinction is between the inner being (οὐσία) of the trinitarian God on the one hand and God's attributes (ἰδιώματα) or names (ὀνόματα) or activities (ἐνέργειαι) on the other. This distinction corresponds to the patristic distinction between *theologia* and *economia*. These distinctions are closely bound up with the patristic notion of salvation as deification (θέωσις). We are destined, according to Maximus the Confessor, to become "everything that God is, except for *essential* identity."[2] Our identity as deified human persons is thus identity with God's nature *ad extra*. But to suggest that we come to be identified with God's nature *ad intra* would be to set our human persons on the same level as the trinitarian hypostases. Even so, our participation in the divine nature (2 Peter 1:4) *ad extra* is on that account no less a real participation in the life of the trinitarian God. God *pro nobis* is no less divine than God *in se*.

The term energy or energies refers to the light of God's glory seen by Moses at the burning bush and by the three disciples who witness the transfiguration. This glory is divine, coeternal with God, and therefore not a part of creation (it is "uncreated"), but neither is it identical with the divine essence. "This light," according to Palamas, "was not a hallucination but will

---

1. Χρὴ τοίνυν ἕκαστον τῶν ἐπὶ θεοῦ λεγομένων οὐ τί κατ' οὐσίαν ἐστί, σημαίνειν οἴεσθαι, ἀλλ' ἢ τί οὐκ ἔστι, δηλοῦν ἢ σχέσιν τινὰ πρός τι τῶν ἀντιδιαστελλομένων ἢ τι τῶν παρεπομένων τῇ φύσει ἢ ἐνέργειαν. *Expositio Fidei* 9, 19, 7–9, in B. Kotter (ed.), *Patristische Texte und Studien*, Vol. 12 (Berlin, 1973). English translation in *NPNF*, vol. 9, *Exposition of the Orthodox Faith*, chap. 9.

2. Πάντα ὅσα ὁ θεός, καὶ ὁ διὰ τῆς χάριτος τεθεωμένος ἔσται, χωρὶς τῆς κατ' οὐσίαν ταυτότητος. *De Ambig.*; PG 91, 1308 B: cited in L. C. Contos, "The Essence-Energies Structure," *GrOrthThR* 12 (1967): p. 294.

remain in eternity, and has existed from the beginning."³ "It is not true," he says in another passage, "that the essence of God is the only unoriginate reality, and that all realities other than it are of a created nature."⁴ The energy is in fact God's uncreated grace, and as such is distinguished from the trinitarian essence. It is through the energies that God relates to the creation, and opens the divine life to our participation. "This grace is in fact a relationship," says Palamas. "Grace is communicated to all worthy of it, while the divine essence transcends all that is participable."⁵ The energy is imparted by the Holy Spirit as a gift, without however, being identical with the hypostasis of the Spirit. "It is properly called 'spirit' and 'divinity' . . . insomuch as the deifying gift is never separate from the Spirit who gives it. It is a light bestowed in mysterious illumination, and recognized only by those worthy to receive it . . . . But the Holy Spirit transcends the deifying life which is in him and proceeds from him."⁶ The energies, in the plural, are associated with the names or attributes of God that can be experienced by and imparted to the creation. John of Damascus had written of the energies as a sort of penumbra of glory that surrounds the divine essence. It is through the energies alone that God is known to us to be God—known in a way that is primarily experiential rather than intellectual. And yet God transcends all names and all manner of knowing. "Since the deifying gift of the Spirit is an energy of God, and since the divine names derive from the energies (for the Super-essential is nameless), God . . . is called 'God' on the basis of his deifying energy."⁷

---

3. Οὐχ ἄρα φάσμα ἦν τὸ φῶς ἐκεῖνο, καὶ γὰρ ἐσαεί τε ἔσται καὶ ἦν ἐκ τῆς ἀρχῆς. Gregory Palamas, Συγγράμματα (ed P. Chrestou: Thessaloniki, 1962), vol. 1, p. 629 (chap. 15, lines 17–18). Translation in Gregory Palamas, *The Triads* (ed. J. Meyendorff, trans. N. Gendle; London, 1983) p. 76.

4. Οὐχ ἕν ἄρα μόνον ἄναρχον, ἡ οὐσία τοῦ θεοῦ, τὰ δὲ παρὰ ταύτην γενητῆς φύσεως ὑπάρχει. Συγγράμματα, op. cit., vol. 1, p. 660 (chap. 15, lines 31–32). Trans. Gendle, op. cit., pp. 93–94.

5.᾿Εκείνη μὲν γὰρ σχέσις .... Κἀκείνης μὲν ἑκάστῳ τῶν ἠξιωμένων οἰκείως τε καὶ καταλλήλως πᾶσι μέτεστιν· ἡ δὲ οὐσία τοῦ θεοῦ καὶ πάντων τῶν μεθεκτῶν ὑπερεξήρηται. Συγγράμματα, op. cit., vol. 1, p. 641 (chap. 29, lines 11–17). Trans. Gendle, op. cit., p. 85.

6. πνεῦμά τε καὶ θεότης προσαγορεύεται δικαίως παρὰ τῶν ἁγίων, ἅτε δωρεὰ θεοποιὸς τοῦ διδόντος πνεύματος ἥκιστα χωριζομένη, φῶς δέ ἐστι, δι᾿ ἀπορρήτου ἐλλάμψεως χορηγουμένη καὶ τοῖς ἠξιωμένοις ἐγνωσμένη μόνοις ....῾Υπέρκειται δὲ τῆς ἐν αὐτῷ καὶ ἐξ αὐτοῦ θεουργοῦ ζωῆς τὸ πνεῦμα τὸ ἅγιον. Συγγράμματα, op. cit., vol. 1, p. 623 (chap. , lines 2–12. Trans. Gendle, op. cit., p. 71.

7. Οὐ μὴν ἀλλ᾿ ἐπειδὴ ἡ θεοποιὸς δωρεὰ τοῦ πνεύματος ἐνέργειά ἐστι θεοῦ, ὁ δὲ θεὸς ἀπὸ τῶν ἐνεγειῶν ἔχει τὰς ἐπωνυμίας, — ἡ γὰρ ὑπερουσιότης ἀνώνυμός ἐστιν αὐτοῦ, ... οὐκ ἂν θεὸς ὡς ἔχων θεοποιὸν ἐνέργειαν ἐκαλεῖτο ὁ θεός. Συγγράμματα, op. cit., vol. 1, p. 643 (chap. 31, lines 14–19). Trans. Gendle, op. cit., pp. 86–87.

This distinction between the essence and the energy of God became in the fourteenth century one of the basic principles of the trinitarian thinking of the eastern church. But it runs directly contrary, it seems, to one of the basic principles of the western trinitarian tradition, viz. "that we have no formula for the being of God in Godself other than the being of God in the world."[8] It is a function of God's faithfulness, God's moral and ontological integrity, that God reveals Godself *as God is* and not otherwise. Our knowledge of God *a se* rests on our experience of God in the history of salvation.

This apparent clash between the two approaches is not to be dismissed as something of no significance, because it underlies the debate between the eastern and western traditions on the question of the *filioque* clause. As far as the western tradition is concerned, the correspondence between the inner divine nature and the economic activities means that the economic sending of the Spirit by the Son is carried over into the inner-trinitarian relations as a procession of the Spirit from the Son. Although the interpolation of the *filioque*, historically, is not the result of this theological principle, the *filioque* is now inextricably bound to it. The *filioque* carries its own authority as a hallmark of an entire model of trinitarian thinking. The basis of this model is the close correspondence between the inner procession and the outer mission of the Holy Spirit.

In Eastern Orthodox theology we find a similar phenomenon—though in the reverse direction. Although the *filioque* is denied on other grounds, this denial bases itself within a total model of trinitarian thinking, a model that both has its own consistency and stands directly opposed to the equally consistent western model of trinitarian thinking. Eastern Orthodox theology posits a "real distinction"[9] between essence (οὐσία) and energy (ἐνέργεια). This is not a sharp division, but neither is it merely a nominal or "rational" distinction with its basis in the limits to human understanding. It entails, in other words, a certain lack of symmetry between the inner being of God and God's economic activities. The missions do not exactly correspond to the

---

8. F. D. E. Schleiermacher, *Der christliche Glaube*, vol. 2, 1831 (ed. M. Redeker, Berlin, 1960), p. 589.

9. B. Krivochein, "The Ascetic and Theological Teaching of Gregory Palamas," in *ECQ* III (1938–39): 152: "Trying to concretise his thought, Gregory called this distinction 'πραγματικὴ διάκρισις'—'real distinction,' contrasting it on the one hand with that 'real division'—which destroys unity and simplicity (πραγματικὴ διαίρεσις), and on the other with 'rational distinction,' i.e. (διάκρισις κατ' ἐπίνοιαν), existing only in the mind of the apprehending subject." Qv. G. Barrios, "Palamism Revisited," *SVThQ* 19 (1975): p. 223: "The distinction between essence and energy may be called a real one, not as if it were a distinction between two self-standing realities, *ut res a re*, nor as the distinction between substance and accidents, but an actual distinction of formalities."

processions. The Holy Spirit may well be sent by the Son within the dimension of the economy of salvation, but we may not deduce from this that the Spirit proceeds eternally from the Son. The *filioque* is, in other words, untenable not only on historical, but also on theological grounds, because it oversteps the distinction between the inner and the economic trinity. The *filioque* problem is thus the visible symptom of a deeper difference of understanding concerning the nature of God and God's activities.

This difference of understanding is the theme of this book. The attempt will be made to throw light on both sides. The western position I call a *principle*, the identity principle; and the eastern position a *doctrine*, the doctrine of energies. This is because the two positions are not directly comparable. In looking at the western position we are dealing with an *a priori*, though not always acknowledged, methodological principle.[10] In the East we are concerned with a recognized doctrine,[11] confirmed by ecclesiastical synods, that has in turn certain methodological ramifications. The theological tradition in which the doctrine of energies plays an important role can be called "Palamite" (or—in reference to its contemporary representatives—"neo-Palamite"), in honor of Gregory Palamas, the fourteenth century archbishop of Thessalonika who first developed a systematic formulation of the doctrine.

It could be asked here whether it is not too simplistic to set a western identity principle over against what we could call a "difference principle" involved in the eastern doctrine of energies. Surely the time for making sharp contrasts between eastern and western theological traditions is well past. It is possible to ask whether the doctrine of energies is a necessary feature of Eastern Orthodox theology. It is also possible to point to individual western theologians (for example, Dietrich Ritschl,[12] Anna Marie Aagaard,[13] and George Maloney[14]) and even to major strands in western

---

10. D. Ritschl, *The Logic of Theology: A Brief Account of the Relationship between Basic Concepts in Theology* (London, 1986), p. 146.

11. Although it is true that this doctrine was often neglected, and even contradicted, by the Orthodox themselves, especially in the period between the sixteenth and the twentieth centuries when Orthodox theology was heavily influenced by Thomistic scholasticism. See P. de Halleux, *Patrologie und Oecumenisme* (Löwen, 1990), p. 814.

12. D. Ritschl, "Historical Development and Implications of the Filioque Controversy," in L. Vischer (ed.), *Spirit of God, Spirit of Christ: Ecumenical Reflections on the Filioque Controversy* (London/Geneva, 1981); D. Ritschl, "Warum wir Konzilien feier - Konstantinopel 381," *Theologische Zeitschrift* 38 (1982): 213–25; D. Ritschl, *The Logic of Theology* (London, 1986).

13. A. M. Aagaard, "Christus wurde Mensch, um alles Menschliche zu überwinden," in *StTh* 21 (1967): pp. 164–81; A. M. Aagaard, *Helligånden sendt til Verden* (Aarhus, 1973); A.

theology (process theology comes to mind here) quite critical of a doctrine of God regulated by the identity principle. The question about the doctrine of energies can be dismissed, I think, at least in relation to the Byzantine tradition, simply by referring to the Palamite councils of 1341 and 1351 in Constantinople, where the doctrine of energies was given an official endorsement that is still in effect. The question as to just how representative the identity principle is in the West is more difficult. What I would say is that the identity principle represents the majority tradition in post-Reformation western theology.[15] As Dietrich Ritschl has pointed out, "The theologies of the Western churches oscillate between this identification of the economic and immanent doctrines of the Trinity and deep scepticism over the concept of the Trinity generally."[16] It is for this reason that I have chosen not to deal with even major alternatives like process thought, but have focused on a methodological principle that can be seen clearly at work in the two undoubtedly most influential western theologians of the twentieth century.

The first chapter is an introductory sketch of the background to the separation of the two models. Apart from this first chapter, I want to deal primarily with thinkers of the present century, and the divergence as it finds expression within the works of contemporary theology. With this intention I look at the identity principle as it appears in the thought of Karl Barth (1886–1968) and Karl Rahner (1904–84); and the doctrine of energies as it appears in the thought of Georges Florovsky (1893–1979) and Vladimir Lossky (1903–58). I will then focus on certain questions that have arisen in the course of the recent debate about Palamism. After this I move on to set out certain common concerns and interests that seem to underlie both positions. The central question in all this is: What can each of the traditions learn and accept from the other without losing its own fundamental insight into the truth about God? Because I write from within the western tradition, my own major interest is to discern what the West can learn from the eastern tradition. Thus I discuss the more familiar territory of the western position first, and then go on to discuss the eastern position. In this context it is helpful to recognize the acknowledgement in recent ecumenical dialogue[17]

M. Aagaard, "Der Heilige Geist in der Welt," in H. Meyer et. al., *Wiederentdeckung des Heiligen Geistes* (Frankfurt aM, 1974); A. M. Aagaard, "Die Erfahrung des Geistes," in O. A. Dilschneider (ed.) *Theologie des Geistes* (Gütersloh, 1980).

14. G. A. Maloney, *Inscape: God at the Heart of Matter* (Denville, N.J., 1978); G. A. Maloney, *A Theology of "Uncreated Energies"* (Milwaukee, 1978).

15. On this I am fully in agreement with Prof. Dorothea Wendebourg, and am very grateful for a conversation in 1985 during which she made this point.

16. Ritschl, *The Logic of Theology*, op. cit., p. 146.

17. Between the Chalcedonian and non-Chalcedonian Orthodox (Geneva, 1970) and

of a distinction between the language of dogmatic statements and their underlying intention. On this basis it may be possible to uncover, beneath apparently divergent traditions of dogmatic formulation, a level of common intention. We should be careful, however, not to ignore Lossky's warning against simplistic attempts at synthesis.[18]

It should also be acknowledged that we do not necessarily live in the most favorable climate for an attempt to learn from Palamite theology. W. Ullmann, in a review of Wendebourg's critique of Palamism, notes a reaction against the sense of discovery of Eastern Orthodoxy in the 1960s on the part of western theologians. The more recent trend is no longer to seek to throw off what Dietrich Ritschl called "the burden of the Augustinian heritage."[19] We do not need to go back to the classic critiques of Palamism by Martin Jugie[20] earlier this century to find evidence of a renewed—or perhaps, at a deeper level, continuing—western dismissal of Palamite thought.[21] I intend to enter into debate with some of these recent western critiques of Palamism, but in a way that will, I hope, also take seriously the insights of the western tradition.

---

between Anglicans and Orthodox (Moscow, 1976). See K. Ware and C. Davey (eds.), *Anglican-Orthodox Dialogue: The Moscow Statement* (London, 1977), p. 49, which refers to the distinction between "the true intention of the dogmatic definition of a Council" and "the particular terminology in which it is expressed, which latter has less authority than the intention." Cf. one of the ten basic rules for ecumenical dialogue suggested by M. Kinnamon: "Be willing to separate essentials from nonessentials and to require agreement only on the former. This follows, of course, from all that we have been saying about diversity and the 'hierarchy of truth.' Dialogue should try to determine which issues demand consensus if we are to know that we worship and serve the same Jesus Christ, and which issues do not" (M. Kinnamon, *Truth and Community: Diversity and its Limits in the Ecumenical Movement* [Grand Rapids and Geneva, 1988], p. 31).

18. "Dogmatic temptation most often consists of false synthesis in a certain primordial confusion; and on the contrary, Christian dogmas are presented most often in the form of *distinctions*." V. Lossky, "The Personality and Thought of Patriarch Sergius," *Diakonia* 6 (1971): 167.

19. W. Ullmann, "Geist oder Energie: Buchbesprechung," in *ThLit* 108 (1983): 607–10.

20. M. Jugie, "Palamas, Gregoire," in *Dictionnaire de Theologie Catholique* (Paris, 1931), and M. Jugie, *Theologia Dogmatica Christianorum Orientalium ab Ecclesia Catholica Dissidentium.* (Paris, 1933).

21. E.g., Mackey, in *The Christian Experience of God,* op. cit., p. 295, n. 155, dismisses the whole eastern position without discussing it; and C. Gunton, in *The Promise of Trinitarian Theology* (Edinburgh, 1991), p. 14, n. 3, reveals an uncritical acceptance of Wendebourg's argument.

Chapter 1
BACKGROUND TO THE DIVERGENCE BETWEEN THE IDENTITY PRINCIPLE AND THE DOCTRINE OF ENERGIES

The distinction between God's inner being and God's activities arises from the biblical experience of God as the one who is both *Deus revelatus* and *Deus absconditus*. This God is encountered at the burning bush, in the liberation of the Hebrew slaves from captivity in Egypt, and in the death and resurrection of Jesus Christ. But the witnesses to these events are always aware that there is more to God than is revealed in the events themselves. In fact it is an act of grace that God is revealed with such reserve, and not in God's full and awesome holiness. "Who sees God's face, that is selfe life, must dye," said the seventeenth century English poet and theologian John Donne,[1] echoing the words of Exodus 33:20. Thus there is a certain bipolarity[2] in God, and to this corresponds a bipolarity in our human speech concerning God, between nominative and vocative,[3] between descriptive and analogical language *about* God and ascriptive and doxological language addressed *to* God.[4] Often these two types of speech stand very close to one another in the biblical text. One type can slide into another in midsentence. Each has its own purpose. The one attempts appropriately to describe our human experience of God's actions; the other attempts appropriately to praise God, or indeed struggle with God, on account of events that have been experienced as God's actions. One type of discourse relates to God in relation to us (*pro nobis*); the other relates to God in Godself (*a se*). The relationship between these two "aspects" (for want of a better term) of God is the central theological issue in this divergence between the identity principle and the doctrine of energies. Behind the divergence of traditions lies both a difference in the usage of certain philosophical terms and also differing theological concerns and questions.

---

1. "Goodfriday 1613 Riding Westward." Cf. Exodus 33: 20.

2. J. Moltmann, *The Trinity and the Kingdom of God* (London, 1981), pp. 25ff., citing A. J. Heschel, *The Prophets* (New York, 1962).

3. H. Gollwitzer, *Die Existenz Gottes* (München, 1963), p. 118, n. 176, citing E. Rosenstock-Huessy.

4. D. Ritschl, *Memory and Hope* (New York, 1967), pp. 167 ff.

The Philosophical Terminology

It is important to note at the outset that the philosophical terminology through which the doctrine of energies finds expression is not always used unambiguously. The Palamite doctrine of energies was developed on the basis of experience. It is in essence not a metaphysical or philosophical theory.[5] The early church fathers did not employ philosophical terminology in an uncritical way, but adapted it and interpreted it creatively in order to convey their experience of life in Christ. It would be wrong, therefore, to regard the use of philosophical terminology in either theological system as simply a reversion to pre-Christian thought forms. Even so, it is also a matter of fact that this philosophical terminology has a pre-Christian history. It is to this history that we now turn.

The Greek philosophical (and especially Aristotelian) usage of the terms essence (οὐσία), power/potential (δύναμις) and energy/efficacy (ἐνέργεια) is often cited as the basis of the essence-energy distinction in Palamite thought.[6] While there is certainly a truth in this, it is also the case that the same concepts lie behind the later western identification of essence with energy. What we find, I think, is emerging differences in the usage of the same technical terms.

For Plato, essence (οὐσία) denotes a particular being, a particular thing whose idea, or source of being as a particular thing, is located "beyond the essence" (ἐπέκεινα τῆς οὐσίας).[7] The Platonic notion of participation also becomes important here. A thing receives its actuality to a greater or lesser extent, depending on the degree to which it participates in the form or idea that lies behind it. Two ontological planes are established, that of the particular thing (the plane of the "sensible"), and that of the idea behind it (the plane of the "intelligible"). Essence and energy may be identified on

---

5. K. Ware and C. Davey (eds.), *Anglican-Orthodox Dialogue: The Moscow Statement Agreed by the Anglican-Orthodox Joint Doctrinal Commission, 1976* (London, 1977), pp. 45f.: "The Orthodox delegates at Moscow insisted that the essence-energies distinction rests not upon philosophical but upon experimental reasons; it is not a 'metaphysical theory,' but an attempt to express in words the living experience of the Saints, alike in the past and in our own day." See also W. Ullmann, "Geist oder Energie: Buchbesprechung" in *ThLit* 108 (1983): 607–10, who emphasizes quite rightly the very limited appropriateness of comparing spirituality with (academic) theology. Palamas was not trying to set up a theological distinction, but defending a spiritual praxis from the suspicion of heresy.

6. J. Meyendorff, *Byzantine Theology* (New York, 1974), pp. 185f.; D. Wendebourg, *Geist oder Energie: Zur Frage der innergöttlichen Verankerung des christlichen Lebens in der byzantinischen Theologie* (München, 1980), pp. 29f.

7. R. D. Williams, in his unpublished dissertation, *The Theology of Vladimir Nikolaievich Lossky: An Exposition and Critique* (Oxford, 1975), writes "Being something *determinate* hence ... the source of determinate existence is ἐπέκεινα τῆς οὐσίας." (p. 169).

the level of particular things, but there is also a dimension of beyondness in Plato's ontology. This Platonic notion "beyond the essence" will later become extremely important for the mystical writings of the eastern church, especially through the influence of Pseudo-Dionysius.

Aristotle, on the other hand, does away with the Platonic distinction between two different ontological planes, the sensible and the intelligible.[8] "Energy," for Aristotle, signifies the attributes or the form of a thing, an οὐσία. The energy is the power that gives life or efficacy to a thing in a practical, human sense. It denotes its significance for human beings.[9] In this limited sense, energy can be be distinguished from essence.[10] But the far more important distinction in Aristotle is between power (δύναμις) and energy (ἐνέργεια), in which power (δύναμις) denotes the potentiality of an essence (οὐσία), and energy (ἐνέργεια) its actuality.[11] A real thing (ἐνέργειαν οὐσίαν)[12] can thus be distinguished from something that is merely potential—that is to say, something that already exists but as yet has no real significance for human beings. In actual things, essence and efficacy (οὐσία and ἐνέργεια) are, according to Aristotle, one and the same. Further, the essence (οὐσία) of an incorporeal thing is in its activity (ἐνέργεια).[13] Aristotle's identification of essence and energy will later become a feature of western scholasticism, which identifies God's essence or substance as pure actuality (*actus purus*). If God is thought of as both incorporeal and fully actual, the stage is set, on the basis of Aristotelian philosophical assumptions, for a theological identification of essence and energy in God; in other words, for an identity principle. Rowan Williams notes that "Aristotle's God is οὐσία, and it would make no sense to speak of Him as ἐπέκεινα τῆς οὐσίας."[14] Here we also have the groundwork for the later philosophical distinction between essence and existence.

For both Plato and Aristotle there is a certain identity of essence and energy in actual things. For both Plato and Aristotle, "a real thing in the

---

8. H. Schaeder, "Die Christianisierung der aristotelischen Logik," *Theol.(A)* 33 (1962): 5f.
9. Aristotle, *Metaphysics* (ed. W. Jaeger, Oxford, 1957), 1043a, 12ff.
10. As in *Metaphysics*, op. cit., 1043a, 27–28.
11. *Metaphysics*, op. cit., 1048b, 9–17; 1065b, 5–7. R. D. Williams writes: "For Aristotle . . . it (sc. ἐνέργεια) means purely and simply 'actuality'; more precisely, an ἐντελεχεία, a kind of activity which includes its own end, or *is* with its own end (an activity such as seeing or understanding, as opposed to one like learning or building, which is directed towards some external end or limit" (op. cit., p. 172).
12. *Metaphysics*, op. cit., 1042b, 10–11.
13. Williams, op. cit., p. 170.
14. Ibid., p. 170.

fullest sense is an οὐσία or an ἐνεργείᾳ ὄν."[15] But the term "essence" carries a different significance for Plato, for whom it can be transcended, than it does for Aristotle, for whom there can be nothing "beyond the essence." Further, in Aristotle, it is possible to see both an ambiguity in the concept of essence,[16] and, more importantly, the roots of two differing ways of combining the terms οὐσία, δύναμις, and ἐνέργεια. There can be an identification of the near synonyms ἐνέργεια and δύναμις, both of which are contrasted to οὐσία. This is the usage that will later find expression in the doctrine of energies. Or there can be a contrast between an essence (οὐσία) that has actuality (ἐνέργεια) and an essence that merely has potentiality (δύναμις). This usage, which follows Aristotle's own distinction between δύναμις and ἐνέργεια, finds its logical extension in the identity principle.

Theological Concerns in the History of Western Trinitarian Thinking

There are other elements in the philosophical world of late antiquity that prepare the way for the identity principle. Plotinus[17] explained the structure of the cosmos in terms of three "hypostases": the One (ἕν), intellect (νοῦς) and soul (ψυχή). Plato had distinguished two ontological levels, the world of ideas, the "intelligible," or the true world of being, and the world of experience, the "sensible," or the world of becoming and change. For Plotinus "soul" represents the level of sensory perception in the domain of becoming; "intellect" the plane of intuitive recognition in the domain of being. But even this higher plane must be transcended, in Plotinus' schema, because there is still a plurality in the world of ideas. Beyond this ideal world lies the fundamental simplicity of the One. Intellect and soul are elements of a cosmos that unfold themselves in successive circles. The procession of the intellect from the One, and of the soul from the intellect, are acts of will. The natural tendency of the cosmos in its plurality is toward a return to the One. Thus it is possible to speak of a movement of procession (πρόοδος) and return (ἐπίστροφη) of the soul—from the One and back to the One. This movement in Plotinus' schema brings together the Godhead and the cosmos. There is no room for the biblical polarity of God in Godself on the one hand and God for us (or God in history) on the other. History has no place in the cosmos of Plotinus. Instead what we find is a hierarchy of

---

15. E. Zeller, *Bericht im Archiv für Geschichte der Philosophie*, 2, 1889, pp. 270f., cited in J. Owens, *The Doctrine of Being in the Aristotelian Metaphysics* (Toronto, 1951), p. 309, note. 74.

16. Zeller sees an "ambiguity in the concept of οὐσία, which runs through the whole of the *Metaphysics*" (ibid.).

17. See E. v. Ivánka, *Plato Christianus: Übernahme und Umgestaltung des Platonismus durch die Väter* (Einsiedeln, 1964); A. H. Armstrong, "Plotinus," GMP, pp. 193 ff.; A. Louth, *The Origins of the Christian Mystical Tradition* (Oxford, 1981).

emanations consisting of the One, the intellect, and the soul that combine together to make up the cosmos. At the end of this schema, at the lowest level in a hierarchy of ideas (λόγοι), are material things. These have less actuality than the ideal, the Logos, from which they take their origin. This Logos is in turn a function (or an energy) of the intellect.

Plotinus' schema gives rise to a new type of mystical praxis, involving the turning inward to the inner self. The return of the soul to the One, by which it finds its true identity, corresponds to the prior outgoing of the One from itself into the world—its self-unfolding, so to speak. The schema is to be understood as an exercise in self-understanding—a practical response to the imperative "know yourself" that stood carved over the portal of the temple of Apollo at Delphi, and which still stands as the unspoken imperative behind so much of western intellectual endeavor. The principle elements of Plotinus' schema are a description of reality by way of analogy to the structure of human thought, and an emphasis on the fundamental simplicity of the One. These elements are to reappear in the trinitarian thinking of Augustine.

A central concept for Augustine, who stands to some extent under neo-Platonic influence, is the unity of God, understood in terms of the simplicity of God.[18] Basically, this means an identity of essence and attributes. It is a function of this simplicity of God that God's trinitarian activities constitute God's trinitarian being. There is no hint here of the distinction between essence and energy that will later be developed in Eastern Orthodox theology. In fact we find ourselves much closer to the basic distinction in Aristotle between potentiality (δύναμις) and actuality (ἐνέργεια) and the identification of essence (οὐσία) with actuality (ἐνέργεια). Any idea of movement would suggest potentiality, and this is banished from this concept of divine being. For Augustine, then, there is not just a correspondence between the unity of God's being and the unity of God's actions (this necessarily follows from the principle that *one* essence has *one* energy or effect or function),[19] but an identity of being and action.[20]

This is necessarily the case in a system in which the unity of God constitutes the "point of departure and the goal of all considerations."[21]

---

18. M. Schmaus: *Die Psychologische Trinitätslehre des Heiligen Augustinus* (Münster, 1967), p. 86: "It is the hallmark of the Augustinian notion of God that God is absolutely simple being. He allows no real distinction between substance and accidence, between accidence and accidence, between being and being-active, between activity and activity. Augustine never tires of emphasizing this simplicity."

19. Meyendorff, *Byzantine Theology*, op. cit., p. 185.

20. Schmaus, *Psychol. Trinitätslehre*, op. cit., p. 151.

21. Ibid., p. 416.

That means, for Augustine, a unity of the trinitarian acts *ad extra* corresponding to the unity of the trinitarian essence *ad intra*. Any possibility is lost of distinguishing between the trinitarian hypostases on the basis of their economic actions.

The Aristotelian identification of essence (οὐσία) and energy (ἐνέργεια) was thus taken on board by the western tradition of trinitarian thinking. Substance and activity are brought together in God under the notion of God's actuality (*actus purus*). The important distinction for western theology remains the distinction that Aristotle himself had emphasized, that between potentiality (δύναμις) and actuality (ἐνέργεια). This Aristotelian distinction is later to find expression in a distinction between essence and existence—a distinction that the Orthodox theologian Christos Yannaras[22] considers as being of fundamental significance for western European thought as a whole.

There was nothing new in Augustine's use of analogies drawn from creation for the holy trinity. The Cappadocians had followed earlier church fathers in explaining the trinity with the help of analogies to the source, stream, and mouth of a river, or to the root, trunk, and branch of a tree. Marius Victorinus, who borrowed from the neo-Platonist Porphyry the triadic model *existentia–vita–intelligentia*,[23] is also the first Christian thinker to derive a trinitarian model of God *directly* from an analogy from creation.[24] That is to say, he is the first to develop his trinitarian thinking without the need for any reference to the biblical history of salvation. While I would not want to suggest a direct path from Plotinus, Porphyry, or even from Marius Victorinus to Augustine,[25] it remains the case that Augustine, in his book *De Trinitate*, comes to explain the trinitarian doctrine through the use of very similar analogies to the human thought process, viz. *mens–notitia–amor* or *memoria–intelligentia–voluntas*. It may well be that Augustine intended these analogies as a trinitarian basis for anthropology rather than the other way round, that is, as an anthropological point of departure for understanding the doctrine of the trinity.[26] However, perhaps because Augustine himself

---

22. C. Yannaras, *De l'absense et de l'inconnaissance de Dieu d'après les écrits aréopagitiques et Martin Heidegger* (Paris, 1971), p. 97.

23. J. P. Mackey, *The Christian Experience of God as Trinity* (London, 1983), p. 121. In Tertullian we also find roots of the later western psychological trinity: Schmaus, *Psychol. Trinitätslehre*, op. cit., p. 417.

24. P. Gerlitz, *Ausserchristliche Einflüsse auf die Entwicklung des christlichen Trinitätsdogmas: Zugleich ein religions- und dogmengeschichtlicher Versuch zur Erklärung der Herkunft der Homousie* (Leiden, 1963), pp. 248f.

25. R. A. Markus, "Marius Victorinus and Augustine," *GMP*, esp. pp. 339–40.

26. Schmaus (*Psychol. Trinitätslehre*, op. cit., pp. 399) argues that Augustine himself regarded his psychological analogies as "a highly imperfect idea" that one should "not be too cautious in considering." A. Louth, *The Origins of the Christian Mystical Tradition: From*

seems at times to suggest that the psychological analogies are more than just illustrations,[27] they were to become highly influential in the coming centuries. The psychological trinity is what we could call a theoretical trinity, that is, one which develops on the basis of its own inner logic, again without the need for any express reference to the *Heilsgeschichte*. It is possible, of course, to tie this trinitarian model to the history of salvation, as Augustine himself does, but it is not absolutely necessary. From this time on there appears on the horizon an important implication for the whole tradition of western trinitarian thinking. This is, that as soon as one mentions the "inner trinity," there is the suggestion of this "other," theoretical trinity separated from and independent of salvation history. This implication will become highly significant for the effective loss of the doctrine of the trinity in the modern era, because any distinction between an inner and an economic doctrine of the trinity is immediately and automatically associated with this metaphysical and speculative trinity. This association forestalls any serious discussion of such a possible distinction. This is so even after the psychological analogies of the trinity have been dismissed as inappropriate.

In Augustine himself there is no suggestion of such a division between two implicit starting points—one based in the history of salvation and the other speculative and ahistorical. On the contrary, the inner and the outer sides of the trinity are held closely together through the correspondence of the missions to the processions. The economic sending of the Son and the Holy Spirit find their basis in the inner-trinitarian processions to which they correspond.[28]

The conflict with Arianism continued longer in the West than in the East. It was in the West a logical step to use *polemically* Augustine's close nexus between the inner procession and the outer mission of the Spirit, that is, in fact, the nexus between the inner and the economic trinity. The divinity of the Son and his consubstantiality with the Father are strongly emphasized if the close economic relationship of sending between the Son and the Spirit can be applied also to the inner being of the trinity. Thus the Spirit is considered as proceeding from the Father *and* the Son (*ab utroque*). This is exactly what the western tradition emphasized in interpolating the *filioque*

Plato to Denys (Oxford, 1981), remarks: "Augustine is less concerned to illustrate the doctrine of the Trinity from his understanding of man, than to discover the true nature of man by means of the doctrine of the Trinity that he believes by faith."

27. Schmaus, *Psychol. Trinitätslehre*, op. cit., p. 413.

28. Ibid., p. 164: "By 'mission' Augustine understood . . . the eternal procession of one person from another, closely tied to the outer manifestation of the person so proceeding. To proceed from the Father and to come into the world means, for the Son, to be sent (*Ergo a Patre exire, et venire in hunc mundum, hoc est mitti*)."

clause into the Nicene Creed. This clause ensured the close connection between the economic, salvation-history trinity and the theoretical, psychological explanation of the doctrine. The *filioque* thus becomes, for the West, a theological necessity, not only as a defense against Arianism, but also to avoid any suspicion that there might be two and perhaps even mutually contradictory trinities. The *filioque* clause thus serves to retain a place for the psychological trinity. The Augustinian axiom that the outward activities of the trinity are indivisible[29] means that the trinitarian hypostases are not to be distinguished on the basis of their economic activities. That leads to the need to emphasize the psychological model of the trinity. In the West there was the tendency to move from a theoretical, psychological idea of the trinity in itself to a corresponding economic experience of the trinity "for us." The psychological trinitarian speculation was to find its most complete form, as Schmaus points out, in the work of Thomas Aquinas.[30]

Theological Concerns in the History of Eastern Trinitarian Thinking

It was an important turning point in trinitarian thinking when the early church decided against the various subordinationist understandings of trinity, whereby the Father represents the inner, hidden Godhead and the Son and the Spirit carry out the economic activities. These understandings were replaced by the Nicene emphasis on the consubstantiality of the three hyspostases. The turning point was the outcome of a bitter struggle against those who had taken early church subordinationism to its logical conclusion, the Arians and the pneumatomachi. Here we see a shift in the usage of the Aristotelian terms οὐσία, δύναμις, and ἐνέργεια. While the distinction between οὐσία and δύναμις denoted, for Origen, the difference between the Father and the Son, this same terminological distinction, for Athanasius, denoted a distinction within the trinitarian life, between God's being in Godself and God's being for the creation.[31] The Cappadocians, who understand the Father, Son, and Holy Spirit as being equally worthy of praise, consider these as three hypostases having a common essence (οὐσία). Here δύναμις (in the sense of power, and also attributes) is clearly

---

29. "'*Opera trinitatis ad extra indivisa sunt*' operates as a rule of Augustinian trinitarian theology, even though these actual words are nowhere to be found in Augustine." T. Freyer, *Pneumatologie als Strukturprinzip der Dogmatik* (Paderborn, 1982), p. 313. Qv. Schmaus, *Psychol. Trinitätslehre*, op. cit., pp. 151f. and 166ff.

30. Ibid., p. 419.

31. A. M. Aagaard, "Christus wurde Mensch, um alles menschliche zu überwinden," *StTh* 21 (1967): 171: "(Athanasius) formulates his thoughts most clearly in *De Incarnatione* I, 17, where he says that the Logos is outside all created things as being, but in all things as dynamis. The Logos comes to be (ἐγίνετο) in all things, but is (ἦν) outside all things."

distinguished from and also subordinated to the οὐσία (or ὑπερουσιότης in the Platonic sense)[32] to which it belongs. Thus in the East the Aristotelian conceptual schema was taken up, but in such a way as to draw a distinction between οὐσία (or ὑπερουσιότης) and ἐνέργεια.[33] There was also a tendency, perhaps because of the influence of Philo and other neo-Platonists, to take δύναμις and ἐνέργεια as synonyms.[34] This represents a creative reinterpretation of the Aristotelian concepts, so that ἐνέργεια is now identified with the attributes of God, especially God's grace.[35] Instead of a difference between the perfect, that is, actuality (in which οὐσία coincides with ἐνέργεια), and the imperfect, that is, mere potentiality (δύναμις), here we find a distinction within God between the "absolute" and the "relative" sides of the Godhead. (Even this is not quite accurate because the "absolute" side of God is trinitarian, and thus relational, while the "relative" side of God is that side of God that stands in relation to us, and is relational in this sense). The most commonly used analogy for this distinction is that of the sun and its rays. It is the distinction that we come across in John of Damascus, between the divine "nature" (φύσις) and "that which surrounds the nature" (τὰ περὶ τὴν φύσιν),[36] or between "according to the essence" (κατ' οὐσίαν) and "according to the energy" (κατ' ἐνέργειαν).[37] There can be no doubt that the same distinction is present in the thinking of many of the Greek fathers.[38] When Gregory Palamas employs this distinction in the

---

32. R. D. Williams (op. cit., p. 171) refers to a problem in the usage of the two terms οὐσία and ὑπερουσιότης; viz. that the Nicaean ὁμοούσιον in fact served to introduce into Christian theology the expression οὐσία, and indeed introduced it in a technical, Aristotelian sense in reference to God's essence. In contrast to this stood the growing tendency in Christian mysticism (under the influence of neo-Platonism) to refer to God's "transcendence of οὐσία, His ὑπερουσιότης." Williams argues that western theology used a relatively consistent Aristotelian concept of οὐσία, while eastern theology vacillated between two different and mutually exclusive terminologies. Against this viewpoint we can note that it is debatable whether there is in fact a consistent Aristotelian concept of οὐσία, even in Aristotle himself. The Platonic concept of οὐσία is, of course, just as problematic as the Aristotelian (see n. 16, above).

33. Ibid., p. 173.

34. I. P. Sheldon-Williams, "The Greek Christian Platonist Tradition from the Cappadochians to Maximus and Eriugena," *GMP*, pp. 430f.

35. H. Schaeder, "Christianisierung," op. cit., p. 8.

36. John of Damascus, *Exposito Fidei*, pp. 4, 14, 34f., in B. Kotter (ed.), *Patristische Texte und Studien*, vol. 12 (Berlin, 1973).

37. Ibid., pp. 7–9, 19. Qv. H. A. Wolfson, *The Philosophy of the Church Fathers* (Cambridge, Mass., 1970³), vol. 1, pp. 465–68, for a discussion of the Aristotelian concept of ἐνέργεια in the thought of John of Damascus.

38. K. Kern, "Duchovnye predki Svjatovo Grigorija Palamy" ("Spiritual forerunners of St. Gregory Palamas"), in *Bogoslovskaja Mysl'* (Paris), 1942, pp. 102–31; V. N. Lossky, *The Vision of God* (Leighton Buzzard, 1963); E. v. Ivánka, "Palamismus und Vätertradition," in

fourteenth century in his *Defense of the Holy Hesychasts* [39] he was making use of an idea already well known in the Byzantine East.

This is also the case with the concept of energy. Before it was taken up and used systematically in the context of trinitarian thinking, this concept had already acquired a certain technical precision in christology. During the so-called monenergist debate in the seventh century, the notions of energy and will were equated with one another.[40] The notion of will was already important in Aristotelian anthropology, but because will is changeable it could not be attributed to the highest essence.[41] Within the biblical tradition, however, it was possible to speak of God's will. Now God's "will" and God's "energy" (ἐνέργεια, in the sense of activity) were brought together, and the notion of energy was thereby personalized. The energy of God is no neo-Platonic procession, here, but rather an activity directed by God's will to the economy of the creation and salvation. Thereafter the distinction between God's essence and energy is connected to the difference between the divine nature and created nature. It can be said that God really enters into a relationship with, and is present in, creation, without any implication that God's nature is somehow exhausted in this involvement. God is active in the world; God does not remain in some hidden way beyond the world. Even so, both the western and eastern theological traditions take account of the biblical (and indeed, Aristotelian) idea of the ineffability of

---

L. Beauduin (ed.), *1054–1954 L'Eglise et les eglises* (Chevetogne, 1955), vol. 2, pp. 29–46; G. Habra, "The Sources of the Doctrine of Gregory Palamas on the Divine Energies," *ECQ* 12 (1957): 244–52, 294–303, 338–47; L. H. Grondijs, "The Patristic Origins of Gregory Palamas' Doctrine of God," in *TU* 80 (1962): 323–28; L. C. Contos, "The Essence-Energies Structure of St. Gregory Palamas with a brief examination of its Patristic Foundations," *GrOrthThR* 12 (1967): 283–94; B. Krivoshein, "Problema poznavaemosti Boga," *Messager* 61 (1968): 48–55; B. Krivoshein, "Simplicity of the Divine Nature," *StVlThQ* 21 (1977): 76–104; G. Patacsi, "Palamism before Palamas," *ECR* 9 (1977): 64–71; A. J. Sopko, "Palamism before Palamas," *StVlThQ* 23 (1979): 139–47.

39. Ὑπέρ τῶν ἱερῶς ἡσυχαζοντῶν, in Συγγράματα (ed. P. K. Chrestou, Thessaloniki, 1962ff.), vol. 1. French transl. *Defense des saints hesychastes* (ed. J. Meyendorff, Louvain, 1959). Sections of this work have been translated into English by N. Gendle in the Classics of Western Spirituality series, *Gregory Palamas: The Triads* (London, 1983).

40. See. H.-G. Beck, *Kirche und Theologische Literatur im Byzantinischen Reich* (München, 1954), pp. 292–95. This debate, which was closely related to the monotheletism controversy, was concerned with the question as to whether there were in Christ one or two energies. The one-energy party focused on the movement in Christ from God to humanity; the two-energy party with the independence of the two natures in Christ. The controversy was brought to an end by way of an enforced compromise formula that mentioned neither one nor two energies, but "one actor" (εἷς καὶ αὐτός ἐνεργῶν). Qv. H. A. Wolfson, *Philosophy*, op. cit., pp. 473–93. A principle that was never called in question in this controversy was that one nature has one will, and one will has one energy.

41. H. Schaeder, "Christianisierung," op. cit., p. 10.

God. In the East the notion of ineffability is reserved to God's essence. Energy (or uncreated grace) is distinguished from this essence. God really indwells the creation in this energy or grace,[42] without there being any suggestion of a compromising of the ontological difference between creator and creation. In the West, energy (insofar as the term is used at all) is identified with essence. If the essence of God is ineffable, it follows that God's energy—God's activity—must also be ineffable. Conversely, theophanies are regarded as "natural" revelations or manifestations, rather than forms of real indwelling of God in the creation.[43]

In Maximus the Confessor,[44] the focus is very definitely upon the relationship between God and the creation. Here, the trinitarian nature of God is taken for granted. Power (δύναμις) and will (θέλημα) are to be identified in God. This includes God's will to bring a creation into being, or the *idea* of a creation. God in Godself is beyond "being" in the sense of a world of ideas. The ideas (λόγοι) of a creation are eternally in God's mind, or—if we speak in trinitarian terms—in the second person, the λόγος. The ideas are desires (θελήματα) located in the will of God. They are eternal, but not on the same level of eternity as the trinity. The ideas are, like material things, created by God and contingent upon God. The difference between ideas and material things is that the ideas remain in being. The procession of the *ideas* from essence (οὐσία) to power or potentiality (δύναμις) and then to actuality (ἐνέργεια) is a movement from "being" (εἶναι) to "good being" (τὸ εὖ εἶναι) to "eternal being" (τὸ ἀεὶ εἶναι). The procession of material things is a movement from becoming (γένεσις) to movement (κίνησις) to rest (στάσις). The relationship between the ideas and material things is the relationship between "universal being" (καθόλου) and "specific being" (καθ' ἕκαστον).

The main concern in all this is to clarify the status of creation as the product of the divine will, actualized within the limits of time. Movement (κίνησις) is no longer considered a falling away from the immovable Godhead (as in Plotinus), and therefore as evil. Movement is rather the field

---

42. D. Staniloae, *Orthodoxe Dogmatik* (Zürich-Gutersloh, 1985), p. 151: "The world is . . . encompassed by the divine infinitude, and also permeated by it—it cannot exist without such a relationship with God. Our finitude can exist only within the frame or the womb of the divine infinitude." On this basis, Staniloae argues that eastern theology understands God principally as the one who holds all things (*Allerhalter*), i.e., in a relationship of love to the world, in contrast to the western understanding of God as the almighty (*der Allmächtige*) with its primary connotation of power (p. 203).

43. Schmaus, *Psychol. Trinitätslehre*, op. cit., p. 161.

44. In the following paragraphs I have referred especially to Sheldon-Williams, op. cit., in *GMP*.

in which created wills exercise freedom to decide between "good being" (τὸ εὖ εἶναι) and "evil being" (τὸ φεῦ εἶναι). Movement is itself not negated when the movement of the created world (viz. becoming–movement–rest) comes to its final state of rest. Movement itself is created by God and is accepted into the eternity of God. The purpose (τέλος) of created being is to find rest in God. This is the rest (στάσις) of contingent being. Maximus described this τέλος in paradoxical terms like "eternal movement" (ἀεικινησία) and "eternally moving rest" (ἀεικίνητος στάσις). These ideas are not far from that of Gregory of Nyssa when he speaks of an ever deeper movement of "reaching out" (ἐπέκτασις) into the inner being of God. The λόγος of human beings is the divine λόγος. Here Maximus links the salvation of human beings directly with the second person of the trinity. The divine λόγος is the purpose and also the way through which both the material world and the world of ideas are redeemed. In this way it is possible for the human being to "become God" (θεὸς γίνεται) through being taken up (ἀνάληψις) into the divine energy. This is for the deified human being an experience that is suffered; for the God who takes up (ὁ ἀναλαμβάνων) it is an energy. This deification applies to the whole human being—body and soul, experiences and emotions—so that not only the human being, but also *in* the human being as microcosm, it comes to apply to the whole creation, the cosmos. The whole is invited and taken into the life of God.

Maximus avoids any merely functional concept of the trinity. His concern here is in fact not to explain the trinity, but to throw light on the relationship between the creator and the creation. To this end Maximus takes up the conceptual schema οὐσία–δύναμις–ἐνέργεια and uses it to present a Christian (and thus trinitarian) understanding of the creator-creation relationship. In the process of creation and salvation, the concept of δύναμις carries the idea of potentiality, in that it is the *locus* of the divine will to create. The concept of ἐνέργεια conveys the idea of a realized or perfected action, in that it becomes the *locus* of the divinized creature.

The Aristotelian concept of energy is carefully explored by John of Damascus, who takes up Porphyry's distinction between a substantial characteristic (ἰδιώμα) and an accidental characteristic (συμβεβηκός).[45] The ἰδιώματα of God become energies[46] in the sense of unchangeable self-

---

45. Schaeder, "Christianisierung," op. cit., p. 15.

46. The question as to whether we should speak of the energy (in the singular) or the energies (in the plural) is discussed by K. Kern (*Antropologija Sv. Grigorija Palamy [The Anthroplogy of St. Gregory Palamas]* (Paris, 1950), pp. 288f.). Kern argues that both are appropriate, because, on the one hand, there is a common energy (singular) of the three divine hypostases, and on the other hand, this energy presents itself to us as a plurality; for example, the seven spiritual gifts in Isaiah 11:12 are energies.

expressions or emanations of God, which permeate the creation. It is in connection with these energies that our statements about God are either valid or invalid. The inner being of God remains ungraspable and thus ineffable. So the distinction between essence and energy in God comes to be also the basis for a distinction between positive and negative, cataphatic and apophatic theologies. The identification of God's energy with God's will distinguishes the creative (and divinizing) emanations of God *ad extra* on the one hand from the inner-trinitarian begetting of the Son and the inner-trinitarian procession of the Spirit on the other. The inner-trinitarian processions are of God's trinitarian nature, that is, they are "necessary"; the emanations *ad extra* correspond to and give expression to the will of God.

It is quite correct to say, with Hildegard Schaeder, that "the reinterpretation of the Aristotelian concept of energy, in the service of giving expression to the connections between christology and salvation history, is fundamentally completed with John of Damascus."[47] Gregory Palamas, however, is the first to use this reinterpretation polemically. It is open to debate whether Barlaam, the main opponent of Palamas, represents a type of early humanism within Byzantine church and society,[48] or whether he stands closer to the western, Augustinian tradition.[49] It is agreed, though, that Palamas intends to defend a particular type of spirituality based on silent prayer (thus "hesychasm," derived from the Greek ἡσυχία) practiced by the monks of Mt. Athos. More specifically, Palamas wanted to defend the conviction that the encounter with God claimed by those who practiced this type of prayer was a real vision of God, not merely some natural phenomenon. Barlaam's attack on this conviction was based on the tradition of negative theology and the presupposition of God's aseity. In the course of the debate both Barlaam and Palamas relied heavily on the authority of Pseudo-Dionysius. It was very important for Palamas to emphasize the *bodily* experience of God's presence. Mystical encounter with God required of human beings an ascetic praxis and a type of prayer in which bodily posture and even the regulation of breathing played an important role. The presence of God was, again, experienced bodily as a vision of uncreated light—just as Moses had experienced that presence at the burning bush and as the three disciples experienced it upon the mount of the transfiguration. The transfiguration of nature—both the inanimate nature of the burning bush and the rational, human nature of Jesus—is effected by the divine

---

47. Schaeder, "Christianisierung." op. cit., p. 19.
48. So J. Meyendorff, *A Study of Gregory Palamas* (Leighton Buzzard, 1976).
49. So J. S. Romanides, "Notes on the Palamite Controversy," *GrOrthThR* 6 (1960–61): 186–205 and 9 (1963–64): 225–70.

energies. It is these same divine energies that become visible in the mystical vision of God—a vision that does not neglect or negate created nature, but in which it is transfigured and taken up into the life of God. This is a recognition of the divine nature of the human Jesus, a recognition also of the true end of all human beings, to be transformed into his likeness (1 John 3:2), a recognition also of the end and purpose of the whole creation to become new creation. The light of the transfiguration belongs, according to Palamas, neither to the world of ideas nor to the world of material things, because the light is uncreated, or divine, that is, beyond the categories of created being.

The main emphasis of Palamas's argument is on the *unmediated nature* of the self-revelation of God experienced mystically by human beings, as opposed to any need for a created mediator. To this end he took up the, by this stage, well attested distinction between the inaccessible inner being of God (κατ' οὐσίαν) and the economic activities of God (κατ' ἐνέργειαν). The course of the debate between Palamas and his opponents was influenced by political factors—a factor not unknown in other doctrinal decisions in church history, and therefore not something that can be condemned out of hand by any theology that claims to look back to a consensus of the first five centuries. The Synods of Constantinople in the years 1341 and 1351 decided in favor of Palamas, and in 1368, only nine years after his death, Palamas was canonized. Although the Palamite position was certainly neglected in Greek theology in the following centuries, largely as a result of Turkish conquest and western theological influences, it continued to hold an important place in the piety of many Orthodox,[50] not least the lay people and the monastics.

Let us try to sum up thus far. We find divergences appearing both between varying usage of the philosophical terms οὐσία, δύναμις and ἐνέργεια, and also between differing clusters of theological concerns or interests. In the West, there was the philosophical tendency to distinguish between δύναμις (in the sense of potentiality) and ἐνέργεια (in the sense of actuality). This later developed into a distinction between existence and essence. In the East the tendency was to treat δύναμις (understood as power) and ἐνέργεια (energy) as synonyms and to contrast both to essence (οὐσία).

Theologically, westerners tended to take the unity (or indeed simplicity) of God as an *a priori*, and with it an understanding of creation as ontologically other than God. The theological challenge was to prove this

---

50. G. A. Maloney, *A History of Orthodox Theology since 1453* (Belmont, 1976), pp. 131, 138, and 166.

simple divine unity to be a *trinitarian* unity. In the East the theological task was to clarify the relationship between God and the creation. This was the central question in the christological debates that were, generally speaking, taken more seriously in the East than in the West. For easterners it was the triunity of God that was taken as an *a priori*.

In the West, there was a tendency to treat the biblical bipolarity of God (God *a se* – God *pro nobis*) as a function of God's triunity, just as it generally had been in the East before Nicaea. By contrast, in the East any tendency to subordinationism was strongly resisted from the fourth century onward. The biblical bipolarity of God could therefore *not* be regarded as principally a function of God's triunity.

We could put it briefly in these terms: In the East, the trinitarian nature of God was taken for granted, and the task was to clarify the relationship between creator and creation. In the West the radical difference between creator and creation was taken for granted, and the task was to clarify how God could be trinitarian. The age from which we might have expected from Orthodox theology a vigorous defense of the trinitarian doctrine is the age of Islamic-Turkish hegemony, conveniently dateable from the fall of Constantinople in 1453. But this is also generally acknowledged as a time in which Greek theology was relatively stagnant. The need for a theological defense of the trinitarian doctrine becomes increasingly urgent also in the West from the beginning of the modern era. The reason is, by contrast, to be found in the effective loss of the doctrine of the trinity as such in modern western theology.

The distinction between the essence and the energies, or in other words, between the inner being of God the trinity and this God's economic activities, is thus since the time of John of Damascus a constant, if not always strongly emphasized, feature of Eastern Orthodox theology. In the West we do not find quite the same consistency. What we do find, since the time of Marius Victorinus, is the possibility of a speculative inner-trinitarian process without any *necessary* connection to the economy of salvation. Often, perhaps under the influence of the patristic distinction between *theologia* and *economia*, western theologians found it expedient to discuss the inner (or "immanent") trinity and the economic trinity under different headings. The ongoing debate with "the Greeks" about the *filioque* clause demanded, for the western position to remain fully coherent, a close correspondence between the trinitarian processions *ad intra* and the missions *ad extra*. As a consequence, this identity of economic and immanent doctrines of the trinity remained, in the West, the dominant position. The exception is the increasing area of thought where, in the words of Dietrich Ritschl, a "deep skepticism over the concept of the Trinity generally" obtained.[51] It is to this skepticism over the trinity generally in modern western thought that we now turn.

The Effective Loss of the Doctrine of the Trinity in the Modern Era

It is significant that a number of recent contributions[52] to trinitarian theology have opened with a discussion of the atheism, or the critique of the idea of God as such, that has been a feature of the modern era. Since the early seventeenth century there has been a growing tendency in western society to live, in Dietrich Bonhoeffer's words, *etsi Deus non daretur*,[53] as if there were no God, as if God were not one of the givens of life. This development has been well described by the authors cited, so no further sketch will be given here. But notice that nothing of this development implies that God is the trinitarian God. In fact, modern discussions of the God-problem from the seventeenth century onward do not seem to involve a doctrine of the trinity at all. The debate between theists and atheists, despite the great variety of positions taken under these broad headings, is conducted on the assumption of what David Brown has called a "unity model" of the trinitarian God. For the most part, it is effectively a unitarian God that is under discussion.

The modern era saw the beginnings of an effective loss of the doctrine of the trinity as such. After the Reformation, which gave only passing attention to this theme,[54] the Protestant scholasticism of the early seventeenth century took up the discussion of the trinity on the foundations of medieval scholasticism. The method was to demonstrate the existence of the one God, making use of the traditional proofs, and then to identify this God as a trinity of persons. Trinitarian speculation was regarded as secondary to and dependent upon the primary datum of God's existence as such. It was in no way seen as constitutive of God's being, nor was it regarded as having any

---

51. See Introduction, n. 16, above.

52. E.g., J. Moltmann, *The Crucified God* (London, 1974); E. Jüngel, *God as the Mystery of the World* (Grand Rapids, 1983); W. Kasper, *The God of Jesus Christ* (New York, 1991); J. O'Donnell, *The Mystery of the Triune God* (London, 1988). C. M. LaCugna (*God for Us* [San Francisco, 1991]), following D. Wendebourg ("From the Cappadocian Fathers to Gregory Palamas: the Defeat of Trinitarian Theology," in *TU* 17, no. 1 [1982]: 194-97), speaks specifically of a "defeat" of the doctrine of the trinity. Veronica Brady, in her book *A Crucible of Prophets: Australians and the Question of God* (Sydney, 1981), has shown how this modern critique of the concept of God is very much part and parcel of the Australian experience of God.

53. D. Bonhoeffer, *Letters and Papers from Prison* (3d ed. London, 1971), p. 360 (letter to E. Bethge, 16 July 1944).

54. F. C. Baur, *Die Christliche Lehre* (Tübingen, 1841), vol. 3, p. 47.

great bearing on the central themes of creation and salvation. The trinity was a matter of revealed information about God's inner being. Certainly it was an article of faith, but in a purely propositional sense. The nature of the inner relationships between the trinitarian persons did not really affect the things that were important for us human beings, the matter of Christ's life, death, and resurrection for our justification and the Spirit's indwelling for our sanctification.

At the same time, during the seventeenth century, deism in England called all speculative knowledge in question. It is hardly surprising that this whole dogmatic understanding of the trinity should come to be regarded as unnecessary speculation. Deism was an attempt to prove that Christianity was "not mysterious" (John Toland). It understood itself as a form of apologetic that salvaged that which it considered tenable, and gave up everything else. That which was not considered tenable in the light of modern reason was considered not to belong to Christian faith. The basic problem was that the western tradition had severed the psychological analogy of the trinity from the history of salvation, making it both independent and, in the last analysis, without soteriological significance.

This sense of the irrelevance of trinitarian doctrine found its clearest expression in the words of Immanuel Kant: "From the doctrine of the Trinity, taken literally, nothing whatsoever can be taken for practical purposes."[55] In other words, a trinitarian doctrine is not only an unnecessary, speculative addition to the doctrine of God, but an unhelpful one, from Kant's point of view. In fact the doctrine of the trinity, like atheism itself, could stand under suspicion of being morally and politically harmful. In the early modern absolutist state, one God corresponded to one monarch and one national loyalty. To talk of a possible threeness of persons was not only unnecessary speculation, but also politically risky. If God is a community of equals, might this not suggest that civil society should also be a community of equals? But the dissenters of the seventeenth and eighteenth centuries either failed to see this possibility or preferred not to explore it.

Kant's skepticism about the doctrine of the trinity as such is the background to Schleiermacher's denial of any speculative doctrine of the trinity beyond the economy of salvation. "We have no formula for the being of God in Godself other than the being of God in the world."[56] It is a

---

55. Cited in O'Donnell, *The Mystery of the Triune God*, op. cit., p. 128; Kasper, *The God of Jesus Christ*, op. cit., p. 371, note. 166.
56. F. D. E. Schleiermacher, *Der christliche Glaube*, vol. 2, 1831 (ed. M. Redeker, Berlin, 1960), p. 589. Cf. LaCugna: "We have no access to the immanent life of God that goes beyond what has been revealed" (op. cit., p. 211).

function of God's faithfulness, God's moral and ontological integrity, that God reveals Godself *as God is* and not otherwise. Our knowledge of God *a se* rests on our experience of God in the history of salvation. Even if this process did not lead to a total abandonment of the doctrine of the trinity, it implied nevertheless a thoroughgoing agnosticism with regard to any innertrinitarian relationships apart from those that may be deduced from the economy of salvation.

The trinitarian formula had, it seemed, been reduced to an example of pure speculation, in the negative sense of this word. The second half of the nineteenth century sees no significant systematic contributions to trinitarian thinking.[57] This situation changed in 1908, with a call by Reinhold Seeberg for a renewed discussion of the doctrine of the trinity, one which would be based on the doctrine of revelation.[58] Seeberg was building on Schleiermacher's work, not in the sense of reducing the status of this doctrine, but rather insisting on the need to set it on a firmer epistemological foundation. Seeberg's call was not taken up immediately, but it undoubtedly was a significant factor behind Karl Barth's, and somewhat differently, Karl Rahner's points of departure. Concealed in this new movement toward the recovery of trinitarian thinking was the old western theological axiom of the "denial of any separation between God in Godself and God in God's revelation."[59] This is still one of the ground-rules for most contemporary western commentators on the doctrine of the trinity.

---

57. I.e., after the three volume work by F. C. Baur, *Die christl. Lehre*, op. cit. Exceptions are perhaps the studies by H. B. Swete, *The Early History of the Doctrine of the Holy Spirit* (Cambridge, 1873) and *On the History of the Doctrine of the Procession of the Holy Spirit* (Cambridge, 1876); and by J. Langen, *Die Trinitarische Lehrdifferenz zwischen der abendländischen und der morgenländischen Kirche* (Bonn, 1876). Both Langen and Swete are concerned mainly with pneumatology, and specifically with the *filioque* question. An answer to this modern critique is supplied by Hegel's bold appropriation of a trinitarianism which is not only based on the analogy of human thought, but in which this analogy is understood really to explicate the life-history of what Hegel calls "absolute Spirit." This inner history in three distinct moments is also God's mission into the domain of human history, so that for Hegel, not only does the inner-trinitarian being of the Spirit become a fully economic trinity, but it is also the trinitarian structure of the world, insofar as this world is constituted by human history. Hegel's system, which regards eternal and temporal reality alike as the self-unfolding of absolute Spirit, assumes a very close correspondence between the inner and the economic trinity, and this forms a link between the western scholastic tradition and the trinitarian theologies of Barth and Rahner. See W. Pannenberg, "Die Subjektivität Gottes und die Trinitätslehre," *KerDo* 23 (1977): 30; and W. Schachten, "Das Verhältnis von 'immanenter' und 'ökonomischer' Trinität," *FranzS* 61 (1979): 15, n. 33.

58. *Zum dogmatischen Verständnis der Trinitätslehre* (Leipzig, 1908), p. 29.

59. K. Rosenthal, "Bemerkungen zur gegenwärtigen Behandlung der Trinitätslehre," *KerDo* 22 (1976): 138.

Even though the received wisdom about the priority of the economic doctrine of the trinity had in fact been convincingly challenged some years earlier in a book by Georg Kretschmar,[60] H. Mühlen, for example, writing in 1965 can say:

> The scriptures have nothing explicit to say about the inner-trinitarian procession of the Holy Spirit, though there is clear witness to the mission of the Spirit through the Father and the Son. From this, the tradition has developed the "inner trinity" on the basis of the "economic trinity." If the "economic trinity" were not in this specific perspective identical with the "immanent trinity," this development would be inappropriate, and we could make no statement whatsoever based on the scriptures about the inner-trinitarian procession of the Holy Spirit.[61]

However, already by the 1920s it had become impossible to ignore the renewal of Eastern Orthodox theology, and with it the Palamite distinction between essence and energy. The St. Sergius Institute in Paris was founded in 1925, and in the same year R. von Walter introduced hesychast spirituality into the world of western spirituality through his German translation of *The Way of a Pilgrim*.[62] In 1936 Georges Florovsky delivered an address in Athens[63] in which he urged upon Orthodox theologians a rediscovery of their own patristic roots. By using the term "patristic" Florovsky included the thought of Gregory Palamas.

Conclusions

The attempt has been made here to sketch the development of two diverging traditions of trinitarian thinking. Both look back to the

---

60. G. Kretschmar, *Studien zur frühchristlichen Trinitätstheologie* (Tübingen, 1956). Kretschmar's thesis has recently found support (apparently quite independently) in the quite similar findings of Margaret Barker (M. Barker, *The Great Angel: A Study of Israel's Second God* [London, 1992]). In light of Kretschmar's thesis we need to acknowledge the following point: We can speak of a pre-Nicene "economic" trinity only in the sense that this pre-Nicene model refers to the second and third persons of the trinity in order to speak of God's activities in the world. (The terms "persona/personae" had been in technical theological use at least since Tertullian). But this is not an economic trinity in the sense of a triadology that is consititutted by and works itself out within a process of going out and coming to some sort of fulfillment in relation to the world. It is not the economic trinity suggested by the (admittedly various) triadologies of Plotinus, Augustine, Hegel, and more recently, of Barth and Rahner. Rather this pre-Nicene triadology involves an immanent (though subordinationist) understanding of the trinity, regulated not by the history of salvation, but by the structure and language of worship.
61. H. Mühlen, "Person und Appropriation," *MThZ* 16 (1965): 51.
62. *Ein russisches Pilgerleben* (Berlin, 1925).
63. G. Florovsky, "Patristics and Modern Theology," in *Procès-verbaux du premier congrès de théologie orthodoxe a Athènes*, 29 Novembre–6 Decembre 1936 (ed. H. S. Alivisatos, Athens, 1939), pp. 238–42.

Aristotelian schema οὐσία–δύναμις–ἐνέργεια. The eastern model tends to draw a dividing line between οὐσία and δύναμις (in earlier writers) or between οὐσία and ἐνέργεια (in later writers). By οὐσία is meant the ineffable being of God in Godself; by δύναμις or ἐνέργεια the characteristic activity of God in relation to the creation, and in which the creation can participate—thus participating in the life of God. From this point of view any confusion of the essence with the energies of God would destroy either the ineffability of God (because God would be "brought down" to the level of creation) or the possibility of a real participation in the life of God (because God would be regarded as totally beyond us). The former alternative reduces God to little more than a creature; the latter tends to necessitate a created intermediary between God and ourselves. The theological emphasis in this eastern model is to clarify the status of the creation in relation to God, both in its existential predicament and with regard to its way to deification.

The western understanding of the trinity tends to follow Aristotle's major distinction between δύναμις and ἐνέργεια. This leads to a concept of God as pure actuality (*actus purus*), in which essence is not distinguished from attributes. There is also the tendency to understand the trinity by analogy to the structure of human thought, and this means, in the last analysis, the development of a speculative trinity independent of human concerns. In the wake of the effective loss of a trinitarian doctrine of God in the modern era, the only way to preserve a relevant doctrine of the trinity was to telescope together the concepts of God in Godself and God in relation to us. This is the theological emphasis of the western tradition as a whole.

It should be clear by now that we are not dealing with any false dichotomy here. Both the doctrine of energies and the identification of the inner and the economic trinity arise out of legitimate concerns. The Palamite position emphasizes the ineffable transcendence of God and, at the same time, a real possibility of the divinization of the creature. Western theology attempts, through the identity principle, to emphasize the faithfulness of God so that there can be no suggestion of another God beyond that God whose saving activity has been experienced in the life of the church.

Chapter 2
THE TWO POSITIONS IN TWENTIETH-CENTURY THEOLOGY

The Identity Principle in Barth and Rahner

Karl Barth holds closely together both the unity of essence in God on the one hand, and on the other the encounter between God and ourselves in Jesus Christ. "What is God as God, the divine individuality and characteristics, the *essentia* or 'essence' of God, is something which we shall encounter either at the place where God deals with us as Lord and Saviour, or not at all."[1] The divine essence, which is equated with characteristics, can be encountered. Even though it is neither visible not graspable, it can be experienced as grasping us. Barth takes from Polanus a description of the divine essence *a se*, without reference to creatures: *"essentia Dei est ipsa Deitas, qua Deus a se et per se absolute est et existit."*[2] One condition that is applied, however, is that we are not permitted to abstract this description from the trinity—and that means, for Barth, "from the act of divine revelation."[3] This in effect rules out any possibility of an idea of the trinitarian divine essence that might be distinguished from the economy of revelation. Barth's objection is to the possibility of an impersonal fourth element of divinity located beyond the three hypostases.

Thus God's essence is inaccessible to us. God *a se et per se* is greater than God in relation to us. Barth cites, with approval, the words of John Chrysostom that we do not know God immediately, according to his essence, in the way God knows Godself, or in the way the Son knows the Father.[4] Thus God has a certain aseity, in the sense of the freedom either to create or not to create a world, either to enter into dialogue with creatures or to refrain from such dialogue. For Barth, God's inaccessibility arises from the distinction between God's freedom and God's love. Although God's love is always given freely, and God's freedom is such that it always finds expression in love, it remains the case that God's freedom pertains to God in Godself,

---

1. K. Barth, *Church Dogmatics* (Edinburgh, 1936ff.), vol. 2/1, p. 261.
2. Ibid., citing Polanus.
3. Ibid.
4. *CD* 1/1, p. 202.

and God's love pertains to God for us. Freedom in God is a positive characteristic that refers to God's transcendent inaccessibility. It is God's necessary aseity.[5] The economic side of God, the side turned toward ourselves, is a function of God's love—which, of course, is also free in that it is not necessitated.

This essence, this "divine selfhood," is, however, encountered by human beings. For Barth, essence denotes divinity in general—albeit a personal divinity. "It is to the one single essence of God, which is not to be tripled by the doctrine of the Trinity, but emphatically to be recognized in its unity, that there also belongs what we call to-day the 'personality' of God."[6] And God's essence can include God's actions. "God's essence and His operation are not twain but one. God's operation or effect is His essence in its relation to the reality distinct from Him, whether about to be or already created."[7] Barth then introduces a notional distinction between essence and operation:

> All we can assert of God, all attributes we can assign to God, relate to these acts of His. And not to His essence as such. Although the operation of God is the essence of God, it is necessary and important to distinguish His essence as such from His operation: in order to remember this operation is a grace, a free divine decision, also to remember that we can only know about God, because and so far as He gives Himself to our knowledge. God's operation is, of course, the operation of the whole essence of God. God gives Himself to man entirely in His revelation. But not in such a way as to give Himself a prisoner to man. He remains free, in operating, in giving Himself.[8]

Here the notion of "essence as such" refers to the aseity of God, and Barth retains this element of God's aseity—as God's freedom. At the same time, however, Barth also insists that the God who reveals Godself to us could be no other than the God who lives in perfect freedom. God—in faithfulness—reveals Godself exactly as God is, and not otherwise. Thus it is that the divine essence can be experienced or encountered by human beings. Essence includes, for Barth, "essence as such" (*Wesen als solches*) and acts (*Wirken*). Essence means Godhead, albeit personal, trinitarian, self-revealing Godhead.

> We may unhesitatingly equate the concept of the lordship of God, with which we found the whole Biblical concept of revelation to be related, with what in the language of the ancient Church is called the essence of God, the *deitas* or *divinitas*,

---

5. Ibid., p. 426.
6. Ibid., p. 403.
7. Ibid., p. 426.
8. Ibid.

the divine οὐσία, *essentia, natura*, or *substantia*. The essence of God is the being of God *qua* divine being. The essence of God is the godhead of God.[9]

Human encounter with God, and thus our knowledge of God, is consequent upon the actions of God as our Lord and Savior. We have no natural access to God, no natural capacity to know God or to speak of God. This point of Barth's must be understood within the context of his polemic against natural theology. We can speak of God only within the church, that is, only within the community of those who have been encountered and brought together by God's word, and who continue to be moved by it. In contrast to any system that postulates a natural point of contact (*Anknupfüngspunkt*) between God and humanity, Barth insists that it is possible to know God only where God graciously reveals Godself as Lord and Savior; that is, as the one who has absolute ontological priority in relation to us, who reconciles us[10] and sets us free.[11] God reconciles us to Godself and sets us free, *for Godself*.

The point is, for Barth, that God gives not just *information about* Godself, but gives God's *self*. It is a result of God's exercise of absolute freedom, "that God can become so unlike Himself that He is God in such a way as not to be bound to His secret eternity and eternal secrecy, but also can and will and really does assume temporal form—this ability, desire, and real action of God we might now regard as a first confirmation of our sentence, God reveals Himself as Lord."[12]

Barth's understanding of revelation allows him to pose certain questions, especially in the light of this emphasis on our natural incapacity to hear God's word.[13] *Who* is this God, who overcomes our natural incapacity to hear God's word? How does it come about, how is it actualized, that this God reveals the divine self? What effect does this self-revelation have on the human person who is encountered by it? These questions have to be answered together, according to Barth,[14] and his discussion of these essentially methodological questions opens up the way to his trinitarian thinking.

> God reveals Himself. He reveals Himself through Himself. If we wish really to regard the revelation from the side of its subject, God, then above all we must

---

9. Ibid., p. 401.
10. Ibid., pp. 457ff
11. Ibid., pp. 513ff.
12. Ibid., p. 367.
13. Ibid., p. 255: "The possibility of knowing the Word of God lies in the Word of God and nowhere else."
14. Ibid., pp. 339–40.

understand that this subject, God, the Revealer, is identical with His act in revelation, identical also with its effect. This is the at first merely indicative fact from which we get the hint to begin the doctrine of revelation with the doctrine of the Triune God.[15]

Correspondingly, revelation, or rather, self-revelation, is for Barth "the root of the doctrine of the trinity." Revelation occurs insofar as God speaks. "Revelation is *Dei loquentis persona*."[16] The word of God which is spoken in the act of revelation is identical with Godself; it is God's self-expression. Because we have no natural capacity to hear the word, the capacity to hear must itself be received from God. There must therefore be an objective and a subjective side to revelation—the objective word and the subjective reception, where God, in the act of coming to the human being, comes to Godself and encounters Godself in the human person.[17] God is thus the one who makes Godself present in the event of revelation—not merely objectively, in the word, but also subjectively, in that God effects a response to the word. Only in this way do we become capable of hearing the word of God (*capax verbi divini*).

This process of revelation reflects an inner-trinitarian self-repetition, a *repetitio aeternus in aeternitate*[18] within Godself. Revelation thus occurs in an order of three moments which in turn reflect the inner-divine order of three "modes of being" (*Seinsweisen*).[19] Barth allows the term "person" to be applied to the trinitarian modes of being only out of respect for the traditional use of this term in trinitarian theology. The concept of the personhood of the trinitarian persons becomes problematic from the moment Barth speaks of God in terms of *a* person, the *"persona Dei."* But the three modes of being are not to be reduced to the level of mere economic activities. They are modes of *being* or *existence*,[20] not merely modes of God's economic activity.

Barth's understanding of the trinity bases itself on a particular concept of revelation. God goes out of God's eternal hiddenness in a twofold movement, objectively in the Word and subjectively in the Spirit. But this understanding of revelation remains unsatisfactory at a fundamental level, because we remain incapable—of our own human nature—to receive God's word. In other words, God remains absolutely, not merely relatively,

---

15. Ibid., p. 340.
16. Ibid., p. 349.
17. Ibid., pp. 516ff.
18. Ibid., p. 406.
19. Ibid., p. 407 (K. Barth, *Die Kirchliche Dogmatik* [Zürich, 1932ff.], vol. 1/1, p. 374).
20. Ibid., pp. 412ff.

inaccessible. It is despite this absolute inaccessibility that God has, however, revealed Godself. The economy of revelation corresponds to the inner-trinitarian "economy"[21] or order. To the two basic economic acts of God in self-revelation correspond the inner-trinitarian activity in the two distinct processions.[22]

If the identity principle is in Barth the implicit methodological principle, in Rahner it becomes quite explicit. "The 'economic' Trinity *is* the 'immanent' Trinity," and vice versa.[23] With the help of this so-called basic thesis or axiom (*Grundthese, Grundaxiom*) Rahner attempts both to overcome the division between the unity and the triunity of God, and thus to establish the doctrine of the trinity firmly on the basis of the history of salvation. Rahner identifies the New Testament term ὁ θεός with the trinitarian hypostasis of God the Father.[24] The Son—Rahner prefers the term "Logos"—and the Spirit are the "distinct modes (or manners) of subsisting" (*Subsistenzweisen*),[25] or "modes of God's givenness" (*Gegebenheitsweisen*)[26] through which the Father ("God as such")[27] expresses himself outwardly. God thus communicates Godself in a threefold way, with the incarnation of the Word and the sending of the Spirit understood as moments of the *one* self-communication of God.[28] These two moments both refer to one another and distinguish themselves from one another. Although the incarnation of the Logos and the sending of the Spirit have their basis in a free decision of God, there is between these two events a necessary relationship so that there can be no comparison of the moments, no reduction of the two events to *mere* events without significance for salvation history.[29] Thus to become incarnate should be regarded as the *proper* mission of the Son; to be sent is the *proper* mission of the Spirit.[30]

---

21. Ibid., p. 407.
22. Ibid., pp. 426ff.
23. K. Rahner, *The Trinity* (Burns and Oates, 1970), p. 22. (K. Rahner, "Der dreifaltige Gott als transzendenter Urgrund der Heilsgeschichte," in J. Feiner and M. Löhrer [eds], *Mysterium Salutis: Grundriß Heilsgeschichtlicher Dogmatik,* Band 2 [Einsiedeln, 1967], p. 328).
24. K. Rahner, *Theological Investigations* (London, 1961ff.), vol. 1, pp. 79–148, esp. pp. 125ff.
25. Ibid., vol. 16, p. 258 (*Schriften zur Theologie* [Einsiedeln, 1954ff.], vol. 12, p. 323); and Rahner, *Trinity,* op. cit., p. 109 (*Myst. Sal.,* p. 389).
26. Rahner, *Foundations of Christian Faith: an Introduction to the Idea of Christianity* (London, 1978) p. 137 (*Grundkurs des Glaubens: Einführung in den Begriff des Christentums* [Freiburg im Breisgau, 1976], p. 142).
27. K.Rahner, *Trinity,* op. cit., p. 64.
28. Ibid., pp. 84–85.
29. Ibid., pp. 85–86.
30. *Investigations,* vol. 4, pp. 77–102.

God communicates Godself as a person,[31] with two moments of self-communication on the part of this one person. In this way Rahner's system distinguishes between God in Godself and God for us. God the Father is God in Godself, and God in relation to us is located in the Son and the Spirit. But this means neither that God the Father fails to communicate himself (this self-communication takes places in the two moments), nor that the Son and the Spirit are confined to the economy of salvation (because the missions *ad extra* presuppose the processions *ad intra*). Rahner goes on to explain the divine self-communication by way of four "double aspects" (*Doppelaspekten*),[32] which are also of symbolic importance for the human person. These are past and future; history and transcendence; offer and acceptance; knowledge and love. In a difficult piece of argumentation, Rahner connects the concepts of past, history, offer, and knowledge on the one hand, and on the other, the concepts of future, transcendence, acceptance, and love. Thus the four double-aspects are reduced to two "fundamental modalities of divine self-communication" (*Grundmodalitäten göttlicher Selbstmitteilung*),[33] or "basic activities of the Spirit" (*Grundvollzüge des Geistes*).[34] These are then identified as the self-communication as knowledge (in the Logos) and as love (in the Spirit).

Because God communicates Godself as a person, this self-communication presupposes a personal recipient or addressee.[35] God has made human beings in such a way as to be capable of receiving God's self-communication. The four double aspects are marks not only of the self-communicating God but also of the human person. The one side of the coin (past, history, offer, and knowledge) represents that element of personality that steps beyond itself. The other side (future, transcendence, acceptance, love) represents the open, receptive element of human personhood. Thus the double aspects give us a duality of word and response, of going out and return. They correspond to Barth's objective and subjective sides of revelation; and even more closely they resemble the second and third moments of Absolute Spirit in Hegel's system.[36] Though in other places[37] Rahner is highly critical of the Augustinian psychological trinity, and has attempted to return to the pre-Augustinian trinitarian schema, here he connects what amounts to the

---

31. Rahner, *Trinity*, op. cit., p. 89.
32. Ibid., pp. 88ff. (*Myst. Sal.*, pp. 374ff.).
33. Ibid., p. 98 (*Myst. Sal.*, p. 381).
34. Ibid., p. 116 (*Myst. Sal.*, p. 394).
35. Ibid., p 88.
36. G. W. F. Hegel, *Phänomenologie des Geistes* (ed. J. Hoffmeister, Hamburg, 1952), p. 533.
37. Rahner, *Trinity*, op. cit., pp. 115ff.; Qv. *Foundations*, op. cit., pp. 135ff.

psychological model very closely with Barth's concept of revelation—with which Rahner is in fundamental agreement. The major difference between Barth and Rahner is to be found in the area of anthropology; specifically the question of the natural human capacity or incapacity to hear the word of God. Rahner's doctrine of the trinity is to be located firmly within the tradition that runs from Augustine to Aquinas to Hegel to Barth.

Rahner gives equal weight to the aseity of God the Father, to the self-communication of the Logos as offer of the truth, and to the self-communication of the Spirit as reception of love. The self-communication of the triune God reveals God *as God is* in and for Godself. That is, the Father is also revealed through the Son and in the Spirit. The Son and the Spirit are not confined to the economy of salvation, but also subsist in God *a se*. Teaching about the inner being of God (θεολογία) is determined by the economy (οἰκονομία) of salvation. God *a se* gives Godself "in a most radical manner."[38] Thus Barth's understanding of the trinity is brought to a logical conclusion by Rahner, and given expression in Rahner's often repeated "basic axiom"—of the identity of inner and economic trinity.

God communicates Godself because God is merciful. Revelation is a function of God's grace, God's generosity. But grace is not simply to be identified with God's self-communication. Rahner discusses the question of grace in dialogue with the Roman Catholic scholastic tradition. In accord with this tradition he allows a concept of created grace, but contrary to the tradition he gives priority to uncreated grace.[39] Uncreated grace is the indwelling of the Spirit—indeed it is the property of the Spirit (*Besitz des Pneumas*).[40] Created grace is no presupposition for this indwelling of the Spirit. There is no supernatural but created *habitus* to bridge the gap between God and humanity. Created grace is simply the outworking of God's indwelling in the "graced" human life. It *is* the indwelling of God in the creature. This distinction between uncreated and created grace allows Rahner to postulate a uniting of God and the human subject without endangering the fundamental ontological difference between creator and creature. Rahner can thus hold together the ongoing creatureliness of even the divinized creature.

Mystical experience plays a role in Rahner's theology. It is the result of the working of grace within human life, and is therefore nothing unusual.[41]

---

38. *Investigations*, vol. 9, p. 130.
39. Ibid., vol. 1, pp. 322–25.
40. Ibid., vol. 1, p. 334 (*Schriften* 1, p. 362). But note also that Rahner, in this essay and elsewhere, is careful to deny any *simple* identification of grace and the Holy Spirit.
41. Ibid., vol. 17, pp. 98–99.

Uncreated grace embraces the human person, so that created grace can grow within the human life. But these two forms of grace are not strictly to be distinguished—and certainly not within the event of being graced with mystical experience. In this way Rahner seeks to establish a western mystical theology that can enter into a genuine dialogue with that of the eastern tradition.[42]

The Doctrine of Energies in Florovsky and Lossky

In his address to the 1936 gathering of Orthodox theologians in Athens, Georges Florovsky pointed to the doctrine of energies as one of the truths that needed to be rediscovered by Orthodox theology.[43] The major part of Florovsky's work on this theme is to be found in three papers: *"Tvar' i Tvar'nost'"* (1928),[44] "The Idea of Creation in Christian Philosophy" (1949),[45] and "The Concept of Creation in Saint Athanasius" (1962).[46] The first and the last of these papers will be examined here.

The starting point of *"Tvar' i Tvar'nost'"* is the argument that the idea of a contingent world arises out of the biblical doctrine of creation. The world does not have to exist. In fact the creation finds its basis in the *will* of God, not the nature or essence of God.[47] This distinction between nature/essence and will becomes the basis, for Florovsky, for a defense of the distinction between essence and energy. That which is of God by nature, or essence (e.g. the generation of the second person of the trinity) is necessary; that which is in accordance with God's will (viz. the creation of the world) is contingent. The former *must* be; the second *may* be, but need not.

The anti-Arian argument of the fourth century depends, according to Florovsky, upon this distinction.[48] To see the begetting of the Son as dependent upon God's will would be to make the Son contingent and thus, in the end, a creature. To suggest that the creation takes its being from an act of the nature or essence of God would be to view the creation as necessary. Either way the difference between creator and creature would be

---

42. Ibid.
43. G. V. Florovsky, "Patristics and Modern Theology" in H. S. Alivisatos (ed.) *Procès-verbaux du Premier Congrès de Théologie Orthodoxe a Athènes* (Athens, 1939), p. 239.
44. First published in *Pravoslavnaja mysl'* 1 (1928): 176–212. Quotes here are from the English translation, "Creation and Creaturehood," in *Collected Works* (Belmont, 1972 ff.), vol. 3.
45. Florovsky, "The Idea of Creation in Christian Philosophy," *ECQ* 8 (1949; [Supplementary Issue: Nature and Grace): 53–77.
46. Florovsky, "The Concept of Creation in Saint Athanasius," *TU* 81 (1962): 36–57.
47. Florovsky, "Creation and Creaturehood," op. cit., p. 48.
48. Ibid., p. 47.

lost. The former alternative reduces the Son to the status of a creature. The latter raises the creation to the status of an emanation of the Godhead, as in neo-Platonism, and though this creation may indeed stand at a lower level, it is ontologically no different from the Godhead itself. The difference between essence and will is thus indispensable for a correct doctrine of creation. Further, the difference must be a "real" distinction, if we are to characterize the difference between creator and creature as "real." Florovsky thus sets the parameters for the doctrine of creation that avoid either a Platonic denial of the world's reality on the one hand or, on the other, a pantheistic divinization of the world.[49] God constantly seeks to invite and draw the creation into a community with Godself. The actualization of this community is no foreordained necessity, but rather manifests the freedom of the creature,[50] for the creature can exist without any such community. The creature can exist, but not exactly *live*. Its decision not to embark on a journey of ever deepening communion with God would mean for the creature a type of "metaphysical suicide,"[51] an existence without life. The creative activity of God is thus characterized, on several levels, by freedom. First there is the freedom either to create or not to create a world and, corresponding to it, the freedom of the creature either to live or not to live. *This* is the question for the creature. The eternal activity of God that brings the creation into existence limits the freedom of the creation on one side. From God's side, the creation is contingent. But from the creation's side it has no choice but to be; its choice is one between mere being and life. On this basis the creation is seen to be preserved beyond the limits imposed by temporality. Its preservation is assured by the divine "let there be" (Genesis 1:3)—an eternal *fiat* that holds the power to preserve the creature beyond the limits of time and into the dimension of eternity.[52] Life—which the creature is free to reject or embrace—means for Florovsky the attaining of one's proper perfection, the completeness that has been foreseen by God and that exists, as an ideal, already in the mind of God. This life is participation in the life of God. Here we touch on the domain of the energies—which is also the domain of creaturely freedom. It stands in contrast to the inner being of God, the domain of necessity, to which the begetting of the Son and the procession of the Spirit belong, for God is trinitarian not by will but by *nature*.

---

49. Though these two positions are, as Florovsky himself points out, not so different from one another; ibid., pp. 61–62.

50. Ibid., p. 48.

51. Ibid., p. 49.

52. Ibid., p. 45.

The second part of the article is a discussion of Origen's doctrine of creation. Although God has created the world in perfect freedom, that is, the act of creation is conditioned by God alone,[53] it is not quite so simple to prove the absence of any *inner* necessity on God's part—even within this self-conditioned action of God *ad extra*.[54] Is there perhaps an inner dynamic within the processions that necessarily leads into missions and demands the creation of a world? To posit such an inner necessity is precisely the error of Origen, according to Florovsky. Florovsky's argument is based on the metaphysical concept of God's immutability. Origen's system must involve a certain necessity in relation to the economic activities, the missions. Otherwise the creative act would introduce a new element—that of mutability—into the Godhead, and God would not essentially be creator and preserver. But Origen starts from the opposite *a priori*, viz. that God is immutable. God must always have been creator, therefore there must always have been a creation. God must always have been the holder of all (παντοκράτωρ)—therefore there must always have been an *all* (τὰ πάντα).[55] Florovsky critiques Origen—or at least the position he attributes to Origen—by calling in question such a logical connection between processions and missions, or in other words, between the essence of God and God's economic actions.

We could easily argue against the eternity of the creation itself, but can we, Florovsky asks, so easily deny the eternal *idea* of a creation?

> The difficulty is only shelved, but not solved, if we limit ourselves to the chronological beginnings of the actual existence of the world, since, in this case, the *possibility* of the world, the *idea* of the world, God's design and will concerning it, still remains eternal and as though conjointly everlasting with God.[56]

In the face of this difficulty, Florovsky insists that the denial of any suggestion of a *necessary* actual creation must also be extended to include the eternal possibility of a creation. The idea of a creation may be an eternal idea, but it cannot be an idea that demands its own necessary actualization.

---

53. Ibid., p. 52: "God creates in perfect freedom . . . . In Creation God is determined only by Himself." It is to be noted, however, that this distinction between nature and will *within God* is historically not totally unproblematic. It was first developed by Athanasius in his highly questionable polemic against the Eusebians. See L. Abramowski, "Die dritte Arianerrede des Athanasius: Eusebianer und Arianer und das westliche Serdicense," in *ZKG* 102 (1991): 389–413.

54. C. V. Florovsky, "Creation and Creaturehood," op cit., p. 52: "But it is not so easy to demonstrate the absence of any *internal* necessity in this self-determination, in the revelation of God *ad extra*."

55. Ibid., p. 53. Qv. Florovsky, "Maximos und der Origenismus," in *Diskussionsbeiträge zum XI. Internationalen Byzantinistenkongreß*, München, 1958, p. 39.

56. Florovsky, "Creation and Creaturehood," op. cit., p. 56.

> The idea of the world, God's design and will concerning the world, is obviously eternal, but not *co-eternal, and not conjointly everlasting* with Him, because "distinct and separated," as it were, from His "essence" by His volition. One should say rather that the Divine idea of the world is eternal by *another kind* of eternity than the Divine essence.[57]

That is to say, God *becomes* creator. The attribute "creator" is an eternal, not merely a temporal, attribute. In this way Florovsky is able to characterize God as—in some sense—eternally creative. But it does not belong to God's essential nature; rather to God's economic nature. So there is another sense in which we *cannot* say that God *became* creator.

> No outward revelation whatever belongs to the 'necessity' of the Divine nature, to the necessary structure of the intra-Divine life. And creative revelation is not something imposed upon God by His goodness. It is executed in perfect freedom, though in eternity also. Therefore it cannot be said that God began to create, or "became" Creator....[58]

The argument makes sense only in the light of a distinction between the divine essence and the eternal attributes of God, attributes which find expression, *ad extra*, in the creation. This is the only possible way through the apparent contradictions of "*eternal* but in some sense not *coeternal*"; and "eternal by another kind of eternity than the Divine essence."[59] If essence were simply to be identified with attribute, this way of speaking would not be possible. The eternal freedom of God either to create or not to create a world, this eternal freedom is located in the domain of the energies. It is the energies that are *eternal* but not *coeternal* in the sense that the Son and the Spirit are coeternal with the Father. The eternity of the energies is other than the eternity of the divine essence. "'To be Creator' does not belong to those definitions of Divine nature which include the Trinity of Hypostases."[60] We are dealing here with a distinction within God between the plane of the trinitarian hypostases and the—so to say, subordinate—plane of the divine names or attributes.[61] Thus there is a hierarchy within the trinitarian nature between the inner being and the subordinate, freely-willed activities of this same trinity. The doctrine of energies has its basis in the distinction between necessity and will. Florovsky expands on this point in his 1959 lecture on Gregory Palamas, delivered in Thessalonika.[62] The

---

57. Ibid.: "He as it were 'becomes' Creator."
58. Ibid., pp. 57–58.
59. Ibid., p. 56.
60. Ibid., p. 58.
61. Ibid.
62. Florovsky, "St. Gregory Palamas and the Tradition of the Fathers," *CW*, vol. 1, p. 118.

distinction between essence and energy *is* in fact the distinction between necessity (or nature—as Florovsky would prefer to call it) and will. This in turn becomes the foundation for a proper ontological differentiation between God and the creation. The begetting of the Son and the spiration of the Holy Spirit are of (God's) nature (κατὰ φύσιν); the creation of the world is an act or energy of the will—a βουλήσεως ἔργον.[63] This means, in general, that the—for Florovsky—very important distinction between necessity and will[64] cannot be considered in isolation from the doctrine of energies. The idea of the world is fully *in* God, but the actual, created world is not. The actual world is thought of as being "beside" or "outside of" God.[65] The idea of the world exists in a "free" or contingent eternity, not an eternity of nature or necessity[66] like the three trinitarian hypostases. A "kind of contingency"[67] is thus attributed to the *idea* of creation. In turn, the eternal idea of a world is distinguished from the actual, created world. In this way a pantheistic continuity between the Godhead and the world is avoided.[68]

---

63. Ibid., p. 119.

64. That is, within God. There is another distinction between necessity and will in human beings and in the creation, whereby the energy or will of God can have a necessary effect in the world. See Florovsky, "Redemption," *CW,* vol. 3, p. 98; and "The 'Immortality' of the Soul," *CW,* vol. 3, p. 233. Human nature is of necessity taken up by God and made whole in the incarnation. Human sin, however, that is based in the human will, is borne by Christ out of free love. The human will is called, but not compelled, into a correspondence with Christ's will.

65. Florovsky, "Creation and Creaturehood," op. cit., pp. 46–47. Qv. p. 58: "the idea of the world and the world of ideas are totally *in God,* ἐν τῷ θεῷ, and in God there is not, and there cannot be, anything of the created."

66. Ibid., p. 59: "a free eternity"; but "not an eternity of essence."

67. Ibid.

68. Ibid., pp. 61–62. Cf. Florovsky, "Idea of Creation," op. cit., p. 65: "The idea of the world *is in God,* and the world itself is *outside God.* The fundamental error of the pantheists consists exactly in their identifying the *idea* and this existential itself: then it would be the Divine idea as such which would be developed in time and be the *subject* of the temporal processes; then again, the 'substance' of things would be a 'substantial' revelation of God's own being and existence; then God *Himself* would be involved in the process of the world. On the contrary, we have to insist on the basic fact that *the idea is not the germ* of things at all. The 'germ' of things comes precisely out of nothing, i.e. is created. The idea of things is their *transcendent* 'image' or *exemplar,* and their norm—not an immanent one. Creation consists in God's calling 'out of nothing' (ἐξ οὐκ ὄντων) into existence a new reality, which becomes the bearer or carrier of His idea, without being ever existentially identified with it—which must and can actualize the idea, in the creaturely order of existence, by its own proper becoming what it was meant and foreordained to become. The created world is an 'exterior' object of the Divine thought, and not this thought itself. It participates in the idea, in so far as it is conformed to it. But even in this participation there is no confusion of the orders of existence. Thus the own reality of the created world is fully secured." Cf. J. D. Zizioulas, *Being as Communion:*

In the third section of the article—a section which could not be rightly understood without the earlier sections—Florovsky discusses the doctrine of energies itself. He begins by distinguishing two types of attributes or names of God,[69] both of which have their basis in activities. First there are the inner attributes, viz. Father, Son, and Holy Spirit, who receive their being from the inner acts of generation and procession. Second, there are the outer attributes, which receive their being from outer acts of the entire trinity. Thus we have the distinction between divine nature or essence on the one hand, and the divine will, which is located "beyond the essence."[70] This distinction (Florovsky insists that it is not a separation) is, of course, that which underlies all Palamite theology.

Florovsky criticizes any trinitarian thinking that suggests a link between the aseity of God and the hypostasis of the Father alone, and locates the economic revelation of God in the Son and the Spirit. This, according to Florovsky, opens the door to subordinationism and, worse, allows "cosmological motifs"[71] a place in the doctrine of the trinity. Behind such a grounding of the Son and the Spirit in God's economic activity would lie the suggestion that the trinitarian processions are contingent. This, for Florovsky, is the decisive problem with every attempt to develop a doctrine of the trinity on the basis of the economy. In the place of the earlier economic models,[72] the fathers of the fourth century developed a new model in which the general attributes of God lie in the domain of the energies, while the aseity of the trinity lies within the domain of the essence. The energies constitute a divine presence, a "providential ubiquity," that is neither the specific, "charismatic" presence of God, for example in the eucharist[73] (though presumably this must be a type of "energetic" presence), nor the being of God in Godself. The *energetic* being of God and the being of God in Godself are the two divine "forms of existence."[74] The energy is

---

Studies in Personhood and the Church (New York, 1985), p. 91.
69. Florovsky, "Creation and Creaturehood," op. cit., p. 62.
70. Ibid., p. 63.
71. Or "motives"—Florovsky, or perhaps his translator, uses both terms interchangeably.
72. Qv. chapter 1, n. 60, above. Florovsky's article predates Kretschmar's *Studien zur frühchristlichen Trinitätstheologie* (with its critique of the older understanding of early trinitarianism as being fundamentally economic) by almost three decades. In any case, Florovsky is referring to the subordinationist trinitarianisms of Irenaeus and Origen, in which the Son and the Spirit are seen to function economically as agents of God the Father.
73. Florovsky, "Creation and Creaturehood," op. cit., pp. 65f.
74. Ibid., p. 66: These two "forms of existence" *in God* are not to be confused with the two *fundamental* "forms of existence," viz. the uncreated and the created. Both the energy and the essence of God are *uncreated*.

understood as a "procession"⁷⁵ from Godself—not like the personal or "hypostatic" processions of the Son and the Spirit, but rather as the procession of grace and, indeed, particular graces. These graces are the attributes of God which become the fundamental life-giving principles of all created things. The energy is "that aspect of God which is turned towards creation."⁷⁶ It is "essence-producing" (οὐσιοποιὸς),⁷⁷ in that it creates the essence of creatures. Florovsky again here connects the distinction between essence and energy with a corresponding understanding of creation. If the distinction becomes unclear, then the difference between generation and creation is lost. The distinction maintains a dividing line between God's being and God's possessing. "God is Life, and has Life; is Wisdom, and has Wisdom; and so forth. The first series of expressions refers to the incommunicable essence, the second to the inseparably distinct energies of the one essence, which descend upon creation."⁷⁸

The inner being of God must, accordingly, be considered outside of any connection with created being, either creation or new creation:

> God is free in His operations and acts. And therefore for a dogmatic confession of the reciprocal relations between the Divine Hypostases, expressions must be found such as will exclude cosmological motives, any relation to created being and its destinies, any relation to creation or re-creation.⁷⁹

Florovsky admits that this is very far from the intentions of the pre-Nicene fathers, and sees a real danger in their economic subordinationism. "The ground of Trinitarian being is not in the economy or revelation of God *ad*

---

75. Florovsky, "St. Gregory Palamas," op. cit., p. 117: "Energies 'proceed' from God and manifest His own Being. The term προιέναι (proceed) simply suggests διάκρισιν (distinction), but not a division."

76. Florovsky, "Creation and Creaturehood," op. cit., p. 67: "The divine energies are that aspect of God which is turned towards creation."

77. Ibid., p. 66.

78. Ibid., p. 68. Cf. Florovsky, "Idea of Creation," op. cit., p. 65–66: "The Idea of Creation, of a Divine 'outside,' a Divine 'non-ego,' obviously does not belong to the intrinsic plenitude of the Divine being—it is not produced in virtue of the 'natural fecundity' of God, for in this case it would be a sort of 'fourth hypostasis'—a supposition impious and sacrilegious. It has been produced from all eternity, but in a supreme freedom, by an act of will. We can dare to say that this idea might not have been produced as well. Certainly it is for us a *casus irrealis*, a wholly formal possibility. But it helps us to understand the full meaning of the idea of Creation. We may say also that the Trinitarian being is an intrinsic revelation of the Divine essence, that it is eminently necessary—and perhaps, there is nothing necessary, in the strict and ultimate sense, except the Holy Trinity, consubstantial and indivisible. God *is* Trinity. And He *has* His idea of the Creation—from all eternity. Still, there is an ultimate difference between the 'is' and the 'has.' Otherwise we would deny His creative freedom."

79. Florovsky, "Creation and Creaturehood," op. cit., p. 69.

extra. The mystery of the intra-Divine life should be conceived in abstraction from the dispensation."⁸⁰ Thus the Son and the Holy Spirit may be characterized only in terms of their trinitarian relations. Any relation to the world comes later. "The predicates referring to the economy of salvation do not coincide with those predicates by which the Hypostatic Being of the Second Person is defined."⁸¹ The divine intention for creation and new creation is indeed a *divine* intention, but this does not mean it belongs to the essential necessity of the divine nature. On the contrary, it is a freely willed external intention. If this were not so, God's grace would not be grace and God's love would not be given freely.

At the end of the article Florovsky offers an interpretation of this divine intention. The idea of participation in God is the final purpose of creatures. All things are in God, that is, in the energy of God, ἐν ἰδέᾳ καὶ παραδείγματα. And the energy embraces the ideas of all things.⁸² The idea surpasses created nature and calls it to the fullest harmony with itself.⁸³ This is the deification (θέωσις or θεοποίησις) of which the Greek church fathers speak. It is not some sort of transubstantiation of the creature into the essence of God in Godself. Rather, deification is spoken of as becoming a child (υἱοθεσία) through adoption and grace, in contrast to being a child by nature. Christ alone is God's child by nature. The doctrine of deification is not to be understood without the qualifier supplied by the doctrine of energies.

The article as a whole is concerned with the relationship between creator and creation. The new creation is the fulfillment of God's eternal intention for creatures. It comes about through the free act of God, according to Florovsky, but not without a corresponding free act on the part of the creature. This is not to say that the movement between God and creature

---

80. Ibid.
81. Ibid., p. 71.
82. Ibid., p. 73.
83. Ibid., p. 75. Cf. Florovsky, "Idea of Creation," op. cit., p. 74: the "goal (sc. of the human being) is exactly to surpass himself and to rise towards God, and even more than that—to partake in the Divine Life. It is only by this participation that man becomes fully himself. . . . However, for the full realization the free effort of man must be corroborated by the condescendence of grace. . . . The free effort and the grace are not separable in this ontological ascent or growth of the 'reasonable beings'—yet there is no confusion, nor composition—as it were, no 'transubstantiation' of the creature. The 'deification,' θέωσις, is precisely, so to say, an impregnation with grace, ἐκ χάριτος, κατὰ χάριν. . . . At this level of his ascent man becomes truly conformed with these uncreated prototypes, with the idea that God has of him from eternity—conformed, but never identical." The idea of creation, for Florovsky, is not some Platonic form, but rather the promised final purpose of creation.

runs equally in both directions. The trinitarian hypostases may not be characterized on the basis of their economic relationships, but only on the basis of their relationships to one another.

To introduce "cosmological motifs" into the doctrine of the trinity—that is, any reference to the world—would merely serve to undermine the distinction between the second person of the trinity and the final status of the deified creature. In other words, it would mean either a reduction of the Son from his status as "only Son of the Father," or else—especially in the context of the doctrine of deification—it would make the creature eternal, without beginning. Florovsky's horror at such possibilities goes some way to explaining his constant polemic against what he calls "Origenism." In this article, Florovsky argues that the doctrine of energies is indispensable both for an appropriate doctrine of creation and for an appropriate doctrine of the trinity.

Many of the themes from "Creation and Creatorhood" are repeated in the 1962 article, "The Concept of Creation in Saint Athanasius."[84] This later article is not only a discussion of the Athanasian concept of creation, but also a systematic argument to the effect that being and act must, in God, be sharply distinguished. Once again the argument here is this: if speech about the inner being of God is identified with speech about the economy, or made dependent upon it, the distinction between that which is generated and that which is created will be lost.

Florovsky begins with the assertion that the notion of *creatio ex nihilo* was totally foreign to ancient Greek thought: "The idea of Creation was a striking Christian innovation in philosophy."[85] This meant that the cosmos was no longer to be understood solely on its own terms, but as having its basis in the will of God.[86] It is significant that Florovsky introduces the notion of will here. The "Creation of the world was conceived as a sovereign and 'free' act of God, and not as something that was 'necessarily' implied or inherent in God's own Being."[87] Florovsky argues further that Greek philosophy had to undergo a creative transformation if it was to bring to expression the new Christian revelation. Again he stresses the dangers inherent in the earlier economic trinitarian model that led directly to Origen. In particular, Origen is criticized for his identification of the economic name παντοκράτωρ with

---

84. Op. cit. (*TU* 81 [1962]: 36–57).

85. Ibid. p. 36.

86. Ibid., p. 37: "The cosmos was no more regarded as a 'self-explanatory' being. Its ultimate and intrinsic dependence upon God's will and action has been vigorously asserted."

87. Ibid.

the inner-trinitarian name πατήρ. "Παντοκράτωρ means just κύριος, the ruling Lord. And God could not be παντοκράτωρ eternally unless τὰ πάντα also existed from all eternity."[88] The Greek word παντοκράτωρ denotes the energy of the trinity, and does so more precisely, according to Florovsky, than the Latin *omnipotens* and its modern translations. "These latter terms emphasize just might or power. The Greek word stresses specifically the actual exercise of power."[89] The suggestion here is that already implicit in the Latin term *omnipotens* is a dangerous confusion of God's being and God's act.

In the long middle section of the essay, Florovsky discusses the specific contribution of Athanasius. Athanasius' sharp distinction between creator and creation places the Logos firmly on the side of the creator. The transcendence of the Logos is also distinguished from its creative economic activities. "The Logos is present in the world, but only 'dynamically', that is, by His 'powers.' In His own 'substance' He is outside of the world."[90] The conceptual schema of "essence" and "power," which was used in earlier Christian thinking to distinguish between the Father and the Logos, has been used systematically by Athanasius to a new end, viz. to distinguish between the inner being of God and God's economic activities:

> In St Athanasius it (sc. the distinction between essence and power) has a totally new connotation. It is never applied to the relationship between God and Logos.... It serves now a new purpose: to discriminate strictly between the inner Being of God and His creative and "providential" manifestation ad extra in the creaturely world.[91]

The energies represent God's will and grace by which the creation is held in existence. "God" here means the trinitarian God, because the inner-trinitarian processions have achieved an ontological priority to the non-hypostatic processions of the energies. The Son is no longer an economic instrument of the Father. "In creation He (sc. the Son) is not just an 'instrument,' ὄργανον. He is its ultimate and immediate efficient cause. His own Being is totally independent of creation, and even of the creative design of the world."[92] Thus the energy must be understood theologically as the energy of the whole undivided trinity. "God's 'Being' has an absolute ontological priority over God's action and will."[93] Athanasius' great

---

88. Ibid., p. 40.
89. Ibid., p. 39.
90. Ibid., p. 46. Florovsky speaks here in terms of "the energies of the Logos."
91. Ibid., p. 47.
92. Ibid.
93. Ibid., p. 48.

achievement was, according to Florovsky, the establishment of true θεολογία, that is, the doctrine of God as such; the doctrine of the inner trinity in contrast to the economic trinity. "What needed correction, in the age of St. Athanasius, was the total theological perspective. It was imperative to establish "Theology," that is—the doctrine of God, on its proper ground. The mystery of God, "Three in One," had to be apprehended in itself."[94] Only after this had been achieved could the creation come to be understood correctly as a reality distinct from God,[95] while at the same time essentially dependent upon God's grace. On the other hand, only when the doctrine of creation was firmly established could the doctrine of God satisfactorily give expression to the experience of God's people.[96] The divine and the created are two distinct "modes of existence,"[97] which can be described as necessary and contingent, or as unconditioned and conditioned. "The two modes of existence, the Divine and the creaturely, can be respectively described as 'necessary' and 'contingent,' or 'absolute' and 'conditional.' . . . This corresponds exactly to the distinction between the Divine Being and the Divine Will."[98] The distinction between the two "modes of existence" thus corresponds to the distinction in God between the two "forms of God's existence,"[99] viz. the essential and the energetic. In a short, closing section of the article this parallel is developed explicitly with reference to the Palamite terminology.

The heart of the matter for Florovsky is to oppose any trinitarian thinking that begins from God's action in the world. "There is nothing necessary, in the strict and ultimate sense, except the Holy Trinity."[100] This understanding of the trinity, developed without any reference to the economy of salvation, would seem every bit as questionable as Augustine's psychological trinity. But this inner trinity is also, for Florovsky, the dogmatic substantiation of (or

---

94. Ibid., p. 53.

95. That is, as a *reality*, as opposed to a mere phenomenon or illusion, as in Platonism. Florovsky, "Creation and Creaturehood," op. cit., p. 51: "Creation is neither self-existent being, nor transitory becoming; neither eternal 'substance,' nor illusory 'appearance.'"

96. Florovsky, "Offenbarung, Philosophie und Theologie," ZZ 9 (1931): 475: "A clear knowledge of God is impossible for us if we hold a false understanding of the world and of ourselves. There is nothing surprising in this. The world is God's creation, and if we attribute to God a work that he has not created, then we pass a faulty judgement on God's act and will."

97. Florovsky, "Concept of Creation in St. Athanasius" op. cit., p. 54.

98. Ibid., pp. 54–55.

99. Florovsky, "Creation and Creaturehood," op. cit., p. 66. Cf. "the ontological and cosmological dimensions" of God (Florovsky, "Concept of Creation in St. Athanasius," op. cit., p. 39); and the inner-trinitarian and economic "sets of names" (ibid., p. 48).

100. Florovsky, "Idea of Creation," op. cit., p. 66.

witness to) Jesus' identity as the incarnate Lord: "The Trinitarian invocation is required (that is, at baptism) because outside Trinitarian faith it is impossible to know Christ, to recognize in Jesus the Incarnate Lord, 'One of the Holy Trinity.'"[101] This doctrine of the trinity is thus a necessary intellectual formulation of the church's experience of Jesus as Lord. It is "dogma," and "dogma is in no way a new revelation. Dogma is merely witness."[102] The formulation of dogma, however, is a necessary byproduct of the translation of Hebraic revelation into the Greek language and way of thinking. "We can simply say: with the formulation of dogmas the church gave expression to revelation in the language of Greek philosophy. Or, if you prefer, the church translated revelation out of the poetic, prophetic Hebrew speech into Greek."[103] Thus for Florovsky the doctrine of the trinity refers not merely to the being of God; rather, it is intimately bound up with that which the church has experienced, and gives to this experience systematic formulation. Although the trinitarian nature of God may not be explained on the basis of the economy, there is a definite relationship between this trinitarian nature and the economy.

Florovsky understands this relationship as an analogy between the trinity and the church, or more precisely, as an analogy between the relationships of the trinitarian hypostases to one another and the relationships of human persons (or hypostases) to one another in the church. The passages[104] that develop this analogy are concerned not with the trinity but with the church, in particular its catholicity or *sobornost'*.[105] The, for want of a better word, "sobornic" unity of the church always reflects the perichoretic unity of the trinity. This unity consists in neither a collective "general consciousness," in which individual personality is lost, nor does it consist in an egoistic individual self-consciousness in which each member seeks to overcome the others. Catholic or "sobornic" individuality finds fulfillment in a mutuality in which the individual member, in finding his or her own fulfillment, brings to expression the wholeness or completeness of the community. Another

---

101. Florovsky, "Redemption," *CW*, vol. 3, p. 149.
102. Florovsky, "Offenbarung," op. cit., p. 470.
103. Ibid., p. 472; cf. p. 475: "Dogmatic theology is the presentation of the revealed truth in the cognitive sphere." Qv. Florovsky, 'Bogoslovskie otryvki" ("Theological Fragments"), *Put'* 31 (1931): 12: "to dogmatize is to formulate."
104. Florovsky, "Catholicity of the Church," *CW*, vol. 1, p. 39, pp. 42–44; Qv. "Bogoslovskie otryvki," op. cit., pp. 21–23.
105. See "Bogoslovskie otryvki," op. cit., pp. 19ff.; and Florovsky, "The Catholicity of the Church," op. cit., where the Russian adjective "sobornij" is equated with "catholic." Florovsky's understanding of catholicity is closely associated with the notion of "sobornost'" as developed theologically by A. S. Khomiakov. Qv. P. Evdokimov, *Christus im Russischen Denken* (Trier, 1977), pp. 76–78.

analogy, for Florovsky, is the genius of a great thinker or artist who is able to bring to expression the mind of his or her own time or people without, however, losing his or her own personality, but on the contrary finding personal fulfillment in this task. This is a sort of *imago trinitatis* for Florovsky; but the best and finally the only true analogy is the church, in which the "sobornic" transfiguration of personality is enabled to take place.[106] This is not to say that the economic aspect of the trinity is grounded in the concept of *sobornost'*. Rather the *sobornost'* that is experienced in the church has its grounding in the trinity, and the *doctrine* of the trinity is the dogmatic formulation that corresponds to this experience.

The distinction between essence and energy is fundamental also in Vladimir Lossky's thought. It is systematically interpreted especially in the chapter on the uncreated energies in his book *The Mystical Theology of the Eastern Church*. This chapter refers to the, on the face of it, self-contradictory citations from the Bible and the church fathers concerning the ineffability of God on the one hand and God's real self-communication or self-giving to creatures on the other. This is not merely a theoretical question, for Lossky, but a quite concrete question with implications for mystical praxis.[107] Lossky approaches this problem from a historical standpoint by looking at the solution offered by Gregory Palamas in the *Theophanies*. We have to take with complete seriousness the promise of a real participation in God (2 Peter 1:4), but this can mean a participation neither in the divine essence nor in a particular divine hypostasis. Either alternative would mean that the human hypostases had the same status as Christ. Christ is Son of God by *nature*; his humanity is bound to God in a *hypostatic* union. The possibility of a unity between human beings and God must therefore locate itself in the energies. It must be a union of adoption and grace. This does not mean, however, that the energies are somehow dependent upon the creation. On the contrary, Lossky sees them as "rays of divinity, penetrating the created universe."[108] They are there irrespective of the existence or nonexistence of a creation, because God is not limited, but streams endlessly outwards from the inner essence. Lossky, like Florovsky, describes the energies as the "modes of existence" of the trinity in which God is God outside the essence.[109] The

---

106. Florovsky, "Catholicity of the Church," op. cit., p. 43: "in the fullness of the communion of the Church the catholic transfiguration of personality is accomplished."
107. V. N. Lossky, *The Mystical Theology of the Eastern Church* (New York, 1976), pp. 68–69.
108. Ibid., p. 73.
109. Lossky, *In the Image and Likeness of God* (New York, 1974), p. 54: "a mode of existence that is proper to Him and according to which God exists not only in His essence, but also outside His essence." The distinction between the two "modes of Being" is understood here as a real distinction, i.e. not dependent upon anything created, such as the capacity

energies must neither be identified with the essence nor separated from it. If the energies were to be separated from the essence, they would be reduced to the status of creatures, and God would be reduced to the status of an abstract, philosophical concept of essence. This, according to Lossky, is the error of Palamas's opponents, and indeed the error of western trinitarian thinking as a whole,[110] viz. that western theology allows a theoretical trinity but tends to replace this trinity with an impersonal divine essence. An apophatic or antinomic (and the two terms are virtually synonymous for Lossky) perspective allows Orthodox theologians, by contrast, both to emphasize the self-communication of God and to retain the ineffability of God, so that the οἰκονομία is not allowed to swallow up the θεολογία, nor vice versa. The same perspective makes it possible also to hold together the notions of one essence and three hypostases.[111] The notion of divine simplicity can therefore not be used as an argument against the essence—energies distinction, as it would also undermine the trinitarian distinctions between the hypostases.[112] On the contrary, the notion of divine simplicity must be tested by the rules of apophasis. The limits of language, including speech about the *simplicitas Dei*, must be respected.[113]

The energies constitute the eternal glory of God. They are not separable "parts" of God. Particular energies cannot be appropriated to particular trinitarian hypostases,[114] for that would subordinate the divine essence to particular attributes. Lossky argues that Bulgakov's sophiology and the traditional western psychological trinity both fall into the same error here. Bulgakov understands God, in principle, on the basis of *one* of the many energies, namely, Wisdom; the psychological doctrine of the trinity

---

or incapacity of the human intellect: "the antinomy between the positive and negative theologies has a real foundation in God. Like all theological antinomies—like that of unity and trinity, which postulates a distinction between nature and persons—the antinomy of the two ways discloses to our spirit a mysterious distinction in God's very being. This is the distinction between essence and divine operations or energies" (ibid., p. 53). If the distinction were understood as dependent upon creation, then the distinction itself—and with it the notion of grace—would be reduced to the status of creatures.

110. There is thus, for Lossky, a connection between western theology and the opponents of Palamas, who were "eastern theologians who had been strongly influenced by Aristotelianism" (*Mystical Theology*, op. cit., pp. 76–77). (The German translation reads "strongly influenced by *Thomism*"—"orientalische Theologen, die einen starken thomistischen Einfluß erfahren hatten" (Lossky, *Mystische Theologie*, p. 99).

111. Lossky, *Image and Likeness*, op. cit., p. 51.

112. Lossky, *Myst.Theol.*, op. cit., p. 78: "Simplicity does not mean uniformity or absence of distinction—otherwise Christianity would not be the religion of the Holy Trinity."

113. Lossky, *The Vision of God* (Leighton Buzzard, 1963), p. 127.

114. Lossky, *Myst. Theol.*, op. cit., pp. 80–81.

understands the two inner-trinitarian processions (of Son and Spirit) on the basis of the attributes of "will" and "love," which are in fact the possession of the *whole* trinity. Of course we can attribute wisdom, will, and love to God, but we may not seek to describe God (or a particular trinitarian person) on the basis of one such attribute. Were we to say God is love or wisdom, we would be speaking on the level of the economy, or in other words, we would be speaking of God in relation to us. We are not to suggest that these (or any other) names constitute a *definitive* description of God in Godself.

The doctrine of energies, for Lossky, mediates between the domains of θεολογία and of οἰκονομία. The energies are eternal and inseparable from the trinity, and they are independent of the creation. But they constitute that side of God through which God is revealed in and to the creation. It is "somewhat inexact"[115] to speak of an economic trinity, according to Lossky. But there is an order (τάξις) by which the trinity is revealed in the world, the order ἐξ πατρός, διὰ υἱοῦ, ἐν ἁγίῳ πνεύματι. We are not permitted, however, to attribute this order to the trinitarian essence as such.[116] It is an "order of manifestation" in which the Father appears as possessor of the attribute, the Son *as* the attribute (because the Son, insofar as he reveals the invisible nature of the Father, becomes—in the economy—almost identical with the energy),[117] and the Spirit is the one who reveals the Godhead. Thus we can, for example, name the Son "wisdom," and the Spirit "the Spirit of wisdom." These names, however, are merely economic. They in no way determine the inner relationship of the Son to the Father or to the Spirit. In the inner being of God, the Spirit takes its origin from the Father alone. In the outer activities, the three persons have a common will so that in each of the missions, all three persons are active. The Son becomes human in being sent from the Father, and is manifested by the work of the Spirit; the Spirit is sent from the Father through the Son.[118] Neither the Son nor the Spirit is sent against its own will, for the will of each is also, always, the will of the entire trinity. Here[119] Lossky thus argues that there is a *direct connection* between the essence-energy distinction and the Orthodox refutation of the *filioque* clause. Both are concerned with the same question, but from different perspectives.

---

115. Ibid., p. 82.
116. Lossky, *Image and Likeness*, op. cit., p. 92.
117. Lossky, *Myst. Theol.*, op. cit., p. 84: "The Son who renders visible the hidden nature of the Father is here almost identified with the manifesting energies."
118. Lossky, *Image and Likeness*, op. cit., pp. 95–96. Lossky allows here an *economic filioque*. Cf. V. Rodzianko, "Filioque in Patristic Thought," in *TU* 64 (1957): 295–308.
119. Lossky, *Myst.Theol.*, op. cit., pp. 84–85. Cf. Lossky, *Image and Likeness*, op. cit., pp. 90ff.

Lossky closes the chapter by sketching the significance of the doctrine of energies as the concrete dogmatic foundation for real mystical experience, or in other words, for the real indwelling of grace. Grace *is* energy. It is the trinitarian God insofar as this God acts *ad extra*, and is communicated to us through the Holy Spirit, thus coming to dwell with us and in us. In mystical experience both the vision and the invisibility of God, both the approachability and ineffability of God are at the same time affirmed. The tension between opposites, the antimony, is retained.[120] Mystical experience arises, for Lossky, out of a sort of gracious self-limitation on God's part. God limits Godself in God's glory, leaving room for the awakening of the creation and its entry into dialogue with its creator.

The chapter on the uncreated energies follows the chapter on the trinity in Lossky's *Mystical Theology*. After that comes the chapter on creation. This order mirrors Lossky's understanding of the energies. They build a connection between God and the creation while at the same time remaining uncompromisingly divine, that is, on the God-side, or the uncreated side, of the dividing line between uncreated and created reality. We have seen that for Florovsky the idea of a creation is located in the energy, in close connection to the will. Not only the creation itself but even the idea of a creation is freed from any suggestion of necessity. Lossky takes this model and sets it up as an alternative to the Augustinian model in which the divine ideas are located in the divine essence.[121]

In contrast to that typically western model, in which grace comes into its own in the salvation of the world, Lossky insists that grace is involved equally in the world's creation. Sin, however, sets up a hiatus between the world and the domain of grace. "From the fall until the day of Pentecost, the divine energy, deifying and uncreated grace, was foreign to our human nature, acting on it only from outside and producing created effects in the soul."[122]

---

120. Lossky, *Myst.Theol.*, op. cit., pp. 87–88. Cf. Lossky, *Image and Likeness*, op. cit., p. 68.

121. Lossky, *Myst. Theol.*, op. cit., pp. 94–95: "the term θελητικὴ ἔννοια ('thought-will,' or, more accurately, 'volitional thought') is very important. It is a perfect expression of the Eastern doctrine of the divine ideas, of the place which the theology of the Eastern Church gives to the ideas of created things in God. The ideas are not, according to this conception, the eternal reasons of creatures contained within the very being of God, determinations of the essence to which created things refer as to their exemplary cause, as in the thought of St. Augustine which later became the common teaching of the whole Western tradition and was more precisely formulated by St. Thomas Aquinas. In the thought of the Greek Fathers the divine ideas are more dynamic, intentional in character. Their place is not in the essence, but in 'that which is after the essence,' the divine energies: for the ideas are to be identified with the will or wills (θελήματα) which determine the different modes according to which created beings participate in the creative energies."

122. Lossky, *Myst. Theol.*, op. cit., p. 133.

Deification through grace can no longer take effect through a human ascent to God. It must be a salvation, a rescue—an act of the powerful God over against a powerless creature. Thus the economic action of the Son has become necessary. The incarnation cannot be replaced by the disembodied action of the energies. In fact they belong together. The indwelling of Godhead in the humanity of Christ is an energetic indwelling.[123]

The Son is not sent into the world without the co-working of the Spirit. In the same way, the Spirit is not sent without the co-working of the Son. The salvific activity of the Son was never absent from the world, even from the first day of creation, but is made present in a new and perfected way in the incarnation. In the same way, the Spirit, though never absent, since Pentecost is present in a new and perfected way. There is thus a mutual interconnectedness between the economic activities of the Son and the Spirit. "Intimately linked as they are in the common work upon earth, the Son and the Spirit remain nevertheless in this same work two persons independent the one of the other as to their hypostatic being."[124] In the order of manifestation the Spirit follows the Son and bears witness to him in precisely the same way that the Son bears witness to the Father. But who or what follows the Spirit and bears witness to the Spirit? Or does the Spirit remain anonymous and unrevealed, perhaps? Lossky's answer is that the gifts of the Spirit, although they belong as energies to the whole trinity, are imparted by the Spirit and so bear witness to the Spirit.[125] According to Lossky, there is thus a special relationship between the Spirit and the energies. The energies, which are present in the whole creation from the beginning, are present in a new way after Pentecost,[126] a way that is capable of deifying the creature. Therefore we cannot say that the energies somehow replace the hypostasis of the Holy Spirit. On the contrary, the energies are the energies *of* the Spirit: the relationship is very clearly stated. Lossky insists that eastern and western Christianity have rather different understandings of the indwelling of the Holy Spirit and the gifts of the Spirit. The gift of the Spirit is "is not a created effect, an accidental quality whose existence would depend upon our created substance, but an uncreated gift, a divine and deifying energy in which we really participate in the nature of the Holy Trinity, by becoming partakers of the divine nature."[127] Just as the Father is

---

123. Ibid., p. 146: "The humanity of Christ is a deified nature that is permeated by the divine energies from the moment of the Incarnation."
124. Ibid., p 159.
125. Ibid., p. 163. Cf. Lossky, *Image and Likeness,* op. cit., p. 57.
126. Ibid., p . 66: "The work of our deification is accomplished by the Holy Spirit, Giver of grace." Grace and energy are for Lossky one and the same.
127. Lossky, *Myst. Theol.* op. cit., pp. 213–24.

revealed in the hypostasis of the Son, and the Son in the hypostasis of the Holy Spirit, so the Spirit is in turn revealed in the host of deified human hypostases.[128]

In this penultimate chapter Lossky returns to the hesychastic controversy. The debate between Palamas and Barlaam centered on the question of the so-called divine light. This light "can be defined as the visible quality of the divinity, of the energies or grace in which God makes Himself known."[129] This light fills the senses as well as the intellect. It is not hostile to the human body, but embraces it in all its senses—in the end, however, surpassing both sense and intellect.[130] It makes itself known both to the senses and to the intellect, although it belongs to the domain of the uncreated. At the transfiguration the energy that was and is always present became visible to the bodily eyes of Peter, James, and John.[131] It was no atmospheric disturbance—that is, it was not simply what we could call a sensual light; but neither was it simply an awakening of insight on the part of the apostles; that is, it was not simply a Platonic intellectual light.

In his book *The Vision of God*, Lossky suggests that the western tradition has become quite incapable of understanding the Palamite doctrine of energies. The history of this growing incapacity is outlined in the first chapter. After this, Lossky gives an account of the patristic background to the doctrine. The Palamite synthesis is not described as a new development, but rather as the clarification of a hitherto unexpressed presupposition of the part of the church fathers. Whereas in the *Mystical Theology* the doctrine was presented as an indispensable part of a whole theological system, in the later book Lossky focuses on the specific question of the face-to-face encounter between human beings and the invisible God. This question is raised in both eastern and western theologies but, according to Lossky, in quite separate ways. In the East the Councils held in Constantinople in 1341, 1351, and 1368 all affirmed the Palamite distinction between the invisible essence and the self-revealing energies. This was also an affirmation of the hesychastic method of prayer leading often, it was claimed, to the vision of God's glory, the energies. The hesychasts did not claim to see God's essence, however. In the West the question was different. Do the saints see the essence of God first in heaven, or is this essence visible this side of death, in

---

128. Ibid., p. 173.
129. Ibid., p. 221.
130. See Lossky, *Image and Likeness*, op. cit., pp. 58–59 for these three types of light: the light of the transfiguration here is distinguished from both "sensible" and "intellectual" light in the Platonic sense.
131. Lossky, *Myst. Theol.*, op. cit., p. 223.

mystical experience? Here the assumption is that the divine essence becomes itself the object of vision. In the light of the western debate and its solution, namely that the saints can in this life be shown a vision of God's essence,[132] the Palamite distinction between essence and energies appeared to imply a reduction or even a denial of the reality of the vision of God in mystical experience. It appeared, further, to postulate an intermediary between God and humanity, and to compromise the unity and simplicity of God in that the light was attributed to this intermediary. From the eastern point of view, the western position appeared to dissolve the proper distinction between θεολογία and οἰκονομία. The western position seemed, on the face of it, to allow a more intimate relationship to God, viz. the face-to-face encounter with God's inner being. But what this actually meant, according to Lossky, was that western theology remained on the level of the energy (because the vision of God is of God's glory, not God's inner being), without itself being aware of its own deficiency.[133] Western theology is incapable of grasping the idea that God is bigger than what is revealed of God—so Lossky argues. The apophatic method has no place in western theology except as a corrective against the supposition that human speech could describe the Godhead. If we use the concepts of "essence" or "being" we reach the limits of this western apophatic corrective, according to Lossky, because the attempt is made to describe God precisely in terms of these concepts. Western theology has no room for a concept of superessentiality.

The problem for the western tradition, in Lossky's view, was that many of the Greek fathers appear to lend support to the later formulations of the so-called Palamite councils of the fourteenth century. Various western writers, above all Petavius,[134] sought to circumvent this embarrassment by concentrating their attack on Palamas alone. Petavius understood the essence—energies distinction as an illegitimate novelty of the Byzantine fourteenth century, without any solid foundation in the thought of the church fathers. So Lossky argues in his book, *The Vision of God*, and his whole endeavor in this book is to contest this argument of Petavius. Lossky does this by highlighting the tension, in the church fathers, between God's ineffability and God's self-revelation.

---

132. Lossky, *The Vision of God*, op. cit., pp. 10–11.
133. Lossky, *Image and Likeness*, op. cit., p. 122: "If I am permitted to speak in the language of the 'Palamite' theology which is natural to me, I will say that Thomas Aquinas, as a metaphysician, attained God and created beings at the level of energy and not at the level of the superessence in Three Hypostases and of the polyhypostasity of the created cosmos."
134. Lossky, *Vision of God*, op. cit., p. 19: "Instead of resolving the difficulty of the Fathers, Denis Petau simply displaced it, directing attention elsewhere."

Lossky still has one other western criticism to overcome, however.[135] This is the argument that any striving for a vision of God this side of the eschaton is an illegitimate platonizing of Christianity. It replaces God's selfless love toward us with a human erotic attraction to and reaching out for God. Lossky's answer is that this human reaching out for God may well be erotic, but that does not make it either Platonic or unchristian.[136] Lossky's argument here resembles Florovsky's critique of the "new monophysitism," which reduces the human being, in his/her relationship to God, to the status of a mere recipient. Again, we touch here on an important difference in tendencies between western and eastern theologies, the East generally giving more role to the exercise of human will than the West, especially where the Augustinian influence has been strong in the West. Lossky later develops his argument against seeing Platonic tendencies at work in eastern theology by mounting a defense of Pseudo-Dionysius against the charge of neo-Platonism.[137] Lossky agrees with Florovsky in seeing the greatest step forward in the doctrine of God occurring in the fourth century. It is the step from a purely economic trinity (in which the Father represents the ineffability of God) to the model in which ineffability is attributed to the trinitarian essence (οὐσία).[138] Only in this more refined model is trinitarian theology set free from any suggestion of subordinationism. This step divides Origen on the one side from Didymus the Blind and the Cappadocians on the other. From here on, θεολογία does not deal purely with God the Father, but with the trinitarian essence.[139] God is no longer to be understood as revealing Godself through the Son and the Spirit, who act as economic instruments of the Father (the two hands of the Father, for Irenaeus). Rather, the trinitarian God is revealed through the trinitarian activities, the energies. Father, Son, and Holy Spirit act together *ad extra*, through their common will. This clarification of the doctrine of God (it is *not* a "development" of doctrine, says Lossky) in the fourth century is, Lossky admits, by no means unproblematic. It is not always clear what a particular early writer intends when speaking of the vision of God. Is it the vision of glory or the vision of essence? In other words, is a particular writer speaking

---

135. Ibid., pp. 26–27.
136. Ibid., pp. 54–55.
137. Ibid., pp. 99ff.
138. Ibid., p. 61.
139. Ibid., p. 67. Cf. A. Heron, "The Holy Spirit in Origen and Didymus the Blind: A Shift in Perspective from the Third to the Fourth Century," in A. M. Ritter (ed.), *Kerygma und Logos: Beiträge zu den geistgeschichtlichen Beziehungen zwischen Antike und Christentum* (Göttingen, 1979), pp. 298–310.

on a "theological," inner-trinitarian plane or an economic plane?[140] Only gradually was trinitarian language clarified and perfected. But there is nevertheless a consistency, according to Lossky, that runs through all the genuinely Orthodox texts. The consistency is that there remains a distinction between creator and creation, between the divine essence and the creature—even after the creature has been deified. It is possible to read Pseudo-Dionysius as a Platonist, but only when one fails to understand his use of the term δύναμις; that is, fails to understand it in the light of the tradition that leads to Palamas.[141]

The Palamite vision of God is, according to Lossky, no mere vision, no mere encounter with a two dimensional datum. This would in effect be an encounter with a "closed door."[142] The doctrine of energies with its accompanying method of mystical praxis means that, on the contrary, a door is opened, an "infinite path beyond knowledge," an "existential communion."[143] This stands in contrast to any mysticism in which God's glory is glimpsed face to face, and in which the beholder then rests satisfied because he or she mistakes this glory for the divine essence itself. The hesychast way, by contrast, sees the vision of glory as the beginning of an ever-deepening relationship of participation, a relationship that stretches beyond the limits of seeing and knowing. In a late article Lossky argues that for the Cappadocians "to know a thing by its essence is to replace the knowledge of the real object by knowledge of a concept."[144] The Greek patristic denial of a vision of God's essence does *not* mean it is impossible to know God as God is. On the contrary, it is *essentialist* thinking that stands in the way of such knowledge. It is impossible to know God other than God in relation to us, other than God's revelation in the economy of creation and salvation.[145] If one must speak of the οὐσία, such speech is invariably allegorical and metaphorical. Thus Lossky understands the doctrine of energies as an affirmation of the concrete, experiential beginning of our whole knowledge of God.

---

140. Lossky, *Vision of God*, op. cit., pp. 90 ff.
141. Ibid., p. 102.
142. Ibid., p. 110.
143. Ibid., pp. 110 and 123: "an infinite path beyond knowledge"; "an existential communion."
144. Lossky, "The Problem of the Vision Face to Face and Byzantine Patristic Tradition," *GrOrthThR* 17 (1972): 241.
145. Ibid.

Chapter 3
COMPARISON OF THE TWO APPROACHES

The Doctrine of the Trinity

How do we know the trinitarian God? Barth's answer is: God reveals Godself.[1] The assumption underlying Barth's understanding of revelation is that God is not limited to God's hidden eternity and eternal hiddenness, but can and does take form in time.[2] This notion of revelation leads directly to Barth's doctrine of the trinity. It is, in fact, the root of the doctrine of the trinity. The order of trinitarian hiddenness, revealedness, and self-giving expresses the inner reality of God. The economic trinity is for Barth the inner trinity. Like every other doctrine, the doctrine of the trinity is based solely on revelation. "If we have to do with His revelation, we have to do with Himself and not, as modalists of all periods have thought, with an entity distinct from Himself."[3] The trinity of God does not limit itself to the economy of revelation, because who God is in revelation, God is already in Godself (*zuvor in sich selber*).[4] It is an outworking of God's absolute freedom that God does not reveal Godself other than as God actually is.

Rahner insists even more forcefully on the identity of economic and inner (or "immanent") trinity. Like Barth's doctrine of the trinity, Rahner's trinity is based in the revelation of God. God's economic self-communication in the Son and in the Spirit reveals the Godhead of the Father. The incarnation of the Son and the sending of the Spirit are the two mutually related moments[5] of God's self-communication. This represents an understanding of the trinity not so very different from Barth's understanding. Rahner's hesitation to use the term "person" in connection with the trinitarian modes of "subsistence" or "givenness" betrays his tendency to start from the unity of God. Barth's doctrine of the trinity also

---

1. K. Barth, *Church Dogmatics* (Edinburgh, 1936ff.), vol. 1/1, p. 340. Cf. pp. 441ff., 457ff., 513ff.
2. Ibid., p. 367.
3. Ibid., p. 358.
4. Ibid., p. 441 (K. Barth, *Die Kirchliche Dogmatik*, [Zürich, 1967], vol. 1/1, p. 404).
5. Rahner, *The Trinity* (Burns and Oates, 1970), p. 87.

postulates one reality (or one subjectivity) that repeats itself in a threefold self-repetition.

In contrast to Barth and Rahner, Florovsky nowhere writes about God's revelation of *Godself*. The doctrine of energies emphasizes that God does not reveal the innermost divine being. God reveals not Godself (in this sense), but the eternal glory. God's glory is Godself, but not God's essence. God's glory (δόξα) or energy penetrates, shines through, and transfigures the whole creation—including human flesh. This transfiguration of human flesh is the goal of Christian ascesis. It is this goal that marks Christian ascesis as fundamentally different from the ascesis of the neo-Platonists.[6] The transfiguration of the flesh is no escape from the body, but rather at once its glory and the overcoming of its limitations. Although Florovsky does speak of unveiling,[7] this refers to the uncovering of God's glory. God's glory is revealed not directly over against the human recipient or addressee, but rather in the direction of and through the recipient or addressee. In this way human flesh is glorified and the earth as a whole is honored and brought under God's protection.[8] There is thus a gracious omnipresence, a "providential ubiquity," of the energy of God.[9]

Barth allows no natural point of contact between God and human beings—this was the subject of his famous debate with Emil Brunner. Florovsky by contrast says that God can and does speak to the human understanding because the human being is in the image of God (*imago Dei*). This is not a matter of God limiting the divine word to human capacity. On the contrary, God's revelation can be received by humanity precisely because God has made humanity capable of such a reception. There is an objective and a subjective side to mystical experience. These are not simply to be identified with work of the Son and of the Spirit respectively. Rather this objectivity and subjectivity concerns on the one hand God's revelation of the divine glory, and our human readiness to perceive this glory on the other. The eternal glory of God is not naturally visible. Its perception requires discipline (ἄσκησις) on the part of the human recipient. Revelation is then the way of God to us, the objective element. Ascesis completes this way, in that it is our way to God,[10] the subjective human response to God's encounter with us. It is God's unveiling of glory (that is, of Godself—but not

---

6. G. V. Florovsky, "Redemption," *CW*, vol. 3, p. 114.
7. Florovsky, "Offenbarung, Philosophie und Theologie," *ZZ* 9 (1931): 463.
8. Ibid., p. 464.
9. Florovsky, "Creation and Creaturehood," *CW*, vol. 3, p. 65.
10. Florovsky, "The Work of the Holy Spirit in Revelation," *The Christian East* 13 (1932): 50.

God's essence) that makes possible a direct vision of God (as glory or energy or light, but not as essence) on the part of the human subject. This unveiling is an intentional act of God, and is therefore to be distinguished from any natural "evidences" of God. There is both a natural (or necessary) manifestation of God's glory in creation, and also this intentional revelation by God of the divine glory to the human being who has prepared him- or herself through ascesis. This distinction between necessity and will means that, for Florovsky, natural theology is of no final significance. God is known only through God's way to human beings. This way reaches its high point in the incarnation of the Word.

The vision of God is a major theme of Lossky's theology. But "revelation" is not a prominent concept in his work, and Lossky, like Florovsky, denies any notion of an inner-trinitarian dialectic that would reveal the trinitarian nature of God to human beings. That would signify a retreat to the ante-Nicene triadology with its basis purely in the economy of revelation. The trinity is for Lossky "absolute stability,"[11] because apophatic thinking places the trinity beyond any and every human concept. Lossky will not allow even the concepts of necessity and will to play a part in the discussion of the trinity. The trinitarian God is *beyond*. Even the person of the Holy Spirit "remains as a person unrevealed," veiled and hidden even in its appearing.[12] The Spirit remains behind its energies. It is through the energies that the Spirit works in the economy. Lossky describes the going out of God toward us and the ascetic return of human beings to God in terms similar to Florovsky's. God's going out of Godself takes place primarily in the incarnation (σάρκωσις) of the Son. The return takes place in the deification (θέωσις) of the human being. There is thus a correspondence between the incarnation of God and the deification of human beings: they complete one another. Jesus Christ manifests the glory of the Father most clearly at his baptism and his transfiguration,[13] the two events at which the voice of the Father is heard and the presence of the Spirit is experienced. In these two events, Christ is manifested as he always was and in reality continues to be.

The going forth of God and our return to God are for Lossky the models of the two ways of knowing God. The positive or cataphatic way is based on the Son's manifestation of the glory of the Father. The negative or apophatic way seeks, through an ascetic ascent to God, to respond to God's descent to us. The human subject experiences the power of God as a result of God's movement out of Godself in self-differentiation—that is, through the

---

11. V. N. Lossky, *The Mystical Theology of the Eastern Church* (New York, 1976), p. 45.
12. Ibid., pp. 160–61.
13. Ibid., p. 149.

hypostatic processions of the Son and the Spirit and through the impersonal, energetic processions (or emanations) that are mediated principally through the person of the Holy Spirit. Our knowledge of God remains, however, unsatisfactory if we simply receive this power of God passively. That would be, again, what Florovsky calls a type of "practical monophysitism," which denies the activity of the human subject in the relationship between God and human beings. The knowledge of God that arises out of such passivity remains a purely intellectual knowledge—mere information about God. In God, however, there is not only a proceeding out in self-differentiation but also a unifying movement, namely the perichoresis of the hypostases and the essential unity of the energies. Human beings are invited to take part in this movement toward unity. This is the apophatic way of experiential knowledge, which complements and surpasses the cataphatic way. Where Barth speaks of the way home of the Son of Man bringing about thereby the salvation of our common humanity, Lossky emphasizes the return home of the completed humanity—thereby also the whole creation—in mystical ascent. All people are called to this sanctification through an ascesis by which all the concepts and all the names by which we normally speak of God must be surmounted and left behind by those who "strain forward to what lies ahead" (Phil. 3:13).

Excursus: The Filioque

The difference between the two positions also has implications for the *filioque* debate. In the identity principle, the inner relationship between the Son and the Holy Spirit is very clear and logical. The outer mission of the Spirit corresponds exactly to the inner procession. Here we can leave aside the historical reasons for the interpolation of the *filioque*. The basis for the present defense of the *filioque* clause is that it brings to expression the close relationship between, or even identity of, the inner procession and the outer mission of the Spirit.

In Barth, the trinitarian modes of being appear in a specific order of revelation. The order of trinitarian revelation (that is, the missions) corresponds to the prior order of inner-trinitarian processions. Barth calls this inner, eternal order an *economia*. Barth emphasizes that this inner *economia* is a logical, not a temporal ordering. The three modes of being are coeternal and equally to be praised.[14] In the hiddenness of God there is, however, a logical priority for the unveiling of the Word, and this leads in turn to a logical priority for the imparting of the Spirit. In his threefold order of veiling, unveiling, and imparting Barth thus presents us with a

---

14. *CD*, vol. 1/1, p. 424.

model in which "veiling" is logically involved in the "unveiling," and the "unveiling" in the origin of the "imparting." The second moment (if we may resort to Hegelian terminology here) takes its origin from the first, while the third moment takes its origin from the first and the second moments together. Barth presents us, in other words, with a model of trinitarian thinking we can identify as "filioquist."[15] It simply does not make sense, in the context of Barth's grounding of the doctrine of the trinity in the concept of revelation, to suggest that the third moment could take its origin from the first moment alone:

> This threeness consists in the fact that in the essence or act in which God is God there is first a pure origin and then two different issues, the first of which is to be attributed solely to the origin, the second, different in kind, to the origin and likewise to the first issue.[16]

Like Augustine, Barth considers the first and the second hypostases, the Father and the Son, together as the common origin of the third hypostasis, the Spirit. Barth's defense of the *filioque*[17] is thus the necessary ramification of his positing of an eternal ordering (*economia*) *within* the divine reality. This inner-trinitarian order is in turn the corollary of his grounding of trinitarian thinking in the concept of revelation. Barth supports this understanding of the trinity through his choice of alternative terms for the hypostases: for example, the Father as pure Giver, the Son as Receiver and Giver, the Spirit as pure Receiver.[18]

Rahner's doctrine of the trinity is based on the similar idea of God's self-communication to human beings. This self-communication includes an ordering of the trinitarian "modes of subsistence":

> When treating of the economic trinity, we are concerned with the two distinct yet related ways [they determine each other, yet they constitute a τάξις] of the free gratuitous self-communication of God to the spiritual creature in Jesus Christ and in the 'spirit.'[19]

Rahner endeavors to avoid an exclusively Latin understanding of the trinity. He understands the New Testament term ὁ θεός to denote specifically the person of the Father. The source of Godhead is thus not some impersonal essence, but the hypostasis (or mode of being) of the Father. But it is questionable whether Rahner's model of the trinity really is

---

15. See N. A. Nissiotis, *Die Theologie der Ostkirche im Ökumenischer Dialog: Kirche und Welt in orthodoxen Sicht* (Stuttgart, 1968), pp. 25ff.
16. *CD*, vol. 1/1, p. 418.
17. Ibid., pp. 541ff.
18. Ibid., p. 418.
19. Rahner, *Trinity*, op. cit., p. 83.

the Greek or biblical model (the Greek Orthodox model *is* the biblical model, for Rahner). If, following Rahner's *Grundaxiom*, the economic trinity *is* the immanent trinity, then the economic order has to be carried over into the immanent or inner trinity. This means that Rahner's trinitarian model postulates, like Barth's, a logical relationship of origin between the Son and the Holy Spirit. Rahner's trinitarian model thus includes an implicit inner-trinitarian *filioque*. Rahner certainly allows the two inner-trinitarian processions mutually to condition one another. This "does not deny the τάξις of both processions, nor that the Spirit proceeds from the Father and (through) the Son."[20] The bracketed "through" is intentionally ambiguous. Does Rahner mean the procession of the Spirit *from* the Son or *through* the Son? We can remark in passing that Lossky regards "through the Son" as being in any case an unsatisfactory formula for attempting any reconciliation of eastern and western theologies.[21] Although Rahner, with the best of intentions, seeks to find common ground with the Greek triadology, his trinitarian thinking remains in the end not so far from Barth's position.

The Orthodox authors argue against the *filioque* on specific historical grounds. More important, however, are the systematic-theological grounds. For Florovsky and Lossky, the church is analogous to the trinity, because in the church a plurality of human persons seek to discover their essential unity and at the same time their fulfillment as individual persons. This analogy suggests no ordering of persons. Both Florovsky and Lossky view the trinitarian thinking of the fourth century—especially of Athanasius and the Cappadocians—as a great step forward, because here the older economic triadology, which included an ordering of the hypostases, was left behind. An eternal order of manifestation, however, is retained. But Florovsky (in contrast to Barth) insists that this order is not coeternal with the trinity itself. Lossky's apophatic method emphasizes the ineffability of the trinitarian relations. There is certainly no basis here to champion the cause of an inner-trinitarian *filioque*. Such a *filioque* would in fact be pure speculation. Even the relations of origin (*relationes originis*) are to be understood apophatically. In other words, Lossky goes only so far as to say that there are differences between Father and Son, between Father and Spirit, and between Son and Spirit. The nature of these differences is not to be explained. In the context of Orthodox theology, Lossky insists that speech about the relations of

---

20. Rahner, *Trinity*, op. cit., p. 117, n. 41.

21. Lossky, *In the Image and Likeness of God* (New York, 1974), p. 95. Barth is, from a western standpoint, in agreement with Lossky that the formula "through the Son" is no satisfactory substitute for the *filioque*. Qv. G. Watson, "The Filioque—Opportunity for Debate?" *ScotJTh* 41 (1988): 321.

origin does not attempt to answer the question as to *how* the hypostases are to be distinguished from one another.

The Doctrine of Creation

Both the identity principle and the doctrine of energies oppose any suggestion of pantheism. A clear ontological distinction between creator and creation is essential to the biblical worldview. In the first edition of his *Römerbrief*, Karl Barth asserts polemically that God is not to be understood in terms of categories drawn from the order of creation. This emphasis is developed in the *Church Dogmatics*, where Jesus Christ is seen as the only proper mediator between God and the creation. God's pretemporal will, or decree, to create a world is located in the second person of the trinity. Barth thus seeks to ground the doctrine of creation in the doctrine of the trinity. God's decision to create a world locates itself not within the divine essence in general, but within the trinity.

The doctrine of creation also plays an important role in Florovsky's thought. Florovsky develops his doctrine of creation in the context of a critique of the natural theology of Origen. Origen begins, according to Florovsky, on the basis of the eternity and changelessness of God. God is eternal and changeless; God is also creator of the world. It therefore necessarily follows, to this way of thinking, that God was always creator of the world, and that the world itself must be eternal. Florovsky demonstrates that this represents a confusion of the creator and the creation. But the problem is not quite as simple as the eternity or temporality of the world. The question remains: is there before the creation of the actual world a pretemporal idea of a creation? If there is such an idea, how is it related to the trinitarian God? Florovsky's answer is that the distinction in God between necessity and will, or between being and having, is indispensable here. The trinitarian God *is*; the trinitarian God *has* the idea of a creation. The idea is an act of the eternal divine will. But unlike God's being, neither the creation itself nor the idea of a creation is, of itself, necessary. In this way God's idea of a creation is to be distinguished from the eternal begetting of the Son and the eternal procession of the Spirit. The idea of a creation is an act of the trinitarian will. This idea is eternal but not coeternal with the trinity. The trinity belongs to the domain of *theologia*, that is, the domain of God's essence, while the idea of a creation belongs in the territory of the *economia*, the domain of the energy and the will of God. The difference between Barth and Florovsky, then, in relation to the doctrine of creation, is not that one writer places greater emphasis than the other on the ontological difference between creator and creation; the difference is that Barth posits two ontological levels where Florovsky identifies three. Barth distinguishes God (including God's pretemporal decree to create a world) from the creation. Florovsky distinguishes God in God's eternity, the pretemporal idea of a creation (that is, the aeonic eternity), and the real temporal creation. Florovsky has thus in fact reintroduced the Aristotelian distinction between potentiality and actuality. There is a potentiality, though, in God—something abhorrent to the mainstream western tradition.[22] Without this threefold distinction the doctrine of creation is threatened, according to Florovsky, with the error of Origen's eternal world of ideas.

Lossky also emphasizes that the idea of a creation is not located within the divine essence. Following John of Damascus, he names this idea of a creation a "volitional thought" (θελητικὴ ἔννοια).[23] This means that the basis for creation does not lie in the realm of the necessary, but in the realm of the divine will. If the basis, the idea, were necessary (as it is, according to Lossky, in Augustine and the tradition that follows him), then there are two possibilities. Either the world is denigrated as being a poor imitation of the Godhead or of something within the Godhead; or else the trinitarian God is reduced to become a mere dynamism that is necessarily bound up in the coming-into-being of the created order.

Lossky, like Barth, places the ideas (λόγοι) within the second person, the λόγος of God—with the rather curious condition, however, that the Logos here carries the economic accent that it possesses in ante-Nicene theology.[24] This means that the λόγοι or ideas of a creation are located in the energetic aspect—not the essential aspect—of the Logos. The Logos is essentially beyond the "volitional thoughts" of God. This insight—once again, that within God a distinction is to be made between necessity and will—is for Lossky indispensable for a satisfactory understanding both of the doctrine of God and the doctrine of creation. Florovsky describes a little more precisely the nature of these ideas. They are "aeonic," which is to say neither eternal nor temporal. The aeonic is that which has a beginning, but one that is outside of time and is determined by the beginning of the actual created order. The aeonic is thus not eternal. We could say (*pace* Arius) "there was when it was not." But the aeonic remains, in contrast to the temporal, unchanged.[25]

---

22. The scholastic notion of God as *actus purus* is, however, increasingly being called in question within western theology. For example, see E. Johnson, "The Incomprehensibility of God and the Image of God Male and Female," in *Theological Studies* 45 (1984): 442, for a feminist critique of God as pure actuality. Process theology has also rejected this notion.

23. Lossky, *Myst. Theol.,* op. cit., p. 94.

24. Ibid., p. 98.

25. Ibid., p. 102.

The Doctrine of Grace

Our knowledge of God, for Barth, is closely bound up with grace; "it is by the grace of God that God is knowable to us."[26] Grace is God's good favor, and it is a function of this good favor that God creates us and enters into a relationship with us. "Grace is God's good-pleasure. And it is precisely in God's good-pleasure that the reality of our being with God and of His being with us consists. . . . In His good-pleasure God is among us and for us."[27] It is a miracle of God's grace that we, who by nature are incapable of drawing near to God (*incapax infiniti*) have now been enabled to hear God's word (*capax verbi divini*). It is also an effect of this grace that God hides Godself. It would be too much for us to encounter the living God face to face. Grace has principally come to expression, however, in that God has for us and for our salvation emerged from the eternal divine hiddenness and come to us in the Son and the Holy Spirit. To receive God's grace is to receive Godself; or in Barth's trinitarian language, "Grace is the Holy Spirit received."[28]

God is thus experienced by human beings through (or perhaps, as) grace, and only thus is God experienced; that is to say, only through Godself. In Barth these sentiments are directed polemically against any notion of natural knowledge of God. Even so, it would be quite wrong to think that, for Barth, a person could stand completely outside of God's grace. That would be to deny the objective reality of what occurred for all human beings on Good Friday.

Rahner also argues that our knowledge of God is to be regarded as dependent upon grace. Rahner criticizes the priority given in scholastic theology to created grace, that is, the concept of a created, supernatural grace that can develop as a characteristic (*habitus*) within the human soul. Rahner wants to retain the concept of created grace, but only to characterize the effect of uncreated grace upon the human being. Uncreated grace is, for Rahner, the real indwelling of the Holy Spirit. The doctrine of grace is nothing other than pneumatology from a different perspective. Christology and the doctrine of grace are the "two chapters about either divine procession or mission ('immanent' and 'economic')."[29] Christology and the doctrine of grace together constitute the doctrine of the trinity. In this regard, again, Rahner's thinking is not far from that of Barth.

---

26. *CD*, vol. 2/1, p. 70.
27. Ibid., p. 74.
28. *CD*, vol. 1/1, p. 533.
29. K. Rahner, *Trinity*, op. cit., p. 120.

God's grace is, for Florovsky, God's energy. The energies represent not only God's power but also God's generosity.[30] Salvation has both an objective and a subjective side. The objective side is the sanctification of human nature as a whole—the necessary outworking of Christ's objective work on the cross.[31] The subjective side is the sanctification of the wills of particular human beings through grace. Once again here we catch sight of the, for Florovsky, important distinction between necessity and will, no longer in connection with God's being but in relation to created being. God's grace or energy, mediated through the Holy Spirit, indwells our wills and seeks to conform our wills to the will of the triune God. Our human nature is, of necessity, already saved through the death and resurrection of Christ. But our will is not of necessity saved, for that would be an act of violence on the part of grace. Instead of this, God seeks our co-operation (συνεργία). Through such co-working with God, the human being is able to ascend to the divine nature. New creation is understood as the transfiguration of nature and the deification of human beings. Deification is the process whereby creatures are conformed (or fail to be conformed) to the uncreated ideas that God has had from (the aeonic) eternity. The act of creation, which is regarded, as in Barth, as an act of grace, is also brought to perfection through grace. Florovsky uses the notion of energy to explain what grace is. Grace is identified with energy, not to deify grace, but to point to deification through grace.

Lossky, like Florovsky, understands God's grace as uncreated energy. The act of creation is not accomplished without grace, and the creation is never left without grace. The act of creation is effected by the Son and perfected by the Spirit. The two hypostases here are viewed in their *economic* activities. Lossky's interest is principally in the reconciliation of creation in general and especially the reconciliation of humanity with God. Human beings are called to become divine, but they fail to respond because of their alienation from God. God's answer to this failure is to redeem human nature in general and to sanctify human beings as individuals. The redemption is effected, like the act of creation, through Christ; the sanctification, like the perfecting of creation, through the Spirit. Redemption thus, through the Son, frees us *from* our alienation from God. Sanctification, through the Spirit, frees us *for* participation in the divine nature. Lossky argues that western theology has, in emphasizing the first step so strongly, virtually forgotten the second. The Spirit is, in this imbalance, reduced to the status of a mere agent.

---

30. Florovsky, "St Gregory Palamas and the Tradition of the Fathers," *CW*, vol. 1, p. 116.
31. Florovsky, "Redemption," op. cit., p. 147.

For Lossky, like Florovsky, the redemption of human nature as a whole, and thus of every human being, takes place objectively and necessarily in Christ. Sanctification, on the other hand, is brought to perfection only in particular human beings. To this end a co-operation is needed, "a synergy of the two wills, divine and human, a harmony in which grace bears ever more fruit, and is appropriated—'acquired'—by the human person. Grace is a presence of God within us which demands constant effort on our part."[32] Lossky thus rules out any suggestion of force or necessity on the part of God's grace. The main thing for Lossky, however, is that a doctrine of salvation remains incomplete if it remains merely redemption *from*. The positive element of sanctification or deification is needed for its completion.

There are two additional ramifications of Lossky's treatment of grace. First, grace is clearly distinguished from the Spirit, through whom it is mediated. There is no danger here of confusing the giver, that is, the Spirit, with the gift, that is, the grace or energy.[33] The energy is not thereby seen as a created effect or power—it remains God, but God for us, God active in the domain of the economy. Lossky, quoting Clement of Alexandria, can also say that the Holy Spirit is hidden by grace.[34] This does not mean that the hypostasis of the Spirit has ceased from its economic activities in the world. On the contrary, Lossky stresses that these economic activities of the Spirit are indispensable for a satisfactory understanding of salvation. The hypostasis of the Spirit is, however, itself neither seen nor given. In this way, the ineffability of the Spirit is protected. The second ramification of Lossky's treatment of grace is the idea that grace, or energy, can "shine" or be mediated through material things, for example through particular holy people or things (icons, relics, etc.).[35]

Let us sum up what has been said so far. The identity principle presents us with a principally *functional* doctrine of the trinity, in which God imparts Godself to us as a person in the economy of salvation. Particular divine attributes are associated with, or appropriated to, particular trinitarian persons. The Spirit is itself received by human addressees as a person. The Palamite position presents us with an, in principal, *superessential* doctrine of the trinity, in which the Holy Spirit imparts to us the energy or glory or grace of God in the economy but does not impart the essence of God. The attributes are not associated with particular hypostases, but regarded as particular emanations or energies of the divine nature. The Holy Spirit is

---

32. Lossky, *Myst. Theol.*, op. cit., p. 198.
33. Ibid., pp. 162–63.
34. Ibid. Cf. Lossky, *Image and Likeness*, op. cit., p. 23.
35. Lossky, *Myst. Theol.*, op. cit., pp. 189–91.

not received by human subjects as a hypostasis, but "merely" energetically. The identity principle means that the creation is regarded as dependent upon the voluntary act of God, but without distinguishing this act from the being of God. Palamite theology regards the creation as dependent upon the will of God, but this will is distinguished from the essence of God. In both eastern and western theologies, grace is the Holy Spirit received by human beings. To receive grace is to experience God as Spirit. Western theology understands this either as an experience of the person of the Holy Spirit or as an attribute of God, viz. God's good favor. Roman Catholic scholasticism developed the concept of the *habitus,* or indwelling of created grace, in order to describe the effect of grace *within* the human person. Palamite theology understands grace as energy. To receive grace is to experience the uncreated energy or energies. Here grace remains emphatically *uncreated* grace. Human co-operation with God through the energies is both allowed and encouraged. Knowledge of God and the new creation alike are understood in terms of participation. In this way the subject-object distinction is overcome between God and the creation that participates in the divine nature.

Chapter 4
CRITICAL QUESTIONS ABOUT THE
DOCTRINE OF THE TRINITY

೧⊖–⊖ഗ

In the previous chapters the question of being and activity in God has been considered with reference to the thought of Karl Barth, Karl Rahner, Georges Florovsky and Vladimir Lossky. Despite some differences in emphasis, a broad consistency has been noted between the positions of Barth and Rahner as representatives of what I have called the identity principle, and between the positions of Florovsky and Lossky as defenders of the doctrine of energies. A comparison has attempted to shed light on the similarities between the two western authors on the one hand, and between the two eastern authors on the other, while also exploring the differences between the identity principle and the doctrine of energies. I would now like to take this process further by identifying some critical questions that can be addressed to the two positions. They are in fact questions that are either implicitly or explicitly posed by the alternate way of thinking.

Economy Instead of Theology? A Question to the Western Doctrine of God

The identity principle, as it comes to expression in Barth and Rahner, postulates a *functional* doctrine of the trinity, that is, one that understands the divine modes of being primarily on the basis of their economic functions. The doctrine of energies, as expressed by Florovsky and Lossky, postulates a *superessential* doctrine of the trinity, that is, one in which the trinitarian hypostases are regarded as fundamentally independent of economic functions or motifs.

Both Barth's and Rahner's understanding of the trinity rest on a concept of God's self-revelation in a threefold movement. It is argued, on the basis of God's faithfulness or reliability, that this threefold movement is none other than that of the trinitarian essence itself. It can be asked, then, whether this understanding of the trinity is not a step backward to (or a hesitation to go further than) the economic, functional triadology of the early church, which—according to Florovsky and Lossky—was in principle left behind with the developments of the fourth century. Another way of putting the question would be to ask whether the theology of the identity principle fails to reach the level of genuine θεολογία. In other words, does this theology remain, in fact, merely economy (οἰκονομία), speech not about God but merely about the activities of God? This is the question that underlies Lossky's charge that western theology remains on the level of the energies. To western ears it seems a strange and somewhat arrogant suggestion, but genuine dialogue must take such questions seriously.

For Florovsky the trinity is necessary, while the creation is the outworking of the divine will. In contrast, Barth bases his understanding of the trinity in God's will to reveal Godself. The revealed and known trinity is identical with the trinitarian being of God beforehand in Godself. Is this typically western way of thinking about the trinity vulnerable to the critique made by Florovsky and Lossky? If Barth were merely offering an analogy for the trinity, we could answer the question in the negative. But Barth writes as though he were offering more than an analogy; he is seeking to explain the trinity, or more precisely, to explain how God in Godself *is* the trinitarian God. Rahner also seems to introduce "economic motifs" into the doctrine of the trinity in the same way. Although Barth and Rahner want to discard the psychological analogy, they continue to approach the inner being of God on the basis of an economic order of manifestation. This is the case even despite Rahner's genuine attempt to find the greatest possible common ground with the Orthodox. By looking at the problem of the vision of God, I shall address these two related questions. First, does the identity principle carry with it a pre-Nicene understanding of the trinity? Second, is western spirituality impoverished by its inability to take seriously the idea of participation in God? Then I will look briefly at how these apparently speculative questions touch on the question of the *filioque* clause.

It is in the context of discussing the sanctifying vision of God that Lossky[1] puts the question as to whether western theology remains on the level of the energies, or in other words, retains an essentially pre-Nicene triadology. Perhaps there is no real θεολογία in the West, he suggests, merely an οἰκονομία that goes by the name of theology.[2] The Palamite assertion that we are permitted a vision of God's glory but not of the essence, was, argues Lossky, never properly understood in the West. The reason for the failure to understand this assertion, and hesychastic spirituality in general, is to be found in the Thomistic understanding of the beatific vision, in which the saints (normally—though not necessarily—only after death) are granted a vision of the divine *essence*. In Thomas's thinking, God is simple essence or pure actuality (*actus purus*). A human relationship with God comes about

---

1. V. N. Lossky, *The Vision of God* (Leighton Buzzard, 1963).
2. See W. Kern and F.-J. Niemann, *Theologische Erkenntnislehre* (Düsseldorf, 1981), pp. 41–42, for the varying understandings in East and West of the term "theology."

through the action of created, indwelling grace—a grace that is, because it is created, other than God. This "theology," according to Lossky, deals only with the divine activities, that is, οἰκονομία, not θεολογία. On these grounds Lossky argues that Aquinas, despite his references to the aseity of God, is really only speaking about the domain of the energies.[3] Pure actuality is, if we remember the Aristotelian identification of actuality with energy, another name for dynamism or energy. By definition it is not the superessentiality (ὑπερουσιότης) of which Palamite theology speaks. This Thomist idea of a vision of the divine essence has, for Lossky, two implications. First, the aseity of God is actually lost, because God's essence becomes the visible object of the beatific vision. Secondly, ascetic praxis is impoverished, because the concept of participation in God (θέωσις) cannot be taken with full seriousness. Where participation in the divine nature is taken to affirm participation in the divine essence, it is quite proper that western theology should hesitate. But the result is that Christian ascesis is undervalued and the legitimate Christian claim to participation in the life of God (Christian "maximalism," as Lossky calls it on occasions) is reduced to a passive intellectual vision of the divine essence. There remains very little room for human activity in relation to God. The human subject becomes a passive recipient. It is the same passivity before God that Florovsky has labeled "anthropological monophysitism."

How should we evaluate this criticism of Lossky's? It is quite astounding to think that neither Thomas Aquinas nor Karl Barth have sufficiently emphasized God's aseity! The ontological distinction between creator and creation is a major theme of Barth's theology, a theme that he never modified, even when the humanity of God came more to the fore in his later thinking. The trinitarian self-revelation always has behind it the *a priori* of God's inner-trinitarian being. It is, however, the essence, the reality of God, that is revealed. This essence is explained in terms of personhood or subjectivity, and revelation in terms of "hearing God's word" (rather than "seeing God's essence"). But the fundamental axiom remains that God reveals Godself. This "self" is the essence, an active reality that proceeds out of itself in revelation. So we can agree that, on these terms, despite Barth's real emphasis on the beyondness of God, he gives us a concept of God that does not in the end allow for the ineffability of the divine essence that we find in Lossky's theology.

In relation to Rahner's thought, Bernhard Wenisch[4] has made a very similar criticism. Wenisch argues that we can deduce from John's gospel an

---

3. Lossky, *In the Image and Likeness of God* (New York, 1974), p. 122.
4. B. Wenisch, "Zur Theologie Karl Rahners," *MThZ* 28 (1977): 383–97.

I-Thou relationship within the Godhead that is prior to and independent of the trinitarian self-communication of God in the world. This contradicts Rahner's notion of the Son as merely the "self-expression" of the Father.[5] Such an understand is, for Wenisch, a reduction of the biblical witness. It allows for neither the I-Thou relationship within the Godhead (John 17:5) nor the personal initiative of the pre-existent Logos (Phil 2). Wenisch's criticism is precisely that Rahner fails to allow for a fully developed trinity independent of the economy. This failure means that the aseity of God on the one hand and the possibility of participation in God's nature on the other become lost. Wenisch has in fact stated, from a western standpoint, Lossky's critique of the whole western tradition.

Is there in Barth a theology of pure receptivity? This would perhaps be the logical consequence of Barth's earlier theology, and the older discussion of Barth's work has interpreted it in this way. More recent research has revealed more of Barth's political engagement with the issues of his day. In other words, there is indeed a type of Christian maximalism in Barth, a maximalism of resistance to political "principalities and powers." Further, this resistance stems directly from Barth's theological work, in particular his understanding of God's sovereignty. It is not ascesis in the sense that Lossky understands it (though we shall see that other Orthodox writers like Staniloae are more open to seeing political action as a form of Christian ascesis). In any case it can be, like mystical ascesis, a form of spiritual discipline. Barth's theology does not give rise to a mere passivity on the part of human beings. Lossky's critique also includes the question about deification ($\theta\acute{\epsilon}\omega\sigma\iota\varsigma$), or participation ($\mu\acute{\epsilon}\theta\epsilon\xi\iota\varsigma$) in the divine nature. Barth does not use either of these terms, or at least not in a positive sense. The reason is obvious. "Deification" would mean union with God's essence. On the face of it, Lossky's critique seems to stand. The harm done to the notion of aseity and to spirituality in the West is, however, in my opinion, not quite as simple a matter as Lossky suggests. The problem may be one of terminology.

In his comparison of the theologies of Gregory Palamas and Thomas Aquinas, Jürgen Kuhlmann offers a way through the apparent impasse:

> We stand confronted by an apparent contradiction: Thomas made a differentiation between entitative and intentional participation (we will indeed see God's essence, but not become God's essence), while Palamas saw the two together (and therefore denied any vision of the essence). But now Palamas makes this other differentiation (knowledge is not the same as the vision of the

---

5. Ibid., p. 391, n. 13.

[uncreated] light), but Thomas does not make this differentiation, rather declaring knowledge and the light to be one and the same.[6]

Both theologians make a distinction. Thomas distinguishes entitative from intentional participation, so that creatures will not *become* God, but will *see* God. With Palamas there is no such distinction. Participation in the essence of God is ruled out, for that would be to become *essentially* God. But participation (both intentional and entitative together, without their being distinguished) is possible, for Palamas, on the level of the energies. Thomas Aquinas and Gregory Palamas thus use differing terminologies, or perhaps the same terminology, but in differing ways. Both allow for a conditional participation in God, but the way they state the condition is different. With Thomas it is a matter of "intentional" but not entitative participation; with Palamas it is a matter of participation in the energy but not in the essence.

Kuhlmann thus shows the differing approaches and terminologies used in the East and the West in reference to the beatific vision, but the underlying similarity in intention. Kuhlmann's characterization of Palamas's thinking applies also to contemporary Palamites:

> Palamas thinks in personalist terms: God is seen not in his essence, but as he personally *wishes* to make himself known. Like every relationship, this can grow without limits to depth and trust. The step from this side to that indeed involves an ascent, but nothing finally and radically new.[7]

Kuhlmann's characterization of Thomas's thought is applicable to Barth only in a limited sense, but needs less modification to apply to Rahner. "Thomas by contrast knows that we either see God or do not see."[8] Barth, we could say, knows that we either hear God's word or do not hear. The act of hearing encapsulates for Barth, as seeing does for Thomas, the whole relationship between God and human beings. There is no question here of a growth or a progress in the relationship. There is only the question of the either/or. Either we see/hear, or we fail to.

We began by considering two critical questions that can be put to the identity principle in relation to the beatific vision. The first criticism, as it is expressed by Lossky, that the whole western tradition remains on the level of the energies, is simply untenable. The very terms in which this critique is phrased, which assume different levels within the Godhead, is simply not the language of western theology. Thomas presents the matter of the beatific vision, as Kuhlmann has shown, in quite a different way. The human being,

---

6. J. Kuhlmann, *Die Taten des einfachen Gottes: Eine römisch-katholische Stellungnahme zum Palamismus* (Würzburg, 1968), pp. 98–99.
7. Ibid., p. 100.
8. Ibid.

in experiencing a mystical vision of God, does indeed participate in the life of God, but does not become identical with the divine essence. Even so, Lossky's criticism is a reminder that we in the West need to retain a notion of God's ineffability. We need to take care not to reduce God to the level of our own comprehension—as, in Wenisch's estimation, Karl Rahner is in danger of doing.

The second criticism of the identity principle, again given expression by Lossky, is that western spirituality is impoverished because of the loss of any concept of full participation in God, or deification. To some extent we have to agree. "Intentional" participation without "entitative" participation is indeed something less than full participation! Barth's doctrine of reconciliation is indeed less ambitious than the "maximalism" of Lossky's doctrine of deification. At the same time, however, we have to notice that Lossky does not aim at entitative participation in the divine *essence*. It would be equally possible to argue that the claim to a vision of the divine essence is more "maximal" than a claim to a vision of God's glory. But the argument would be just as futile as the original critique. Both theologies use separate terminologies and make different distinctions. Both, however, seek to safeguard the same underlying intention—to praise God as the trinity, to regard human beings as beloved creatures of God, and to deepen the human relationship with God.

Although I have argued against Lossky's critique, it is important to take note of a strength in Orthodox spirituality, namely that it includes an anthropology that recognizes the whole human being. Deification encompasses the human body as well as the soul. There is no place in this doctrine of theosis for any Platonic dualism.[9] Nor is there any danger of this spirituality becoming intellectualized. The doctrine of energies posits a distinction within God between essence and energy, and goes on to view the human person, biblically, as a psychosomatic unity. Body and soul are deified together. The identity principle, in distinguishing between intentional and entitative participation, distinguishes in effect between participation in God and imitation of Christ. The distinction is anthropological rather than theological. It posits a distinction within the human being, between different human capacities.

The danger in such a distinction within the human person is that it can easily give support to an unbiblical separation between spirit and matter, or body and soul, which in turn can be interpreted as a separation between that in the human person which can be sanctified (or deified) and that which

---

9. See esp. J. Meyendorff, *St. Gregory Palamas and Orthodox Spirituality* (New York, 1974), pp. 174ff.

cannot. Western theology does not go so far as to allow this potential separation.¹⁰ The danger remains, however, precisely because western theology has not ventured as boldly as eastern theology to promote the patristic notion of deification. On these grounds Meyendorff is quite right to argue that Orthodoxy, in canonizing Gregory Palamas, affirmed a biblical anthropology and rejected any neo-Platonic anthropology.¹¹ Kuhlmann puts it this way:

> We stand before two equally developed theologies, one that thinks in a 'personalist' way, the other in an 'ontological' way. For Thomas, 'God' is that which is God in Godself; for Palamas 'God' is that which is God, be it in Godself or be it God for us.¹²

Expressed in this way, the Palamite position sounds more acceptable to our contemporary desire to think in personalist and existentialist rather than ontological and essentialist ways. The Palamite emphasis on the psychosomatic unity of the human person is at once more contemporary and more biblical than any dualism of spirit and matter. Such a dualism was perhaps never officially approved in western Christianity, but it can easily float to the surface from the deep, neo-Platonic collective unconscious of western thought.

A similar critique of the identity principle appears in relation to the *filioque* clause. This interpolation into the western creed denotes for Lossky¹³ a confusion of the outer side of God (the economic missions of the Son and the Spirit) with the inner side (the inner-trinitarian processions). In the economy, the Father and the Son do indeed send the Spirit, who makes known the Son. In the inner being, the Spirit proceeds from the Father alone, without any relationship of origin to the Son. The *filioque* thus means for Lossky that the economic relationships between the trinitarian persons are simply carried over into the territory of θεολογία. In other words, the western creed confuses the levels of θεολογία and οἰκονομία. A western response to this, of course, might be that the western tradition uses the

---

10. See, e.g., Florovsky's treatment of the debate in eighteenth century England about the immortality of the soul: *CW*, vol. 3 (Belmont, 1976), pp. 214ff.

11. Meyendorff, *Palamas and Orthodox Spirituality*, op. cit., pp. 174ff. Cf. K. Kern, *Antropologija Sv. Grigorija Palamy* (Paris, 1950).

12. Kuhlmann, op. cit., p. 101. It is precisely this point that Catherine La Cugna has failed to see in her otherwise very helpful book (*God for Us: the Trinity and Christian Life* [San Francisco, 1991]). For La Cugna, only the western, non-Palamite tradition can in the end give us a God who is "for us."

13. Lossky, *Myst Theol.*, op. cit., pp. 156ff.

terms θεολογία and οἰκονομία somewhat differently from the way they are used in the East.[14]

But Lossky's argument does raise some questions about Barth's defense of the *filioque* and Rahner's implicit defense of it. George Hendry[15] has shown that Barth's identification of the inner and economic trinity is an important reason for this defense. Hendry goes on to point out the ensuing difficulties. Barth binds the Son and the Spirit so closely together through the *filioque* that the Spirit becomes effectively just another form of Christ. Barth's pneumatology becomes a part of his christology. The work of the Spirit in fact became more important in Barth's later theology,[16] but without Barth ever revoking his earlier defense of the *filioque*—and this means that his developing pneumatology remains confined within its earlier limits. In the light of Hendry's discussion we can begin to understand the criticisms made by Orthodox thinkers like Nikos Nissiotis that the western theology as a whole is too strongly christocentric.[17]

There is a similar problem in Rahner's retention of a filioquist understanding of the trinity. In the western tradition, the Spirit is regarded as the unifying principle of the trinity. The Spirit constitutes the bond of love between the Father and the Son. The problem is not that the Spirit forms a bond—this in fact is also affirmed in Orthodox theology,[18] on the grounds that each person of the trinity stands in a perichoretic relationship with both of the others. The problem of a filioquist trinity is that the Spirit *constitutes* this bond. The Spirit becomes an embodiment (or personification) of this bond. The Spirit is then seen as little more than a power or a dynamism of the one God. The filioquist understanding of the trinity may indeed avoid the idea of God as a simple monad; but the "trinity" remains little more than a twoness, a binity of the first and the second persons with the Spirit as a less than fully personal bond of unity between them. The Spirit is reduced in fact to that which in Palamite theology is called an energy. The relationship between the hypostasis of the Spirit and power (δύναμις, ἐξουσία)[19] is recognized alike in eastern and western theologies. But if we identify the Spirit no longer *with*, but *as* this power or

---

14. Kern and Niemann, *Theologische Erkenntnislehre*, op. cit., pp. 41–42.

15. G. S. Hendry, *The Holy Spirit in Christian Theology* (London, 1965), pp. 42ff.

16. See. T. Freyer, *Pneumatologie als Strukturprinzip der Dogmatik: Überlegungen im Anschluß an die Lehre von der "Geisttaufe" bei Karl Barth* (Paderborn, 1982).

17. N. A. Nissiotis, *Die Theologie der Ostkirche im Ökumenischen Dialog: Kirche und Welt inorthodoxer Sicht* (Stuttgart, 1968), esp. pp. 21ff and. p. 51.

18. D. Staniloae, *Theology and Church* (New York, 1980), chap. 1.

19. A. M. Aargaard, "Die Erfahrung des Geistes," in O. A. Dilschneider (ed.), *Theologie des Geistes* (Gütersloh, 1980), p. 15.

energy, the Spirit is in effect subordinated to the Father and the Son. The doctrine of energies avoids this tendency, because the energies are regarded as powers or gifts *of* the Spirit. It could be asked, however, whether the identity principle retains an authentic pneumatology, one that is not simply subsumed into the doctrine of grace. Our misgivings are only increased when we hear Rahner equate pneumatology with grace.[20]

Eastern and western theologies both know the anonymity of the Holy Spirit—that is, the difficulty of evaluating the Spirit as a personal subject. In the East it is because the Spirit is "overshadowed" by the energies, not because—as tends to be the case in western theology—it is reduced to something less than fully personal. The most telling evidence of this latter western tendency is the tradition of speaking of the Spirit as a gift. We need here to recognize the ambiguity of the term "gift of the Holy Spirit" (Acts 2:38). This can mean either that Spirit itself is a gift (objective genitive) or that the Spirit gives a gift or gifts that are different from itself, for example, the energy/energies of the Spirit (subjective genitive). The doctrine of energies, needless to say, tends to protect the, albeit hidden, personhood of the Spirit, precisely by seeing the Spirit as the giver or imparter of God's energies.

A Purely Metaphysical, Soteriologically Functionless Doctrine of the Trinity? A Question to the Eastern Doctrine of God

Eastern theology locates the origin of the Son and the Spirit in the Father, because the Father as a person freely wills the communion that comes with the begetting of the Son and the bringing forth of the Spirit. God is by nature trinitarian because of the personhood of the Father, and because personhood involves communion. The energies are identified with the will of the trinitarian God in relation to that which is not God. The will of God is unchanging but brings contingent things into being and to the fulfillment proper to them. The fulfillment of creation—especially the human creature—is to be deified, that is, to attain, through participation in the energies, to a state of uncreatedness. This is what God wills. Is this not, however, a metaphysical system in which the incarnation of the second person of the trinity—the life, death and resurrection of Jesus Christ— become totally superfluous? In other words, is this not a system without any need of God becoming human?[21] The doctrine of energies thus seems to replace the second person of the trinity and to undervalue the third person.

---

20. E.g., Rahner, *The Trinity*, op. cit., p. 120.
21. Wendebourg, *Geist oder Energie: Zur Frage der innergöttlichen Verankerung des christlichen Lebens in der byzantinischen Theologie* (München, 1980), p. 26, n. 94: (Christ's) "earthly life

This idea has been explored by Dorothea Wendebourg, in a two-pronged critique of the Palamite position. First, Wendebourg argues that the trinity is rendered soteriologically functionless by the essence-energies distinction. It becomes a matter of mere metaphysical information about the inner being of God without any connection to the economic activities or attributes. In practical terms the essence-energy distinction becomes more important than the distinction between the trinitarian hypostases. This means a "soteriological modalism,"[22] whereby the doctrine of the trinity is eclipsed by the doctrine of energies. "The energies 'around the essence' take over the function of the persons on the level of the essence," says Wendebourg.[23] This is exactly the error that both Barth and Rahner seek to avoid, according to Wendebourg, by taking the economic activities of the trinitarian persons as their starting point.

Secondly, Wendebourg is of the opinion that this decline in the soteriological function of the doctrine of the trinity did not begin with the formulation of the doctrine of energies, but earlier, with the distinction between the inner and the economic trinity, a distinction that first emerges clearly in the polemical writings of Photius.[24] This led Byzantine theology into an untenable position in that, on the one hand, it had to deny the *filioque* clause, and on the other it had to deny any suggestion that there is *no* inner-trinitarian relationship between the Son and the Spirit.[25] Wendebourg, then, is not criticizing the "Palamite synthesis" of the fourteenth century so much as the systematic-theological foundation on which it was built. She remarks, though, quite correctly, that these two problems are in the end one and the same problem. This is why the principle that identifies the inner and the economic trinity appears, on the face of it, so irreconcilable with the doctrine of energies. I will leave aside the historical question as to the emergence of the doctrine of energies, as the primary concern here is with present-day theology. The question remains, however, as to whether the doctrine of the trinity becomes soteriologically irrelevant in the thought of contemporary Orthodox writers.

As we have seen, Florovsky's explicit discussion of the doctrine of the trinity is to be found in isolated texts that develop the ecclesial analogy of

---

plays no central role.... The only important thing is the permeation of his human nature by the energies." Wendebourg's book is an important source for C. LaCugna (*God for Us*, op. cit., chap. 6), who, though sympathetic to a Cappadocian model of trinitarian thinking, repeats and endorses Wendebourg's criticisms of Palamas and his followers.

22. D. Wendebourg, *Geist oder Energie*, op. cit., p. 63.
23. Ibid., p. 245.
24. Ibid., p. 84.
25. Ibid., p. 97.

the trinity. Soteriology is seen as a function of God's grace or energy. Thus far we can appreciate that soteriology seems to have no direct connection with the Christian experience of God as trinity. Florovsky's important distinction between nature and will appears again in relation to soteriology as it does in relation to the doctrine of creation. Here it is concerned with the human nature and human will, however. Human nature is saved through the incarnation of Christ, but the human will through grace, or the energy of the Spirit. Thus the hypostasis of the Spirit does indeed play a role in the process of salvation. There still remains the charge that Florovsky sees no role for the incarnate Logos. But again we can distinguish this from the inner being of the Logos which remains within the being of the trinity even during the earthly life of Christ. Indeed, the same can be said of the Spirit—it is in the trinity, while at the same time active (energetic) among and around and within us. The trinitarian persons are ineffable in the same sense in which every human person is ineffable. We can never claim fully to understand another human being, or even ourselves.

Lossky discusses the doctrine of the trinity without any apparent reference to the question of salvation. In the *Mystical Theology* far more space is devoted to the energies than to the trinity. The chapter about the uncreated energies begins with the question: How do we really become "participants in the divine nature" (2 Peter 1:4)? This is a soteriological question, and Lossky asks it here, in relation to the doctrine of energies, rather than in relation to the doctrine of the trinity. Thus far, Wendebourg's criticism seems justified. The trinitarian distinctions between persons seem to be, with Lossky as with Florovsky, of little significance.

In the chapters about the economies of the Son and the Spirit, however, we find Lossky's discussion of the soteriological activities of the second and third hypostases. God descends to us in the incarnation, we ascend to God in deification.[26] Incarnation (σάρκωσις) and deification (θέωσις) correspond to one another. The works of Christ concern human nature as a whole in that they effect our redemption, and the works of the Holy Spirit concern individual human beings insofar as their deification is effected.[27] Particular trinitarian hypostases are thus active in the economy of salvation, the Son's work effecting something on behalf of all, the Spirit's work effecting something for particular people who take upon themselves a life of cooperation with God. The trinity thus has indeed a soteriological function. We notice, however, that this whole theme, in Lossky as in Florovsky, is

---

26. Lossky, *The Mystical Theology of the Eastern Church* (New York, 1976), p. 137.
27. Ibid., p. 166. This distinction between the "economies" of the Son and the Spirit is criticized by D. Staniloae in *Theology and the Church* (New York, 1980), pp. 65–66.

discussed in relation to the side of God that encounters us, that is, in relation to the energies, not the essence. We are not dealing here with the essential persons of the Son and the Spirit, but with their outer activities or energies. Does this render the doctrine of the trinity soteriologically functionless? The answer to this question really depends on where we place the emphasis, on person or work. If we read, in Lossky's book, that redemption is *the work* of the Son, and deification *the work* of the Spirit, we emphasize the activity or energy of these hypostases. Then we can certainly argue that the persons are not sufficiently emphasized. There is then indeed a danger that the trinitarian hypostases might recede into the background—especially when we remember that the activity or energy is that of the common trinitarian will. If, however, we read: redemption is the work of *the Son*, deification is the work of *the indwelling Spirit*, then, clearly, we are emphasizing particular hypostases.

This much we can concede, that there is a danger in Lossky that the doctrine of the trinity may be lost, especially—as Wendebourg emphasizes[28]—when the distinction between being and act, or between inner-trinitarian processions and outer missions, is polemically asserted. But we also have to say just as emphatically that the energy doctrine does not necessarily bring this danger in its train. A distinction between the trinitarian persons on the one hand and the common trinitarian energy on the other can be held without losing an effective doctrine of the trinity. The doctrine of energies need not replace the doctrine of the trinity. It can complete it and bring it to clear and, more importantly, practical expression. So, how are we to avoid making the doctrine of the trinity functionless, and at the same time retain the doctrine of energies? Three arguments suggest themselves.

First, the theological environment in which the doctrine of energies comes to expression is remarkable on several counts in the way it treats the doctrine of the trinity.

(a) Orthodox thinkers work from a social or plurality[29] model of the trinity, in contrast to the western starting point in the unity model, which finds its normative analogy in the human psyche. Eastern theology has thus always emphasized the threeness of the hypostases, as opposed to the western tendency to emphasize the unity of essence (or of the subject, since the Enlightenment). The standing danger of modalism (including any "soteriological" variety of modalism) is therefore less evident in eastern than in western theological thinking. If we hold together the traditional western

---

28. Wendebourg, *Geist oder Energie*, op. cit., p. 79.
29. D. Brown, *The Divine Trinity* (London, 1985), pp. 272ff.

tendency to start from the unity of God and the Augustinian concept of the common activities of the trinity *ad extra*, then there is indeed a danger of soteriological modalism, because then the practical existential significance of the trinity is threatened. The danger exists in connection with the Palamite doctrine of energies. But the danger is lessened by the eastern *a priori* of a plurality model of the trinity.

(b) Where Florovsky sees a significant step forwards in the trinitarian theology of the fourth century, Wendebourg sees only a negative development. For Florovsky, the earlier, purely economic understanding of the trinity was at that time superseded by a genuine θεολογία, that is, a doctrine of God the trinity free of economic motifs. For Wendebourg, the genuine economic foundations of the trinity were lost in this move, and a speculative trinity without basis in the *Heilsgeschichte* was set up. I have no doubt that this process indeed took place in the West, especially in conjunction with the psychological analogy. But in the East? What actually took place in the fourth century was that theological expression was given to the traditional sense that the three persons were equally to be worshipped. That is to say, the equality of the three hypostases was asserted dogmatically as well as doxologically. This dogmatic expression was formulated in the words of the Nicene-Constantinopolitan creed. Why does this theological event receive such different assessments from Florovsky and Wendebourg? Wendebourg's concern is for the soteriological *relevance* of the doctrine of the trinity, which is assured by the trinitarian ordering of sending and worship.[30] This concern for relevance is to be understood in the context of the western unity model. Florovsky's concern, on the other hand, is to insist that divine *identity* of the three hypostases is assured by the trinitarian doxology. This is given expression by the "equally to be worshipped" formula of the creed. This concern for the common divine identity of the hypostases is to be understood in the context of the eastern social analogy of the trinity. Both concerns make sense in their own contexts. Too great an emphasis on the equally divine identity of the hypostases would, in the western context, serve to further the natural tendency to modalism. Too great an emphasis on the autonomy of the hypostases (that is, the autonomous relevance of

---

30. J. Moltmann, "Die versöhnende Kraft der Dreieinigkeit im Leben der Kirche und der Gesellschaft," *Ökumenisches Forum* 6 (1983): esp. 57–59. The order of sending: the Father creates through the Son in the Holy Spirit. The order of worship: the Holy Spirit glorifies the Son, and through the Son and with him, glorifies the Father. The trinitarian doxology: Glory to the Father and to the Son and to the Holy Spirit. For the methodological contrast between relevance and identity I am indebted to J. Moltmann, *The Crucified God: The Cross of Christ as the Foundation and Criticism of Christian Theology* (London, 1974), chap. 1.

each of them) would, in the eastern context, further the tendency to view the three hypostases as being quite independent entities, perhaps even separated from one another. The development of trinitarian thinking in the fourth century, including the emphasis on the equal status of the three hypostases, is very important. The insight, that each of the hypostases is genuinely and person-specifically active in the economy of salvation, is just as important.

(c) We must recognize the way in which Christ's presence is understood in Eastern Orthodox worship and spirituality. Werner Elert[31] has explored this theme in connection with the spirituality of the Oriental Orthodox churches, but his argument applies, at least to some extent, also to the spirituality of the Chalcedonian churches of the East. The Palamite distinction was developed in a context of practical spirituality, as a practical assistance for the hesychast monks of Mt. Athos, and so a consideration of spirituality is relevant here. The picture of the incarnate Christ (*Christusbild*) is, in this context, to be found in the practical ascesis whereby the Christian seeks *to become Christ*. The second person of the trinity becomes present and visible in the human being who, through God's grace, dedicates his/her life to the quest for deification. This quest is the place where the doctrine of the trinity becomes soteriologically relevant, and the Christian life finds its anchoring in the inner life of the holy trinity.

Secondly, the energies are mediated through the Spirit. They are often in fact called the "energies of the Spirit." Dimitru Staniloae tells us that "the fathers regarded the Holy Spirit as the person who brings into souls divine energy, which becomes in them the capacity for knowing God and loving him."[32] This relationship between the Holy Spirit and energy was, according to Staniloae, first formulated by Gregory Palamas himself. In other words, we are not dealing here with a tension, far less a choice, between Spirit *or* energy,[33] but with the mediation of the common energy of the trinity through the Spirit. Despite appearances, this is *not* thought of as an *appropriation* of the energy to one of the trinitarian hypostases, namely the Holy Spirit. Rather, the Spirit mediates or imparts the energies, and is in turn manifested in creatures who/which are transfigured by the energies.[34] The energy of God was, according to Lossky, ineffective from the Fall till

---

31. W. Elert, *Der Ausgang der altkirchliche Christologie: Eine Untersuchung über Theodor von Pharan und seine Zeit als Einführung in die alte Dogmengeschichte* (Berlin, 1957).

32. D. Staniloae, "The Holy Spirit in the Theology and Life of the Orthodox Church," *Sobornost'*, 1975, p. 5.

33. As Wendebourg puts it in the title of her book, *Geist oder Energie*, op. cit.

34. Lossky, *Myst Theol*, op. cit., p. 172–73.

Pentecost, so that the post-Pentecost working of grace is of a different order from the grace that was apparent in the Old Testament. For the people of the Old Testament grace was purely external; Christians, on the other hand, experience grace as the indwelling of the Holy Spirit. Lossky argues, not entirely clearly, that the Holy Spirit is thus now present in the world not merely as activity but also as a person.[35] The main point is that, in spite of anything that can be said of the history of Palamism, contemporary Palamite theologians do not replace the person of the Spirit with the impersonal energies, precisely because the energies are *the energies of the Spirit.* The doctrine of the trinity is thus *not* rendered soteriologically functionless. In one place Lossky remarks that, in the level of the economy, the Spirit is not distinguished from grace, but is overshadowed by grace.[36] We could perhaps see this as a practical replacement of the person of the Spirit by grace. But in the context of Lossky's thought as a whole we can see that this is not the intention. The person of the Spirit is indeed at work, behind the energies of the Spirit. Thus the economic work of the Spirit is not replaced by the energies in contemporary Palamite theology, but rather understood in terms of energy.

Thirdly, it could be asked whether the unity of the energy in neo-Palamite theology is simply another way of expressing the axiom implicit in the Augustinian tradition that the outward works of the trinity are indivisible (*opera trinitatis ad extra indivisa sunt*). This axiom has been strongly criticized by Rahner in his discussion of the doctrine of appropriation. Rahner's concern above all is to base the doctrine of the trinity in the history of salvation. Thus he argues for the real indwelling of the Spirit in creatures and the real relationships between human beings and particular divine hypostases. In other words, Rahner argues against the notion of a relationship between human beings and God-in-general. God's three "modes of subsistence" are modes of God's presence with us. Rahner argues this polemically against any speculative understanding of the trinity, above all against that implied in the psychological analogy. On this basis Rahner criticizes the doctrine of appropriation. If the economic working of God is understood primarily as the activity of God-in-general, which is then appropriated to particular persons of the trinity, then the experience of God as trinity is in effect denied. We are no longer speaking in trinitarian terms, but of God-in-general.

For Palamite thought, the unity of the energies *ad extra* is rather different. It has already been noted that the energies of the trinity are imparted

---

35. Ibid., p. 157–58.
36. Lossky, *Image and Likeness*, op. cit., p. 23.

through the person of the Holy Spirit. Even if we accept Rahner's critique of the doctrine of appropriation, we do not have to conclude from this a denial of the unity of the divine energy. In the context of the eastern model of trinitarian thinking, viz. the plurality model, the unity of the energy means simply that the three hypostases possess a common will. In the economy, the three trinitarian persons work together in perfect harmony of will, perfect consensus. The one will of God corresponds to the one energy, which is imparted, however, in various ways as a plurality of energies by the hypostasis of the Spirit.

God as a Person? A Question to the Western Doctrine of God

The identity principle as it appears in the theologies of Karl Barth and Karl Rahner speaks of God *as a person* who reveals him- or herself in a threefold manner. The doctrine of energies speaks of the *trinitarian essence* of God, which of itself is inaccessible, while God is at the same time accessible in the energies. The notion of God as a person (or subject) rests, it could be argued, on an individualistic concept of God. This individualism is criticized in Florovsky's discussion of catholicity or *sobornost'*. The point is that the trinity cannot be simply a subject. It must be a sort of intersubjectivity. Further, the authentic human person develops only in such intersubjectivity, principally within the intersubjective community of the church insofar as this is understood on the analogy of the (social) trinity. Florovsky sets this notion of intersubjectivity over against both individualism and collectivism—by implication, against the characteristic errors of capitalist and socialist society, respectively. Implicitly the identity principle comes under criticism for its individualistic tendencies.

This critique we can usefully compare to that of Franz Xaver Bantle,[37] who argues that Rahner's understanding of the trinity "comes to completion in revelation and redemption alone."[38] This is in fact a variation on Lossky's critique that western theology as a whole remains on the level of the economy of salvation. The roots of this tendency are to be found, according to Bantle, in an unsatisfactory concept of person. We have already noted the tendency on the part of both Barth and Rahner to speak of God as a person, a term suggesting a single subjectivity or center of consciousness. In fact this suggestion is reinforced by the embarrassment of both writers about the traditional trinitarian term "person," and their substitution of terms like "mode of being" (Barth), "mode of subsistence" or "mode of givenness"

---

[37]. F. X. Bantle, "Person und Personbegriff in der Trinitätslehre Karl Rahners," *MThZ* 30 (1979): 11–24.

[38]. Ibid., pp. 15.

(Rahner). Rahner argues in fact that the term "person" in its contemporary sense can only be applied to God, not to the hypostases of the trinity—presumably because "person" in contemporary speech means an independent individual without necessary reference to other individuals. Jürgen Moltmann has criticized this concept of person by referring to newer personalist thought that sees personhood not in the independent individual but in the relationship between an "I" and a "Thou." In this sense, it can be argued that the term person is particularly suited to the trinitarian understanding of God. Lossky is quite correct when he discerns the roots of modern philosophical personalism in the church's doctrine of the trinity.[39]

One of the generally accepted differences between the eastern and the western understandings of the trinity is, as I have suggested above, the difference between a social or plurality model and a unity model. From this perspective, the trinitarian thinking of Barth and Rahner stands firmly in the western tradition, while Florovsky's ecclesial analogy places his thinking in line with the traditional eastern social or plurality model. Several contemporary authors[40] have argued for the greater coherence of the plurality model, without however casting doubt on the identity principle. But we could ask whether the divergence of these two models of trinitarian thinking is quite such a separate problem from the divergence between the identity principle and the doctrine of energies. The nexus that Bantle draws between Rahner's unsatisfactory concept of person and his strong advocacy of the identity principle suggests the issues are not so completely unrelated.

Bantle shows that Rahner postulates only *one* consciousness in God, a consciousness that communicates itself in a threefold manner. This means that there is, for Rahner, no I-Thou relationship in God.[41] We can see here the tendency noted by Moltmann to regard the Spirit as not fully hypostatized or personified.[42] But Rahner has gone further—not only is the Spirit scarcely a person, but the Son also. The Son is primarily understood as the self-expression of the Father. The first person of the trinity escapes this depersonalization only by being identified with God in Godself.[43] Bantle argues that Rahner's concept of person as *independent person* brings with it a similarly individualistic concept of God. God becomes a single person who

---

39. See Clement, *Orient-Occident*, op. cit., pp. 33 ff. Qv. C. Schwöbel and C. Gunton (eds), *Persons, Divine and Human: King's College Essays in Theological Anthropology* (Edinburgh, 1991).
40. J. Moltmann, *The Trinity and Kingdom of God* (London, 1981); Brown, *The Divine Trinity*, op. cit.
41. Bantle, op. cit., p. 13.
42. Moltmann, *Trinity and Kingdom of God*, op. cit., p. 169.
43. K. Rahner, *Theological Investigations* (London, 1961ff.), vol. 1, pp. 79ff.

imparts him-/herself in three different ways. The three "modes of being" are needed for the economy of revelation. With the exception of this *a priori*, there is simply nothing to say about the inner trinity.[44] Rahner has no choice but to identify the immanent with the economic trinity. This means that there is no "immanence of the trinity beyond the economy of salvation."[45] This in turn means, according to Bantle, that Rahner loses sight of the biblical witness to an I-Thou relationship between the Father and the Son as two complete centers of consciousness or subjectivity. Bantle draws the following conclusion: "All in all it is clear: Rahner's understanding of the divine persons and his thesis, *resultant on this understanding* of the divine persons, that the immanent trinity and the trinity in the economy of salvation are one and the same, is not justified in the light of the biblical passages discussed here."[46]

I am not personally convinced that Rahner's concept of person precedes his basic axiom. The identity principle may indeed be the foundational axiom that Rahner claims it to be, especially since Rahner is so clearly dependent upon Barth on this question. The important thing is, though, that in Rahner's thought the identity principle is closely bound up with an individualistic concept of person. If the triunity of God is understood in the first instance as a type of self-revelation (or self-communication or self-giving), it is very difficult to avoid the corollary that only *one* subjectivity (or *one* center of consciousness) stands behind this self-revelation. From this it is difficult to avoid the reductionist understanding of personhood that Rahner arguably gives us. This is indeed a weakness of the identity principle. If Bantle's critique is valid, Rahner's postulating of this principle is *based on* an erroneous notion of personhood. Bantle's critique is very similar to Lossky's critique of the whole western tradition, that it never actually rises above the level of the energies. Nothing is said about the inner-trinitarian relationships aside from their connectedness to the economy. Lossky's generalization is not valid, of course, precisely because Bantle, writing from within the western tradition, can bring the same criticism to Rahner.

Yves Congar[47] underscores Bantle's critique. Although he expresses high regard for Rahner's contribution to trinitarian theology, Congar does not accept his basic axiom uncritically. Congar accepts the first clause ("the economic trinity is the immanent trinity"), but refuses the second ("and vice versa"). The first clause affirms that our knowledge of God as trinity is

---

44. Bantle, op. cit., pp. 14–15.
45. Ibid., p. 15.
46. Ibid., p. 18.
47. Y. Congar, *I Believe in the Holy Spirit* (New York and London, 1983) Vol. 3, pp. 13–17.

dependent upon the history of salvation, that is, upon God's imparting of Godself to us. But the second clause represents for Congar a claim to know too much about God. "The economic trinity reveals the immanent trinity—but does it reveal it entirely?" God is much more than we can possibly imagine. This "more" is not inconsistent with what we have known and experienced—but it is more. This reservation on Congar's part is similar to Lossky's notion of the inaccessibility of God. If we claim to know the inner essence of God, we deceive ourselves. At most we know God on the plane on which God has entered into our experience, that is, the plane of the energies.

God's Super-Essentiality? A Question to the Eastern Doctrine of God

The doctrine of energies distinguishes between the essence (or super-essentiality) and the energies of God. We can ask whether this position takes us any further than the essentialist (or substantialist) notion of divinity common in western thought till the time of Hegel but now largely replaced by a notion of God's unity as a subject.[48] Is God simply viewed in the end as supreme substance? Speech about God's essence (or superessentiality) seems unavoidable if we seek to work out systematically the Palamite distinction. Here, however, we also need to listen to the neo-Palamite criticism of western essentialism. The doctrine of energies, according to John Meyendorff, offers us the possibility of a Christian existentialism. "If one identifies the being of God with the essence *only*—as it was done in the West since Augustine—this essence loses its absolute transcendence, incomprehensibility, and immutability."[49] In other words, western theology demands of the concept of essence two quite different tasks: that of denoting the unity of God in Godself, and that of denoting the unity of God in relation to us. This leads to a confusion, according to Meyendorff. Eastern theology reserves the concept of essence to denote God's beyondness. But in doing so, it does not simply add another essentialist category, the energies, to the Godhead. Rather, according to Meyendorff, the eastern doctrine offers a nonessentialist approach to the knowledge of God. "The originality of the Palamite response to the essentialist concept of God does not consist in adding another element—the energies—to the Divine being, but in thinking of God Himself in existentialist terms, while holding to His absolute transcendence."[50] God is experienced in God's actions, and these alone.

---

48. Moltmann, *Trinity and Kingdom of God*, op. cit., pp. 10ff.
49. J. Meyendorff, *Christ in Eastern Christian Thought* (New York, 1975), p. 213.
50. Meyendorff, *Palamas and Orthodox Spirituality*, op. cit., p. 126.

Christos Yannaras[51] has developed this idea by viewing the doctrine of energies in close relationship with the thought of Martin Heidegger. We can say nothing whatsoever about the essence of a thing according to Yannaras. We can only speak of its presence (that is, its energy).[52] The being or nature of a thing in the abstract is unknowable. Being or nature can be known only ἐν προσώποις,[53] that is, only insofar as one person is distinguishable, by his/her characteristics or energies, from other persons (or one thing from other things). Yannaras sees parallels here between Heidegger's understanding of truth and the Palamite understanding of the knowledge of God. The truth is "the coming into appearance, the coming out of hiddenness." The *Being* of the existent thing is not identical with its objective reality, that is, with its given "essentiality" (*essentia*, οὐσία), but is grasped as energy, as the concrete event of "coming to light," as coming out of hiddenness into dis-covery, "out of absence into presence."[54] Heidegger in this way overcomes the distinction between essence and existence and replaces this distinction with the idea of existence (*Da-sein*) as ecstatic event, as coming to appearance or as being uncovered.[55] This, according to Yannaras, is precisely the intention of the Palamite doctrine of energies. In mystical experience God is experienced in a sensible or aesthetic (in contrast to an intellectual or noetic) way, precisely because God makes Godself available to us in the energies, while remaining at the same time essentially inaccessible to us. God reveals Godself as event, ἐν προσώποις, insofar as God comes to appearance out of hiddenness. This event, in which we can experience God's presence, is consistent with God in Godself. The distinction between essence and energy is an ontological distinction. It is not a merely functional distinction (like that between one energy and another),[56] nor is it a separation or division. A separation could mean an inconsistency between God in Godself and God in relation to us. Yannaras argues, in other words, that our knowledge of God begins and ends with our actual experience of God—that is, the experience of the history of salvation as it is understood and appreciated for us and in our time. Yannaras is saying exactly the same thing here as Meyendorff, when he argues that for Palamism God is regarded not in an essentialist, but in an existentialist way.

---

51. C. Yannaras, *Person und Eros: Eine Gegenüberstellung der Ontologie der griechischen Kirchenväter und der Existenzphilosophie des Westens* (Göttingen, 1982).

52. Ibid., p. 17.

53. Ibid., p. 26.

54. Ibid., p. 21.

55. Ibid., pp. 39–40. Cf. C. Yannaras *De l'absence et de l'inconnaissance de Dieu apres les ecrites aréopagitiques et Martin Heidegger* (Paris, 1971), p. 97.

56. C. Yannaras, *The Freedom of Morality* (New York, 1984), pp. 100, 111–12.

The question that has been posed is thus to be answered in the negative. Although neo-Palamism does indeed use the term essence (οὐσία), it is not to introduce the essentialist or substantialist notion of God that we find in the older western theological tradition.[57] Palamite theology starts from what Meyendorff calls "the divine *existence* made accessible to us in Christian experience."[58] It does not ask about the *essence* of God. The ramifications of this starting point are huge, according to Yannaras. In the West, God has been regarded as simple essence. Everything other than the divine essence is God's creation. This means that God can be known only intellectually. There is no basis for any sensual knowledge of God, or any notion of bodily participation in the life of God. This in turn leads to an intellectualization[59] of understanding as a whole, and specifically in relation to our understanding of God. In contrast, Yannaras argues that for Palamite theology "the acceptance of this distinction between essence and energies means an understanding of truth as personal *relationship*, that is, as an experience of life, and of knowledge as *participation* in the truth and not as an understanding of meanings that result from intellectual abstraction."[60] The questions as to whether Palamite theology is because of this more humane than the more abstract western theology is a matter we can leave open. It is enough to say here that the Palamite notion of superessentiality is not simply to be likened to the older western concept of divine substance.

An Illogical Distinction? A Question to the Eastern Doctrine of God

A related question is this. Is the Palamite distinction between essence (or superessentiality) and energies a real or merely a rational distinction? In other words, is it a question of ontology or epistemology?[61] Western

---

57. It could be asked whether this question is even relevant in the light of the replacement of "substance" by "subjectivity" as the fundamental concept for the doctrine of God in recent western theology (see J. Moltmann, *Trinity and Kingdom of God* [London, 1981], p. 10–16). D. Staniloae (*Orthodoxe Dogmatik* [Zürich/Gütersloh, 1985], pp. 270–72) points to the idea of trinitarian intersubjectivity, whereby God is thought of, at one and the same time, as a trinity of subjects and also as a single subject: "God is pure subject or a threeness of subjects."

58. Meyendorff, *Palamas and Spirituality*, op, cit., p. 123.

59. See H. Aldenhoven, "The question of the procession of the Holy Spirit and its connection with the life of the Church," in L. Vischer, *Spirit of God, Spirit of Christ* (London/Geneva, 1981), pp. 121–32.

60. C. Yannaras, "The Distinction between Essence and Energies and its Importance for Theology," *StVladThQ* 19 (1975): 241.

61. C. La Cugna, op. cit., pp. 186–97, sees this as one of the three critical issues in relation to Palamite thought. Another is the breach between *theologia* and *economia*, and the third is the primarily historical question of patristic antecedents to Palamas. Qv. K. Ware, "Debate about Palamism," *ECR* 9 (1977): 59.

theology, if it concedes a distinction at all between inner and economic trinity, allows this only as a rational distinction (*distinctio rationalis*), that is, as a distinction that has its basis in the limitations of human thought.[62] Eastern theology on the other hand regards the essence-energies distinction (and thus the distinction between inner and economic trinity) as a real distinction (*distinctio realis*), that is, as a distinction within God, not dependent on anything within the creation, independent even of the existence or nonexistence of a creation. A logical problem arises here. The ineffability of God's inner being must be ineffable *to someone*, someone who is not God. Although the trinitarian distinctions between hypostases may be prior to and independent of a creation, the very idea of a distinction between the inner and the economic seems to demand the existence (at least potentially) of an economic domain, that is, a creation. It seems illogical to regard the distinction as anything more than a purely rational distinction. If this is a *real* distinction in God, as neo-Palamite thinkers consistently argue, then we could ask, is not the simplicity of God—God's absolute and indivisible unity—called in question?[63] Behind this question is the suspicion that Palamas and his followers have introduced a neo-Platonic system of semidivine emanations. This, and other criticisms, have been made independently by Bernhard Schultze[64] and Rowan Williams.[65] Williams characterises the Palamite distinction as a piece of "dubious scholasticism"[66] based on a confusion of Aristotelian and neo-Platonic philosophical terms. This criticism is developed carefully and supplemented by a positive appreciation of the personalist and existentialist elements in Orthodox theology, elements which, in Williams' opinion, overshadow and in the end render the Palamite distinction unnecessary.

Kallistos Ware attempts to defend the Palamite position by reducing the gap between ontology and epistemology. Williams, he argues, has considered Palamas's thought without reference to its historical and intellectual environment, and as a consequence imposes upon it the

---

62. E. Jüngel: "Das Verhältnis von ökonomischer und immanenter Trinität," *ZThK* 72 (1975): 353–64.

63. B. Schultze, "Grundfragen des theologischen Palamismus," *OstKirchSt* 24 (1975): 132.

64. B. Schultze, "Die Bedeutung des Palamismus in der russischen Theologie der Gegenwart," *Scholastik* 26 (1951): 390–412; B. Schultze, *Das Gottesproblem in der Osttheologie* (Münster, 1967); B. Schultze, "Grundfragen," op. cit.; B. Schultze, "Zur Gotteserkenntnis in der griechischen Patristik," *Greg* 63 (1982): 525–58; B. Schultze, "Hauptthemen der neueren russische Theologie," in W. Nyssen, H.-J. Schulz and P. Wiertz (eds), *Handbuch der Ostkirche*, vol. 1 (Düsseldorf, 1984), pp. 391–92.

65. R. D. Williams, "The Philosophical Structures of Palamism," *ECR* 9 (1977): 27–44.

66. Williams, "The Philosophical Structures of Palamism," op. cit., p. 44.

inappropriate categories of western scholasticism. Where Williams argues that the essence-energies distinction is merely a rational distinction, a reflection on the capacity of human thought, that is, a matter of epistemology, rather than an ontological distinction, Ware offers this reply: "If we say, as the Cappadocians for example are concerned to do, that God is unknowable in a unique sense, we are not merely making a statement about the limitations of our human understanding, but a statement about God himself."[67] Ware goes on to set himself against any either/or thinking in this regard, against the suggestion that this must be either one sort of distinction or the other. Ware's argument is not entirely satisfactory. Many Orthodox authors, for example Lossky, emphasize very strongly the ontological status of the essence-energies distinction, often without clearly explaining the reason for this emphasis. Although Palamite theologians insist on the reality of the distinction, this remains a puzzling idea to western thought.

I want to explore this problem area by focusing on two questions. First, does the essence-energies distinction threaten the simplicity of God, so that differing degrees of divinity are introduced? Secondly, is it conceivable to regard the essence-energy distinction as a real, rather than merely, rational distinction?

Florovsky discusses the energies in the context, always, of his exposition of the doctrine of creation. Here the distinction between God's nature and God's will is basic. Should we identify God's will with God's nature, then it follows that we must introduce gradations either into the doctrine of God or into the doctrine of creation. In such a move we hear echoes of Arius, according to Florovsky. Lossky is also careful to distinguish between Christian and neo-Platonic apophasis, and thereby avoid any gradations of deity. If we accept Andrew Louth's[68] criteria for deciding between Christian and neo-Platonic mysticism, we have to agree that the mysticism both Florovsky and Lossky defend is a genuinely Christian mysticism.

The real problem lies in what we could call an oversimplistic concept of God's simplicity. The idea of the absolute and final simplicity of the One is itself essentially neo-Platonic. Christian mysticism seeks not the Alone, the

---

67. K. Ware, "The Debate about Palamism," *ECR* 9 (1977): 60. Cf. D. Coffey ("The Palamite Doctrine of God: a New Perspective," *StVladThQ* 32 [1988]: 329–58), who seeks common ground with Palamite thought by arguing that "Palamas nowhere goes so far as to characterize his distinction as 'real'" (p. 329). This may well be true of Palamas himself, but it does not hold for all contemporary Palamite theologians.

68. A. Louth, *The Origins of the Christian Mystical Tradition: From Plato to Denys* (Oxford, 1981), chap. 10. These criteria, summarized, are: (a) God is regarded not as an abstraction, but as personal; (b) the soul is regarded not as divine, but created; (c) virtue is regarded not as a means of purification, but as a fruit of the Spirit.

absolutely simple One, but the Three-in-One. The trinity is indeed simple, insofar as the hypostases are neither deities in their own right nor "parts" of the Godhead. The fulness of deity indwells each of the trinitarian hypostases. But the same is also true, in Palamite understanding, of the uncreated energies. The energy is a divine emanation. Unlike the processions of the Son and the Spirit, the energy is not, however, a hypostatic procession. Rather, it is an anhypostatic (that is, impersonal) procession, mediated through the hypostasis of the Spirit. Kuhlmann, in the title[69] of his eirenical comparison of the thoughts of Gregory Palamas and Thomas Aquinas, sees no contradiction in speaking of the "acts of the simple God." Bernhard Schultze expresses some understandable anxiety, or perhaps frustration, at the Palamite tendency to speak of a "higher essence" and a "lower Godhead."[70] But it is also important to notice that contemporary Orthodox commentators are fully aware of the dangers inherent in this way of speaking, and seek to avoid these dangers. The simplicity of God is called in question, they quite correctly point out, not only by the doctrine of energies but also by the doctrine of the trinity itself. The God of biblical experience is not as simple as Schultze seems to suggest.

In response to the second of our questions, it is to be noted that neo-Palamite thinkers are quite consistent in arguing that the essence-energies distinction is a real ontological distinction within God, not merely a *distinctio rationalis*. This contention is, in my opinion, an emphasis that the subject of the discussion is not humanity, but God; that the distinction is theological, not anthropological—as it would be if it claimed to say something about *human* intellectual capacity, that is to say, what *we* can or cannot know about God. In this connection the not always clearly defined notion of antinomy comes to the fore. Schultze sees antinomy simply as self-contradiction, and asks how antinomic thinking can possibly relate to logical reason. Rowan Williams poses a very similar question.

Schultze, in attempting to explore this notion of antinomy, fails to go further than the Aristotelian principle of no self-contradiction, viz. "A cannot be B and at the same time and under the same conditions not be B."[71] Schultze asks, "does my dialogue-partner accept the Aristotelian formulation of this principle or not?" The provocative tone of this question shows no openness, at least in the article under discussion, to the idea of antinomy as paradoxical or dialectical truth. For Schultze, the rules of Aristotelian logic seem to be the final criteria of truth. This is quite a

---

69. *Die Taten des einfachen Gottes*, op. cit.
70. Schultze, "Grundfragen," op. cit., p. 107.
71. Ibid., p. 112.

remarkable position after almost three quarters of a century of dialectical theology in the West. Both sides of the argument seem bedevilled by an overly propositional understanding of truth.

Kallistos Ware's answer to this position—as it finds expression in Rowan Williams rather than Schultze—is to try to explain the notion of antinomy not simply in negative terms as contradiction, but positively by reference to dialectic:

> By 'antinomy' in theology I mean the affirmation of two contrasting or opposed truths, which cannot be reconciled on the level of the discursive reason although a reconciliation is possible on the higher level of contemplative experience. Because God lies 'beyond' the world in a unique sense, he cannot be precisely conceived by the human reason or exactly described by human language. But if there are no exact descriptions of God, there are many 'pointers.' In order to reach out towards that which is inconceivable, the Christian tradition speaks in 'anti-nomic' fashion—as Newman put it, 'saying and unsaying to a positive effect.' If we rest satisfied with a strictly 'logical' and 'rational' theology—meaning by this the logic and reason of fallen man—then we risk making idols out of our finite, human concepts. Antinomy helps us to shatter these idols and to point, beyond logic and discursive reason, to the living reality of the infinite and uncreated God.[72]

Theology is thus, for Ware, a reaching out toward that which is ungraspable. It can be understood either as intellectual discipline or ascetic praxis, or both. The antinomic method recognizes the ineffability of God, and Ware demonstrates the role of antinomy in the formulation of the doctrines of the incarnation and the trinity. The main thing is this. Antinomic thinking does not mean incomprehensible or irrational thinking. This is true as much in relation to the doctrine of energies as it is in other areas of theology. Ware distinguishes between discursive reason (διάνοια, *ratio*) and spiritual understanding (νοῦς, *intellectus*). Each has its own legitimate function. The use of "spiritual" understanding (rather than discursive reason) as such is not irrational, he argues. Irrationality occurs only when this spiritual understanding is misused. If we never venture past the limits of discursive reason, we will never transcend the limits of created reality—nor, we could add, plumb its depths.

Behind the criticisms of Williams and Schultze lie several legitimate concerns. First, there is a pre-eminent and understandable concern for definition of terms. This is a matter that strikes any western reader of Palamite theology. Why, for example, is energy spoken of sometimes in the singular, sometimes in the plural?[73] There is a lack of clarity about much

---

72. Ware, "Debate," op. cit., pp. 46–47.
73. Qv. chap. 1, n. 46, above.

Palamite speech about God. But this does not render Palamism a form of scholasticism. On the contrary, it suggests a more poetic, metaphorical way of speaking, one which, though it receives lip-service in western theology, has often been forgotten in the attempt to make clear ontological truth-claims about the deity. Williams's point that Palamite terminology emerges from a synthesis of Aristotelian and neo-Platonic terminologies need not in itself be taken as a criticism. Eclecticism is not a crime, and all theological terms have their origins in language adapted from other contexts, including from philosophical systems. The term "superessentiality" (ὑπερουσιότης) is intended to convey a notion of the beyondness of God. We need not be blinded to this intention either by the fact that the notion of "beyond the essence" has a Platonic origin,[74] nor by the western tendency to speak of God in terms of the *via eminentiae,* by which "superessentiality" might suggest a premodern notion of essence or substance that is then amplified to an infinite degree. God is not seen as "being" in an ideal or perfected state, but rather, beyond any concept of being.

Kallistos Ware's whole discussion is directed to answering Rowan Williams's critique of Palamism as a historical phenomenon. The arguments on both sides are equally applicable to contemporary Palamism, however. The attempt must be made to encounter and listen to contemporary Palamite theologians on their own grounds. For Palamas himself, the central questions were not primarily philosophical or speculative ones but questions arising out of ascetic praxis and experience.[75] Contemporary Palamite thinkers, who work to some extent in a western cultural environment, are seeking to explain this living mystical tradition. The present-day defense of Palamism is consequently not purely an intellectual exercise but a clarification of existential concerns.

---

74. See Plato, *The Republic,* 509b, for the notion of the Good as beyond being.

75. In relation to this methodological question, see G. Podskalsky, "Zur Bedeutung des Methodenproblems für die byzantinische Theologie," *ZKathTh* 98 (1976): 385–99; G. Podskalsky, *Theologie und Philosophie in Byzanz: der Streit um die theologische Methodik in der spätbyzantinischen Geistesgeschichte (14./15. Jh.), seine systematischen Grundlagen und seine historische Entwicklung* (München, 1977); and G. Podskalsky, "Die griechisch-byzantinische Theologie und ihre Methode. Aspekte und Perspektiven eines ökumenischen Problems," in *ThPh* 58 (1983): 71–87.

Chapter 5
CRITICAL QUESTIONS ABOUT THE DOCTRINE OF CREATION

Being and Act in God: A Question to the Eastern Understanding of God in Relation to the World

The identity principle, as represented in the works of Barth and Rahner, identifies God's being with God's activity. God's triunity is completed in the trinitarian self-revelation. It is an axiom of the doctrine of the energies, on the other hand, that God's being (in the sense of essence or super-essentiality) and God's economic activities are to be distinguished from one another. The pretemporal idea of God to create a world is located in the energies, not in the essence.

A question can be put here to eastern theology. Is the doctrine of creation introduced by means of a middle-level of deity? The names or attributes of God are regarded dynamically in both traditions. In Barth they relate to the innermost being of God. God's being in Godself is designated by reference to God's freedom, while God's being in relation to us is designated by reference to God's love. We have already noted Barth's distinction between "being as such" and "works" in God. But Barth does not extend this line of thought further. Barth prefers to speak of the reality of God rather than of God's being or essence, in which "reality" holds together being and act. To speak of being or essence runs the risk of suggesting a static essence, separated from activity. It may even suggest a fourth entity, "being as such," that somehow lies behind the threefold activity of divine self-revelation. God, for Barth, is emphatically *who God is in the act of revelation*. This idea is very clearly expressed in the early *Christliche Dogmatik*. "He who knows the revealed God, he and he only knows also the hidden God. If we say, 'God is totally in his revelation', we also say, 'God is personally not only the revealer, but also the act of revelation.' God's work is identical with his person."[1] God's personhood is identical with God's activity, for Barth.

---

1. K. Barth, *Die Christliche Dogmatik im Entwurf* (München, 1927), pp. 137–38.

For Rahner, speech about the attributes of God is not essentially different from speech about the activities of God in the economy of salvation. These attributes are the possessions of particular modes of being. They are not merely appropriated. This means that for Rahner, like Barth, the attributes/activities are located in what Palamite theology designates as God's essence.

Lossky, in agreement with Rahner, argues that the divine attributes or names are not merely metaphysical characteristics, but represent dynamic activities. God is the one who relates to us as God. Thus far there is no disagreement with either Rahner or Barth. But here the agreement ends, because the energy doctrine distinguishes between, on the one hand, the "necessary" (Florovsky) or "natural" (Lossky) activities of God—the inner generation of the Son and the inner procession of the Spirit—and, on the other hand, the willed activities of God *ad extra*. It is these outer activities that are understood in terms of the divine names or attributes. God's being is thus not *constituted* by God's activity as a whole. God is not *actus purus*. When Lossky speaks of the trinity as an "absolute stability,"[2] he is not suggesting that the trinity is totally static, but rather that the trinity is to be understood as lying beyond any concept of dynamism or energy, and beyond any distinction of potentiality (δύναμις) from actuality (ἐνέργεια), beyond the dynamism not only of the creation itself, but also of God in relationship with the creation. God is not, in other words, in any sense analogous to the creation in which being (in the sense of matter) stands in a logical and even mathematically calculable relationship with energy. God's being stands on a different ontological plane from God's acts. Indeed, if we are to consider the reality of God, or better if we are to praise God—using ascriptive and doxological rather than descriptive and analogical language, then the notion of *being* must also in the end be abandoned. The doctrine of energies thus serves to underscore the insight that God's aseity cannot be grasped through any names. Certainly, the names are eternal and energetic, so God is not inconsistent with what the names suggest. We are not dealing here with some unknown Godhead. But—to remember an analogy used by Palamas himself—the energies function like the rays of the sun, revealing but at the same time concealing their source from our gaze.

Dorothea Wendebourg criticizes what she sees as an abstract, functionless, and unknowable concept of Godhead, hidden behind the accessible, but ultimately impenetrable cloud of glory in which we are deified. Such a concept represents, she argues, a form of modalism. Behind this critique stands Karl Barth's concern that any distinction between God's

---

2. V. N. Lossky, *The Mystical Theology of the Eastern Church* (New York, 1976), p. 45.

being and God's "perfections" (that is, God's attributes, God's names, God's powers) may in fact divide the God whom we know in revelation from another, unknown deity behind this mask of glory.[3] Such a separation would both devalue the attributes and also mean that the being of God could be conceived of, in the end, only in Stoic or neo-Platonic fashion as pure being.

The origin of such a distinction between being and doing is to be found, according to Barth, in a form of nominalism. The alternative is a notion of the divine essence understood in terms of the attributes. It is only by identifying essence and attributes, being and doing, that the doctrine of God is freed from an abstract, basically nominalist, notion of divine essence. Thus the question as to who God is must be answered, according to Barth, through reference to God's perfections or activities—which are in turn essentially identical with God in Godself.

It is in his critique of nominalist reductionism in relation to the attributes of God that Barth also attacks the Palamite distinction between essence and energies, on the grounds that the energies are identified in Palamite theology with the names or activities of God. This critique is the only reference to Gregory Palamas or his thought in the whole of the *Church Dogmatics*.[4] The concept of energies is rather condescendingly characterized as "a middle-level of the divinity," and Barth endorses the criticism made originally by Nicephorus Gregoras that the doctrine of energies means either a fourth hypostasis or else an impersonal manner (that is, not belonging specifically to any one of the trinitarian hypostases) of God's action in and dealing with the world. Barth attributes the victory of the Palamite party in the fourteenth century to, on the one hand, an abstract notion of God's simplicity, and on the other to the demands of a mysticism that emphasizes the unmediated experience of God's presence. The result of this victory was, according to Barth, a separation of being from attributes in God, so that the being becomes formless and God's form becomes insubstantial. The fundamental question for Barth is the possibility—and its apparent realization in Palamism—of a hidden, faceless God who is in reality quite other than what God outwardly pretends to be.

Barth's dismissal of Palamism as a form of nominalism represents a fundamental misunderstanding of the Palamite tradition. Barth's theological system allows no place for mysticism and, as we have seen, locates the roots of the doctrine of the trinity in the economy of revelation. As a form of mysticism Palamism appears, from Barth's point of view, to reduce the distance between God and human beings. But the intention of Palamism is

---

3. K. Barth, *Church Dogmatics* (Edinburgh, 1936ff.), vol. 2/1, pp. 325ff.
4. Ibid., pp. 331ff.

quite different. Mystical participation in the life of God leading to deification takes place for Palamism through the energies, and *in this way* the distance between the deified human being and God's essence is strongly retained. Considered a form of nominalism (or seminominalism), Palamism appears to restrict the names of God to a purely creaturely plane, without any real aplication to God in Godself. But this is not the case. Palamite theology does *not* seek to restrict the names of God to a creaturely level. The energies are an uncreated, therefore eternal reality that also acts in relation to the creation. *Speech about the energies remains speech whose subject matter is God.* We are dealing here not with a merely created manifestation of God. This, in fact, is the common thread that runs through all Palamite writings, the affirmation that the energies are uncreated.

Elsewhere, in a splendidly rhetorical purple passage, Barth sets up an opposition between faith in God on the one hand and any notion of deification of the creature on the other:

> How can this belief in Some Thing be? To believe in supermen and demigods, leader-figures, heroes, personality-cult figures, principalities and powers—a preposterous deification of the creature and reification of God! *Finitum capax infiniti*—this is what the human heart has always wanted, as the whole history of religion bears witness![5]

This attack on the Orthodox (and patristic) notion of deification is valid and sustainable *only* if the Palamite essence-energy distinction is left out of consideration. It is precisely through this distinction that a distance is maintained between God and the deified creature. Palamite theology does indeed defend a notion of *finitum capax infiniti*,[6] but at the same time is careful not to bridge the ontological difference between creator and creature. Barth quite rightly ridicules the idea of the Holy Spirit as a "stream of life or grace" in which the human being can "bathe,"[7] for this would indicate a continuity between God and humanity. Barth's presupposition, however, is the identification of the Spirit with the works of the Spirit. If, on the other hand, we speak of the grace or the energy of the Spirit, the ontological distance is maintained. Grace or energy is no longer identified precisely with Spirit. It has become a gift of the Spirit.

---

5. Barth, *Die christliche Dogmatik*, op. cit., pp. 199–200.

6. A. M. Aagaard, *Helliganden sendt til Verden* (Aarhus, 1972), with abstract in English, p. 284: "The basic distinctions of Eastern trinitarian Theology—as opposed to the Western tradition—allow for an affirmation of the question 'finitum capax infiniti' and at the same time they safeguard the inaccessibility of the triune God."

7. Barth, *Die christliche Dogmatik*, op. cit., p. 293.

Barth's argument must in fact be read as a critique not of Palamite theology but of western romanticism, and its pantheistic divinization of nature. Barth develops his whole theology in dialogue not with the Byzantine tradition but with this western romantic tradition and its theological expressions. It is not unlike Florovsky's dispute with German idealism. It is therefore not so surprising that Florovsky and Barth are fundamentally at one in their opposition to natural theology.[8] Barth's critique of mysticism is that—under the guise of union with God—it ultimately leaves one alone with oneself in empty space.[9] This in fact sounds very similar to Lossky's criticism of *western* mysticism.[10]

Barth's criticism of the essence-energy distinction mistakes Palamism for a form of nominalism. When Barth was publishing these volumes of his *Church Dogmatics*, the rediscovery of Palamism had scarcely begun.[11] A misunderstanding of Palamism at that time is not too surprising. There were also more pressing theological issues to hand. As for the relationship between nominalism and Palamite theology, this was later to become the theme of a debate between John Meyendorff[12] and J. S. Romanides.[13] If Meyendorff is correct, the argument against any similarity between nominalism and Palamism is strengthened. It was the opponents of Gregory Palamas who were, according to Meyendorff, representatives of the new nominalist philosophy.

A solution to the problem of being and act is offered from an unlikely source, the Jewish philosopher Abraham Heschel.[14] According to Heschel, God, in prophetic thought, is not pure actuality (*actus purus*), because this would involve an incapacity to suffer. Rather, the God of the prophets is constantly active (*semper agens*). This means that *in our experience* there is no distinction between God's being and God's activity. "The God of Israel is a God who acts, a God of mighty deeds. The Bible does not say how He is, but how He acts."[15] Being and act are identified with one another in the biblical

---

8. Florovsky, "Offenbarung, Philosophie und Theologie," *ZZ* 9 (1931).

9. *CD*, vol. 2/1, p. 197 (*KD*, II/1, p. 221).

10. Lossky, *The Vision of God* (Leighton Buzzard, 1963), p. 110.

11. KD, vol. 2/1 was published at the beginning of 1938, barely two years after Florovsky's decisive lecture in Athens. Lossky's *Mystical Theology* appeared in French in 1944.

12. J. Meyendorff, *St. Gregory Palamas and Orthodox Spirituality* (New York, 1974), p. 99; J. Meyendorff, *Byzantine Theology: Historical Trends and Doctrinal Themes* (New York, 1976), p. 188.

13. J. S. Romanides, "Notes on the Palamite Controversy," *GrOrthThR* 6 (1960–61): 186–205, and 9 (1963–64): 225–70.

14. A. J. Heschel, *The Prophets* (New York, 1975), vol. 2, esp. pp. 42–44.

15. Ibid., p. 44. Cf. L. Boff, *Liberating Grace* (Maryknoll, 1987), p. 163.

understanding of God, but not in the way in which western theology has traditionally identified them with one another, that is, not as *actus purus*. Heschel argues that the biblical God is beyond any notion of being:

> To Greek philosophy, being is the ultimate; to the Bible, God is the ultimate. There, the starting point of speculation is ontology; in the Bible, the starting point of thinking is God. Ontology maintains that being is the supreme concept. It asks about being as being. Theology finds it imposible to regard being as the supreme concept.[16]

Thus—although in our experience, who God is, is identical to what God does—speech about God's presence is radically set over against speech about God's essence.[17] God is inaccessible in God's holiness and, at the same time, accessible in the world.[18] This is exactly the point that Palamite theology seeks to emphasize. God's being is experienced in God's activity in relation to us, that is, in God's energy. Being and act are *in the context of existential encounter* not to be distinguished. If the neo-Palamite authors seem at times to set up an unbiblical distinction between being and act in God, they are in fact seeking to emphasize thereby that God is essentially beyond any concepts, whether of act or being. This insight they try to protect through the use of the term superessentiality (ὑπερουσιότης). The distinction between essence and energy intends no dualism between two layers of reality. On the contrary it emphasizes that the creation, and its historicity in co-operation with God, is totally contingent. There is nothing strictly speaking necessary, says Florovsky, except the trinity.

The whole question of God's being and God's act is once again, then, the question as to whether God is accessible to us, and if so, how. Is God accessible in God's essence as *actus purus*, pure actuality? If so, then access to God could only be regarded as a variety of pure receptivity—as the capacity either to see the beatific vision or to hear the word of God. Western confessional differences may reflect different understandings of the nature of this receptivity, but there is no real difference in their fundamental attitude toward our passivity in the face of God. God is to be intellectually received, and the fundamental human behavior before God is one of contemplation, θεωρία. If God is accessible to us, however, only in God's activities or energies, then these activities are the proper locus of our access to God. Then the fundamental human way of relating to God is not one of passive contemplation but one of πρᾶξις, practical ascesis. Theory and praxis are of course not mutually exclusive. The one who hears the word of God or

---

16. Heschel, op. cit., p. 44.
17. Ibid., p. 55.
18. Ibid., pp. 136 and 144.

sees the vision of God experiences a call to action. The one who undertakes the ascetic praxis of the hesychasts experiences receiving the energies of the living God. Perhaps it is an exclusive opting for one or the other of the two ways, the active or the contemplative, that gives rise to problems.

The polemics developed by both East and West on this issue can clash in sometimes rather amusing ways. Christos Yannaras[19] attacks the western concept of *actus purus*, which, he argues, tends either to identify the divine energy with the divine essence itself, or else place it completely outside the essence as something separate. This means for Yannaras that the deification of the human person, our participation in the life of the trinity, becomes impossible. This is, according to Yannaras, the source of *western* European nihilism and atheism. Bernhard Schultze attacks the doctrine of energies, which places our access to God in the realm of God's acts but not in the realm of God's essence. This, says Schultze, implies that God is not to be found in receptivity, but only in action. Schultze quotes Michael Bakunin, the nineteenth century Russian anarchist, to prove his point. "God is not experienced through learning or metaphysics, but in deed and in revolution."[20] Ascetic activity is replaced by political, revolutionary activity. This for Schultze is the final source of *eastern* European nihilism and atheism!

One thing is clear, that in our experience of God, act and being are not separate. It is equally clear, though, that God is more than we experience. Our receptivity and our activity, θεωρία and πρᾶξις, both play important roles in our human relationship to God. The significance of the problem of act and being for the issue under discussion can be summarized in this way. Being, for Palamism, denotes more than act. God is both being *and* act, or rather, superessentiality and act. The superessentiality of God is indeed distinguished from the activity of God in this model, but the "being" of God in the more general sense encompasses both. The distinction is exactly the same as that made by Barth between "being as such" (*Wesen als Solches*) and "acts" (*Wirken*), which both come under the larger heading of the "reality of God" (*Wirklichkeit Gottes*). God's being (or "reality") is experienced and known in and as God's activity, and *only* in this way. God is, in Abraham Heschel's words, experienced only as *semper agens*. The doctrine of energies demands no static concept of God, nor does it introduce any "middle-level" of divinity into the doctrine of creation. It offers a way of avoiding both these problem areas.

---

19. C. Yannaras, "The Distinction between Essence and Energies," *StVladThQ* 19 (1975): 242–43.

20. B. Schultze, *Das Gottesproblem in der Osttheologie* (Münster, 1967), p. 57.

Aeonic Eternity? A Question to the Eastern Doctrine of Creation

We have already noticed that Florovsky postulates an order of manifestation whereby the economic trinity is not rendered dependent upon time. This order of manifestation of the trinitarian hypostases is eternal, but not coeternal with the eternal generation of the Son or the eternal procession of the Spirit. Has Florovsky introduced an unnecessary concept here? If the doctrine of energies requires such a difficult concept (eternal but not coeternal), would it be better simply to adopt the identity principle, which operates with the relatively clear concepts of eternal and temporal? Ockham's razor seems to require the simpler solution in this context.

Dimitru Staniloae[21] introduces this notion of aeonic eternity in a discussion of the inner-trinitarian relationship between the Son and the Spirit. While allowing that there is such a relationship, he is careful to rule out any relation of origin. Staniloae starts from the argument of Joseph Bryennios to the effect that each hypostasis has two names. The Father is also the cause of procession; the Son is also the Word; the Spirit is also the one who proceeds. There is nothing remarkable in this so far. Joseph Bryennios draws the conclusion, however, that the Son and the Spirit possess in common the fact that they are both caused. The Son and the Spirit have a hypostatic but not a causal relationship to one another—they shine through one another, flow through one another, eternally. In a sense, this is a reflection on the notion of perichoresis. But this mutual shining through means that neither the Son nor the Spirit act independently of the other in the economy. The Spirit rests eternally in the Son, and vice versa. This argument allows an unusual critique of the *filioque*, namely that it divides the Son from the Spirit because they are necessarily viewed in a relationship of cause and effect. It is equally remarkable when Staniloae, in another essay,[22] claims to discern a filioquist tendency in Lossky's characterizing of the Son and the Spirit as principles of trinitarian unity and plurality respectively. Staniloae argues that the hypostasis of the Son is thereby—because it is considered a cause—confused with the Father. Staniloae, in criticizing this, sketches a correspondence between the inner-trinitarian procession and the economic mission of the Holy Spirit. This correspondence suggests a relationship of mutuality and equality between the Son and the Spirit in the trinitarian essence and in the economy alike. This means in turn that Staniloae can distinguish the inner trinity and the outer activities of the trinity without magnifying this distinction into a separation.

---

21. D. Staniloae, *Theology and the Church* (New York, 1980), chap. 1.
22. Ibid., pp. 65–66.

When the God in Trinity reveals himself to us, he reveals himself as a saviour-God, and a God whom we experience in the saving activity that he exercises upon us and within us. He is revealed to us as an economic Trinity. But in this revelation of itself the Trinity also draws our attention to certain premises about the intrinsic relations between the divine Persons. The theological teaching on the inner reality of the Holy Trinity is based on these indications and on the bond which joins the eternal relations between the divine Persons together with their saving activity.[23]

This presentation of the Palamite position offers us a point of contact with the western understanding of the trinity, which has always emphasized the inner-trinitarian relationship between the Son and the Spirit. Such a point of contact is not entirely unproblematic, because not all Orthodox theologians are fully in agreement with one another on this matter. Yves Congar[24] has shown that while Kallistos Ware also defends a correspondence between the inner and the economic trinity, his colleague A. Radovic, in the same journal, argues for a radical separation. But Staniloae and Ware have opened a door here to a discussion with the West about the inner-trinitarian relationship between the Son and the Spirit. Staniloae in particular has opened this possibility for further discussion without compromising the Orthodox position.[25] His argument makes reference not only to Joseph Bryennios, but has its roots in the thought of Gregory of Cyprus and, in the end, Gregory Palamas himself.

The eternal relationship between the second and third persons, as it is presented by Staniloae, is of significance not only for the *filioque* debate but also for the doctrine of energies as a whole. Because the Spirit eternally rests in and indwells the Son, the Son participates fully in the energy of the Spirit.[26] It could be said that the Spirit radiates forth hypostatically through the Son. The human person can also become the focus of the Spirit's resting and indwelling, but only under two conditions. First, there is no eternal hypostatic relationship between the Spirit and the human being. The Spirit can abandon a human being. Secondly, the shining forth of the Spirit from the believer is conditioned by the Christian maturity of the believer. In other words, the Spirit does not shine through a human person in the fullness of its, the Spirit's, personhood; only through Christ does the Spirit shine forth fully and hypostatically. It is the activity (or energy) of the Spirit that

---

23. Ibid., p. 75.
24. Y. Congar, *I Believe in the Holy Spirit* (New York/London, 1983), vol. 3, pp. 16–17.
25. This stands in contrast, for example, to the work of V. V. Bolotov, "Thesen über das Filioque," in *Revue Internationale de Théologie*, 1898, pp. 681–712. Bolotov offers a useful approach to the *filioque*, but in a way that has not found universal acceptance among his fellow Orthodox theologians.
26. Staniloae, *Theology and Church*, op. cit., pp. 26ff.

transfigures and shines forth through the believer. Staniloae's exposition of the inner-trinitarian relationship between the Son and the Spirit thus has a practical consequence for the doctrine of energies. Staniloae has explained how there can be a qualitative difference between the eternal, hypostatic indwelling of the Spirit in Christ and the energetic indwelling of the Spirit in the believer. Staniloae has presented us with an eternal, hypostatic but noncausal relationship—of "resting in" and "shining forth from"—between the second and third trinitarian persons. This relationship is the consequence of their having a common origin or cause in the first person. In turn, Staniloae's discussion opens up a way to understanding the difficult concept we have found in Florovsky of the "eternal but not coeternal."

The mutual relationship between the Son and the Spirit is logically dependent upon their common cause in the Father (clearly it is not temporally dependent, because the category of time has no place here). This relationship is thus, so to say, eternal but not coeternal in the same way as Florovsky's order of manifestation. The hypostases themselves are mutually coeternal. The inner relationship of Son to Spirit is eternal, but—because caused—not coeternal. This secondary relationship is described by reference to the energies. The Son eternally participates in the energies of the Spirit, and the energies of the Spirit eternally shine through the Son. The "eternal but not coeternal" refers then to the domain of the energies. In his *Orthodoxe Dogmatik*[27] Staniloae explores this concept under the heading of "aeonic eternity." It is in this aeonic eternity that God's pretemporal but contingent idea of a creation is located.

The problem of the Palamite denial of the *filioque* is that it remains unclear whether there is a correspondence between the inner and the economic trinity (as Ware and Staniloae want to argue), or not (as Radovic insists[28]). Radovic's position seems to leave us with an unduly authoritarian understanding of revelation, so that the doctrine of the trinity itself is reduced to a matter of mere information. Dorothea Wendebourg is quite right in questioning such a theology. But the doctrine of energies does not necessarily have to bring with it this authoritarian understanding of revelation. Florovsky explicitly speaks out against it,[29] and so does Staniloae when he contrasts the older understanding of revelation as disclosure of doctrines to the newer understanding of it as an event of new awareness.

---

27. Op. cit.

28. "On the basis of the manifestation of the Trinity in the world, we cannot come to any conclusions about God's mode of eternal existence." Cited in Y. Congar, op. cit, p. 17.

29. G. V. Florovsky, "Offenbarung, Philosophie und Theologie," *ZZ* 9 (1931): 465.

"Revelation is not only a simple communication of teaching but a continuous new state of man achieved by drawing near to God."[30] Lossky, it is true, tends to hold a more propositional understanding of revelation, as disclosure of "primordial fact."[31]

Florovsky's brief and rather unsatisfactory references to a realm of the "eternal but not coeternal" thus receive further explanation in Staniloae's works. Further, this idea can be seen on reflection to lend support, within the context of the Orthodox tradition, to the emergence of a more open understanding of the nature of revelation. Palamite theology understands God as containing the potentiality for a creation, in the form of the idea of a creation. The creation can be deified, that is, attain a state of appropriate actuality—appropriate, that is, to the creature thus deified. In this theology, there is no need for the dichotomies between "supernature" and "ordinary" nature[32] found in the western tradition. God's energy is Godself, albeit Godself as God encounters us, and this energy permeates the whole of nature, energizing it and actualizing it, bringing it to the fulfillment in God's glory that God has intended for it from the beginning. The energy of the Spirit indwells us and the creation; the hypostasis of the Spirit remains, at the same time, essentially beyond us. Given that the energy of the Spirit is uncreated energy, it is no less a real indwelling of the Spirit than were the case if the Spirit as a hypostasis were regarded as a gift, as it traditionally is in western theology. The problem with the western position is that, once it is admitted that the Spirit as a person can dwell in us, various other distinctions become necessary in order to distinguish the Spirit from ourselves: uncreated and created grace, gospel and law, spirit and matter, revelation and reason, and so on. The purpose of these distinctions is to ensure that the Spirit is not somehow brought down to our level, and that our created spirits are not confused with the Holy Spirit. These distinctions are not necessary if the Holy Spirit's indwelling in us is conceived of as energetic rather than essential or hypostatic.

In a sense this criticism is nothing more than an indication that Occam's razor can be wielded as effectively by Orthodox theologians as it is by westerners. The point is simply that western theologians cannot claim, by denying any distinction between essence and energies in God, to present a simpler or more elegant doctrine of God than their eastern counterparts. Both theological systems involve complexity and simplicity. Orthodox theology, from a western perspective, tends to place the complexity in God

---

30. Staniloae, *Theology and Church*, op. cit., p. 124.
31. Lossky, *Myst.Theol.*, op. cit., p. 64.
32. Ibid., p. 88.

and the simplicity in created nature; western theology, from an eastern perspective, simplifies its doctrine of God, but at the expense of importing complexities into its doctrine of creation. In any case, one theological system is not to be regarded as superior to the other on grounds of simplicity.

The Indwelling of the Idea of a World, or of the Actual World, Within God: A Question to the Western Understanding of God in Relation to the World

The existence of a world for Florovsky presupposes the prior *idea* of a world. Without this prior idea in the mind of God, the actual world would be an impossibility. If this idea of a world is located in the essence of God, there are two possibilities. First, the idea would be as necessary as God's trinitarian nature itself, and the actualization of the idea would also become necessary. God would be constrained by God's own nature to create a world. The world itself—at least Origen's invisible world of spirits and angels—would be necessary and coeternal with God. That invisible world would be the real world, and the concrete, historical, material world would be seen as being of less consequence. Florovsky claims to discern this tendency in Augustine.[33] The alternative possibility is this: God's essence would, like the world, become contingent upon God's will; that is, the being itself of God would become the object of God's free will. God could then decide, for example, whether to be a trinity or not, and God could decide quite arbitrarily the nature of God's own attributes. God would be, like the world, strictly speaking, unnecessary. The Orthodox answer to this whole problem area is given expression by Athanasius, according to Florovsky, specifically by Athanasius's basing the ontological difference between God and the creation in the ontological distinction within God, between God's being and God's will. The being of God is necessary and eternal. The will of God is free. It is eternal, but not coeternal, and is revealed within time in the economy of salvation. This "eternal but not coeternal" gives to the divine will a consistency of purpose, without taking away God's freedom. That which is dependent upon the will of God is the temporal and the creaturely. The question to western theology that suggests itself here is this: must the identity principle, which on the terms laid down above does not seem to distinguish *ontologically* between God's being and God's will—must this theological position either render the world necessary or the Logos unnecessary? In the first case it would lead to pantheism, in the second to Arianism. Either way, it appears to collapse the ontological dividing line between creator and creature. It seems a very strange suggestion in the light of, for example,

---

33. Florovsky, "Protivorecija Origenizma," *Put'* 18 (1929): 114. Cf. D. Ritschl, *Memory and Hope: an Inquiry Concerning the Presence of Christ* (New York, 1967), pp. 45–46.

Barth's struggle to emphasize precisely that distinction between creator and creature.

The question can be approached by referring back to the criticism that the theology of the identity principle is not a real θεολογία, but remains on the level of the economy. If this is so, then the idea of a creation finds its basis not in God's trinitarian essence (or superessentiality), but in the trinitarian economy. The idea of a world, or the "eternal decree" (Barth) to create a world, is not located in what Palamism knows as the divine essence, precisely because, in western theology, there is no concept of essence (or superessentiality) in the Palamite sense of the term. The idea of a world is located in what Palamism designates as the energy, even though this term is not used—at least not in the Palamite sense—in the theology of the identity principle. The danger, then, is not the danger of making the world necessary and eternal, though it is true that Aquinas saw no logical reason why this should not be the case. The danger is that the doctrine of God the trinity might become contingent upon God's will and thus, in the last analysis, unnecessary. This tendency we have already noticed in the history of western trinitarian thinking. In deism and the practical unitarianism expressed by Kant, the trinitarian nature of God becomes optional; in modern agnosticism and atheism the very being of God becomes optional.

The problem for Florovsky concerns the real foundation for creaturely existence. Can we simply set up an "ontological dualism"[34] of God (including God's idea of a world) and the actual world, with a sharp, axiomatic distinction between them, without any prior foundation for this distinction within the doctrine of God? Florovsky's answer is a clear "No!" Such a starting point will inevitably lead us to see God and the world as mutually autonomous.[35] The danger in this is that we will in turn lose sight of either the reality of God or the reality of the world. It may be the reality, in the sense of the historicity, of the world that is lost, for history is first taken fully seriously in the biblical worldview, that is, in the worldview that regards the world both as the temporal creation of the ontologically other creator-God, and at the same time as standing in an ongoing relationship with this God.

In eastern theology this ongoing relationship is described in terms of the world being filled with the uncreated energies. The created universe as a whole is regarded as lying within the embrace of God,[36] or even within the

---

34. Florovsky, "Spor o nemetskom idealizme," *Put'* 25 (1930): 71.
35. Ibid., p. 79.
36. D. Staniloae, *Orthodoxe Dogmatik* (Zürich/Gütersloh, 1985), p. 203.

"bosom" or "womb" of God.[37] Our inability to conceptualize God—the aseity of God—is partially analogous here to the inability of an unborn child to conceptualize its mother, but even more analogous to the fact that no human being is fully and finally knowable to another human being, or even to him- or herself. In the western tradition God's indwelling in the creature (or the creation as a whole) is seen as a task of the Holy Spirit, insofar as we can distinguish the activities of the Spirit from those of the other two persons. The imaginative picture here is much more of the Spirit indwelling the individual creature than of the creation as a whole being encompassed by the Spirit, or dwelling ἐν πνεύματι (Acts 1:10; 17:28). Karl Barth[38] characterizes the indwelling of the Holy Spirit as the "subjective self-revelation" of God, corresponding to the "objective self-revelation" that occurs in the incarnation of the Logos. This is a picture of a God who stands over us and outside of us, but who in God's mercy may choose to come to us from the beyond. The aseity of God is the aseity of a stranger. Eastern Orthodox writers have no trouble in laying the blame for a number of undesirable ethical phenomena at the feet of this western mental picture of our relationship with God: a hindering of human development,[39] a tendency to overvalue intellectual abstraction,[40] and a tendency to undervalue a creation that is so far removed from any notion of God's embrace.[41]

A question suggests itself here. How far can western theology begin to imagine God as the one who does indeed embrace the creation, without diminishing the primary ontological distinction between creator and creation? Western theism has tended to see God either as the absolute subject, the one who looks down from the detachment of heaven upon the creation, or else as the absolute object, the one whom the saints encounter in the mystical beatific vision or whose word the congregation hears in the preaching of the church. These are two sides of the one coin. How, in this separation of subject and object, could a notion of co-operation with God, or participation in God's glory, become possible?

It is in the context of these questions that the doctrine of energies seems to have great advantages to offer. Western and eastern theologies alike argue that God is inaccessible, but that it is possible to participate in some sense in

---

37. Ibid., p. 151: "im Schoße Gottes." Cf. Lossky, *Myst. Theol.*, op. cit., p. 92.
38. Barth, *Christliche Dogmatik*, op. cit., sections 14 and 17.
39. D. Staniloae, *Orthodoxe Dogmatik*, op. cit., p. 204.
40. C. Yannaras, "The Distinction between Essence and Energies," *StVladThQ* 19 (1975): 241. Qv. H. Aldenhoven, "The question of the procession of the Holy Spirit and its connection with the life of the Church," in L. Vischer (ed.), *Spirit of God, Spirit of Christ: Ecumenical Reflections on the Filioque Controversy* (London/Geneva, 1981).
41. P. Gregorios, *The Human Presence* (Geneva, 1978).

the life of God. The doctrine of energies offers us a systematic explanation of this notion of participation, and in doing so offers us also a way of understanding God's presence. Western theology (in contrast to eastern) takes very cautiously to the bold patristic language of deification. Participation refers here mainly to the intellectual receptivity that leads to hearing the word of God or else to seeing the beatific vision of God. An ontological participation in the divine nature would suggest a form of pantheism. The human being would be immersed in the divine nature. This essentially intellectual understanding of participation can easily suggest an unbiblical separation within the creature of intellect from body, spirit from matter, and supernature from nature. Unconscious nature is shut out from participation in the divine nature. The identity principle allows only two possibilities, according to Florovsky, either an "anthropological monophysitism"[42] in which the human person is a completely passive recipient of grace, or else an "anthropological Nestorianism" in which God and the human person never actually encounter one another, except in Christ, and even then only fleetingly and tangentially.

In contrast to this the doctrine of energies offers a way of conceptualizing the transfiguration of matter, not only of conscious animate matter but unconscious inanimate matter as well. The transfiguration of Christ exemplifies the former and the similar "transfiguration" of the burning bush (Exodus 3:2) exemplifies the latter. Matter that has become conscious is transfigured in seeking to participate in the divine nature; unconscious matter participates in the divine nature because it participates in conscious matter, because we as human beings are body and soul together, and because we are integrally connected with our animate and inanimate environment. Alexander Schmemann[43] has explored this connectedness by developing an understanding of the human being as priest, standing before God the creator, for the whole created order. The fragility of the natural environment and the threats to it from our civilization are themes of which we have become well aware in this last quarter of a century. Sometimes the biblical worldview is blamed for these threats. If it had not been for the biblical desacralizing of nature, the natural order would never have been so thoroughly investigated or so ruthlessly exploited. The doctrine of energies, including a vision of the universe filled and transfigured by God's healing energies, offers us an alternative insight into the relationship between God and the created world. This insight is no less biblical than the traditional

---

42. Florovsky, *CW*, vol. 1, chap. 1. This article was also published as "As the Truth Is in Jesus," in *The Christian Century* 19, Dec., 1951.

43. A. Schmemann, *The World as Sacrament* (London, 1966), esp. pp. 113ff.

"ontological dualism" of western theology. The energy doctrine may just offer a practical foundation for a new ecological ethic.

Several methodological consequences of the doctrine of energies are to be noted here. First, Roman Catholic scholasticism distinguishes between nature (that is, created matter) and grace (that is, created, immaterial existence). The doctrine of energies makes no such distinction. The terms "nature" and "grace" are indeed used by Palamite theologians but not totally consistently. In the central text concerning participation in the divine nature (2 Peter 1:4 θείας κοινωνοὶ φύσεως), "nature," according to Lossky, has to be understood as God's being in general, essence *and* energy, being *and* act, together. Elsewhere "nature" refers to the divine essence, in contrast to grace or energy.[44] The problem for a dialogue between the two theological traditions is that the same terminology is used in different ways, sometimes even within the one tradition. The western scholastic use of the terms "nature" and "grace," although more exact than the eastern usage of these terms, runs the risk of introducing an unbiblical plurality of ontological levels into the order of creation. More recent Roman Catholic theology distances itself from this older scholastic distinction. The recent critiques of the reification of grace, and Rahner's emphasis on grace as the experience of God's presence, go some way to making common ground with the Palamite concept of grace.[45]

Secondly, the eastern tradition tends to emphasize the ubiquity of the energies, and to make the conscious human perception of these energies dependent upon ascetic praxis. The western tradition tends to emphasize God's gift (or non-gift) of self-revelation, and the passivity of the human recipient. The old western distrust of mysticism is not, in principle, overcome through the notion of God's self-revelation. In this context it is worth noticing that the Enlightenment critique of mysticism has now itself become subject to critique. We can no longer regard a narrow "scientific" method, in which every valid experience is, in principle, repeatable as an appropriate method for the humanities—including theology.[46] The experience that is handed on as tradition, the "wisdom of the elders" (David Suzuki) has again become a legitimate source of knowledge. Despite this, western theology still carries within it the inheritance of the Enlightenment,

---

44. E.g., Florovsky, "Creation and Creaturehood," op. cit., p. 69.

45. See G. Russo, "Rahner and Palamas: a Unity of Grace," *StVladThQ* 32 (1988): 157–80; and D. Coffey, "The Palamite Doctrine of God: a New Perspective," *StVladThQ* 32 (1988): 329–58.

46. H.-G. Gadamer, *Wahrheit und Methode* (2d ed.; Tübingen, 1965), esp. pp. 261ff; C. F. v. Weizsäcker, *Die Einheit der Natur* (4th ed.; München, 1972), pp. 35f.; A. Louth, *Discerning the Mystery* (Oxford, 1983).

while the eastern theological tradition not unintentionally sought to avoid the western cultural movements known as the Renaissance and the Enlightenment. Here it is to be asked, as a methodological question, whether western thought can for much longer hold out against the insights of the mystics into the relationship between God and the world.

Thirdly, Jürgen Moltmann[47] has correctly located the origin of the contemporary ecological crisis in the analysis and objectification of the natural life system and the corresponding subjectification of the human person. The subjectification of the human person is already to be seen in the refinement of feeling on the part of the poets of the twelfth century. Denis de Rougemont[48] has located the roots of contemporary western dualism in the heretical movements of that period. This dualism, which gained philosophical expression in the thought of Descartes, is the basis of a fundamentally individualistic concept of the human person, or of human subjectivity. If we are to overcome the subject-object split that sets the individual over against his/her natural environment, then we must begin with a critique of the individualistic concept of the human person. The notion of personhood has developed, as Lossky has claimed, out of the church's understanding of God as trinitarian community. The critique of the individualistic concept of the human person is essential if we are to develop a notion of personhood-in-intersubjectivity. Such a notion of human personhood in turn finds its analogy in the trinitarian intersubjectivity outlined by Florovsky. But it is equally important to say that the history of modern individualism is not something simply to be renounced or denied. Rather, this history needs to be developed further. The wholeness of the human person (and thus also of the creation as a whole) will be effected by a radicalizing of the concept of subjectivity[49] whereby the division between subject and object is overcome.

The Scientific Concept of Energy: A Question to the Eastern Doctrine of God in Relation to the World

In 1901 Wilhelm Ostwald in his Leipzig lectures on natural philosophy equated energy with susbstance. Albert Einstein was to develop this idea further. "Mass and energy are therefore essentially alike; they are only different expressions for the same thing."[50] Since then energy has come to

---

47. J. Moltmann, *God in Creation: an Ecological Doctrine of Creation* (London, 1985), pp. 23–32.
48. D. de Rougemont, *Passion and Society* (London, 1956), esp. pp. 74ff.
49. Boff, op. cit., p. 183.
50. A. Einstein, *The Meaning of Relativity* (London, 1967), p. 45.

be understood, not only among physicists but also popularly, as unbound mass, and mass as bound or "frozen" energy. This is of course not without theological significance. The fact that contemporary physics has discovered a logical, even a calculable relationship between energy and matter or substance, could perhaps be used in support of the identity principle. Here we should remember Gregory Palamas's concern to distinguish ontologically between created and uncreated light, between the created energy or vitality of the creation and the uncreated energy of God. The theological notion of energy is not to be confused with the everyday notion of energy. In the divine energies we are encountered, according to Palamite theology, by the living God. Thereby we take part in the divine nature, and God's being is revealed and rendered accessible. Thus far we can say that there is a correspondence between the being and the act of God. God is *semper agens*. We could draw an analogy from the physicists' concept of energy. An electromagnetic field could perhaps serve as an analogy for the divine energies, provided we remember the limited nature of every analogy. God is always beyond that which we experience of God. God in Godself is always ὑπερουσιότης. The uncreated energy is ontologically other than the dynamism that corresponds to and constitutes the matter of our universe.

Fridhof Capra[51] has likened the energy-filled universe of current cosmology to the cosmic dance of Shiva, the Indian god of creation and destruction. This dance is regarded as a symbol of *cosmic* energy. It describes the cycle of nature. How are we to respond to Capra's references to energy? The doctrine of energies was developed in the context of a mystical theology which, on the face of it, seems to have some similarities to the Indian mysticism to which Capra refers. This non-Christian mysticism also emphasizes paradoxes or antinomies, without seeking to resolve them.[52] It rests on experience[53] that is not to be understood analytically but that, rather, emphasizes participation.[54] Thus far we can see some similarities, but when we look at the content of what is affirmed, the similarities end. The cosmic energy that is the theme of Capra's analogy is not to be equated with what Palamism considers the energy of the biblical God. We refer again to Abraham Heschel's argument that for nonbiblical thought, the absolute concept is that of *being*, while for biblical thought, *God* is the absolute. Capra is speaking constantly in terms of being, the being of the cosmos; that is, from a biblical point of view, *created* being. "The picture of an

---

51. F. Capra, *The Tao of Physics* (Oxford, 1983^2).
52. Ibid., pp. 56 and 167–68.
53. Ibid., p. 42.
54. Ibid., p. 153.

interconnected cosmic web which emerges from modern physics has been used extensively in the East to convey the mystical experience of nature. For the Hindus, brahman is the unifying thread in the cosmic web, the ultimate ground of all being."[55] The doctrine of energies, by contrast, speaks about God in Godself, that is, the superessentiality of God, which is not to be equated with God's being as a whole, and about the energy of God, which is also not to be equated with God's being as a whole. The uncreated energy is ontologically other than the being of the cosmos, or the created energy system of the universe. The natural dynamism of creation is explicitly distinguished from God's energy. It is through the *uncreated* energy that God is experienced in history. Here, Moltmann is quite correct in saying that "the cyclical element in the Indian concept is broken through."[56] In other words, the basic energy system of the cosmos that is constantly subject to ever deeper research on the part of the natural sciences remains, from the standpoint of Christian theology, essentially *created* energy. When the Palamite theologians speak of uncreated light or uncreated energy, they explicitly seek to transcend any notion of created light or energy. Created energy can be explored and analyzed in the laboratory, uncreated energy cannot.

---

55. Ibid., p. 151.
56. Moltmann, *God in Creation,* op. cit., p. 307.

Chapter 6
CRITICAL QUESTIONS ABOUT THE DOCTRINE OF GRACE

Co-Operation with God? A Question to the Eastern Doctrine of Grace

For the doctrine of energies, the final purpose of the creation is θέωσις, in which creatures come to participate in the divine nature through co-operation. This understanding is problematic for western theology. For Protestantism, grace is the experience of our absolutely undeserved acceptance by God. This conception of grace is fundamental to the whole Reformation polemic against justification by good works. How, in the light of this, are we to approach the Palamite assertion that our relationship to God is not simply a passive, receptive relationship on our part, but an active ascent to God through ascetic praxis? Are we here, to refer back to an older controversy, in danger of a Pelagian understanding of the way to God? Have we, in the Palamite understanding of grace, lost sight of any notion of grace as a free gift, as something that does not have to be earned?

We can attempt an answer to this question by referring to Karl Barth's doctrine of reconciliation.[1] There are for Barth three elements to reconciliation between God and humanity: justification, sanctification, and calling. Justification takes place through grace alone (*sola gratia*), in which the human stance before God is indeed one of pure passivity. The human being is justified. In connection with sanctification and calling, a certain activity is both allowed for and required, an active movement toward God. God's grace is active here as well, of course. Christologically, the justification of the human being corresponds to the self-emptying of God in Christ, while sanctification corresponds to the exaltation of humanity in Christ. The calling of the human being corresponds to the unity (the co-operation, if you like) of divinity and humanity in Christ. Christologically considered, these are acts of God. Reconciliation is a process that can be considered in these three stages. In the stage of justification the human person is passive, but our sanctification and our discipleship as people called by God require a certain activity in co-operation with God. This is not to deny or compromise

---

1. K. Barth, *Church Dogmatics* (Edinburgh, 1936ff.), vol. 3.

the absolute dependence of our salvation upon God's grace. It is simply to note that reconciliation or salvation is more than justification, the element that for historical reasons has received the greatest attention from Protestant apologists and preachers.

Barth's doctrine of reconciliation can be compared with Florovsky's. Florovsky distinguishes between the salvation of human nature as a whole, effected for us without any knowledge or volition on our part on Good Friday, and the salvation of the particular human person, which demands a certain volitional activity or discipline on her or his part. Reconciliation does not take place without the first step being taken by God toward us, that is, not without God's gracious descent to us in the incarnation of Christ. Florovsky emphasizes only slightly more strongly than traditional Protestant theology the role of the second step, that of the human ascent to God. In Palamite thought, the human person is deified through grace. Those who are through grace adopted children of God will become like the eternal Son of the Father (1 John 3:2). This "becoming like" is something Palamite thought takes very seriously. Only here does the distinction between created and uncreated finally disappear—though of course the deified creature is ontologically distinguished from the trinitarian essence of God in the same way that the energies are distinguished from God's essence. Our salvation takes place through God's grace alone—this is taken just as seriously as the reality of deification. The adopted children of God remain children through adoption, through election. The only-begotten Son of the Father remains a child by "nature," that is, by virtue of being one of the trinity.

Does Apathy Play a Role in the Christian Life? A Question to the Eastern Doctrine of Grace

Jürgen Moltmann has drawn out some of the ethical and social-political ramifications of monotheism and the trinitarian critique of monotheism.[2] Could the trinitarian critique of political authoritarianism arise, however, from a theology that regards the human person as invited to participate in the divine energies? What precisely are the ethical implications of a mystical reaching out to God, especially when this reaching out requires apathy as a human virtue? Are we dealing here with a spirituality and a life-style that, in the end, requires of us an isolation from the world, even a contempt of the world, in order to reach further into the inner life of the transcendent God?

We have already considered Dorothea Wendebourg's critique, that the doctrine of energies introduces a soteriological modalism. I have argued that it is in fact the fully trinitarian God, no mere modalist divinity, that

---

2. J. Moltmann, *The Trinity and Kingdom of God* (London, 1981), pp. 129ff.

Palamite mysticism claims is encountered in the uncreated energies. Everything that Moltmann wants to affirm about the pathos of God can also be affirmed, at least in theory, from a Palamite position.[3] Moltmann's notion of the "inviting unity of the trinity"[4] is in fact very close to the Palamite notion of our invitation as human beings to take part in the trinitarian life of God. Lossky's trinitarian thinking, on the other hand, does present us with a picture of the absolute immoveability of the divine essence, beyond any concepts or names. Florovsky also presents us with a trinity that is beyond any economic motif. It is true that this picture of God seems very different from the living and passionate God of the Bible. Deification begins for Lossky in the practice of silence and detachment. We could ask, however, whether this detachment from suffering and passion is at all reconcilable with ethical and political activity in the world. There are three points to be made here.

First, in connection with the passion of God, we again encounter an example of antinomy in Vladimir Lossky's thought. God suffers in the economy; God is, however, essentially—that is, in essence—beyond suffering. Lossky emphasizes that in his suffering, death, and burial Jesus Christ is to be understood as a *deified* human being, in fact as *the* preeminently deified human being.[5] In Christ's sufferings, it is *God* who suffers. This is the point of the incarnation. There would be no possibility of a deification (θέωσις) of human beings unless there has been a prior incarnation (σάρκωσις) of the second person of the trinity. Even so, the incarnation for Lossky is an act of the divine *economy*. The inner life of the trinity is not affected by it. Moltmann puts a rather different interpretation—the Father suffers in eternity the death of the Son.[6] Yet even here there is room for a kind of ἀπάθεια in God. For God the pain remains, but God does not suffer, like creatures, from a deficiency of being. *To this extent* Moltmann can allow that God is apathetic.[7]

I suggest the two positions are not totally irreconcilable. Lossky, like Moltmann, knows the suffering of God in the economy—that is, in the domain of the overflowing love of God. Moltmann, like Lossky, argues that God is not overcome by God's suffering. God overcomes suffering. God is eternally affected by the suffering that affects the economy, but remains

---

3. J. Meyendorff, "Reply to Jürgen Moltmann's The Unity of the Triune God," *StVladThQ* 28 (1984): 183–88.

4. J. Moltmann, *History and the Triune God: Contributions to Trinitarian Theology* (London, 1991), pp. 80ff.

5. V. N. Lossky, *The Mystical Theology of the Eastern Church* (New York, 1976), p. 242.

6. Moltmann, *Trinity and Kingdom of God*, op. cit., p. 81.

7. Ibid., p. 23.

essentially even more than the love that itself necessarily involves suffering.[8] Abraham Heschel gives expression to this idea when he speaks about the pathos of God in prophetic thought. "The prophets never identify God's pathos with His essence, because for them the pathos is not something absolute, but a form of relation."[9] The "essence" of God remains for Heschel beyond God's relationship to us.[10] God's pathos—God's interest in and compassion with the pain of the creation—expresses God's relationship with us. Heschel distinguishes the egoistical passions of the Olympian deities from the com-passion (that is, the suffering with us) of the biblical God.[11] Ancient Greek philosophical monotheism sought to transcend the passions of the pagan deities by asserting the apathy of the deity. There was simply no question here of the biblical alternative, the compassion of God. By contrast, the God of Israel is a God of *pathos*, according to Heschel. God's pathos, including God's jealousy (Exodus 20:5), is the outworking of God's love for the people of Israel. God's passion is always directed to the salvation of the elect creation. It is this purpose of God's that inevitably involves suffering, for God is affected by the suffering of the creation. This emphasis on divine suffering in the Hebrew Bible becomes even more explicit in the trinitarian doctrine of God. Here every suggestion of an egoism (of one person) or a narcissism (of two persons) is explicitly transcended and overcome.[12] We can assent to the patristic notion of God's apathy insofar as it functions as a critique of the egoistic or narcissistic passions of the pagan deities. But we have to recognize the danger that this very limited affirmation of divine apathy can easily be interpreted as a counsel to detachment from every form of passion, including compassion. Taken in this sense, the notion of divine apathy has nothing to do with the passionate God of the Bible.

Secondly, the "way of unification" demands, for Lossky, "a co-operation, a synergy of the two wills, divine and human."[13] This means, as we have found, a coinciding of action (πρᾶξις) and contemplation (θεωρία),[14] leading to detachment from passions (ἀπάθεια). This for Lossky does not mean some sort of ultimate passivity, but rather a vigilance. This difficult idea is explained by George Maloney. "It is a passionate seeking of the loving

---

8. Qv. my article, "Without Parts or Passions? The Suffering of God in Anglican Thought," in *Pacifica* 4 (1991): 257–72, in which I argue for a pretemporal freedom of God from suffering.
9. A. Heschel, *The Prophets* (New York, 1975),Vol. 2, p. 11.
10. Ibid., pp. 263–64.
11. Ibid., pp. 23–24.
12. D. Staniloae, *Orthodoxe Dogmatik* (Zürich/Gütersloh, 1985), pp. 87 and 279.
13. Lossky, *Myst. Theol.*, op. cit., p. 198.
14. Ibid., pp. 202–3.

Father's face in each event and a total *detachment from one's own impetuous control* over such an event."[15] For Lossky this connectedness of theory and praxis becomes a form of knowledge (γνῶσις) of God, not merely an intellectual knowledge, but a knowledge arising out of love, specifically out of loving participation in the life of the trinity. Moltmann also speaks of a union of the *vita activa* and the *vita contemplativa* leading to a knowledge of God that is not overpowering, not the knowledge that is associated with control, but rather the knowledge of love, wonder, and participation.[16] This is not so far from Lossky's concept of apathy if we have understood it aright. It does not call for a passive dissociation from everything worldly, but rather a refusal to regard and use knowledge as an instrument of power. Instead, our knowledge of God is something akin to a sense of wonder, and this is the only sort of knowledge that can give depth to either our human relationships or our relationship with God.

Thirdly, the clear ethical and social priorities that emerge from Moltmann's reflection on the trinity correspond to Florovsky's and Lossky's ecclesial analogy for the life of the trinity and our participation in that life. God is the one who reaches out to us in the economy of the Son. God suffers with us and for us in the world. God is the one who in the economy of the Spirit indwells us and invites us to conscious co-operation with the energetic will of the trinity. This requires of us a preparedness, arising out of ascetic contemplation. Dimitru Staniloae argues that this ascetic co-operation is not only to be understood in traditional terms of spiritual exercises, but can also include social and political action for the benefit of human beings and the whole creation:

> God requires of us today that we join even more closely in spiritual growth through word and self-sacrifice. This is a new form of ascesis, an ascesis that is positive, general and obligatory, and in no sense opposed to the older forms of ascesis, but which is deepened and supported by them. Our responsibility for the natural order God has given us seems to us today to involve a duty, to conserve natural resources caringly, and to avoid destroying or polluting the environment. These circumstances curb our pride and our licentiousness, and call us to seek for the eternal purpose of our existence here in this world.[17]

---

15. G. A. Maloney, *Inscape: God at the Heart of the Matter* (Denville, N.J., 1978), p. 40.
16. Moltmann, *Trinity and Kingdom of God*, op. cit., p. 9.
17. Staniloae, *Orthodox Dogmatik*, op. cit., p. 297.

Participation in the Divine Nature as an Unmediated Experience of God's Grace: A Question to the Eastern Doctrine of Grace

A further problem area concerns the question of participation, which is so central to the Palamite interpretation of 2 Peter 2:4. Human beings are capable in the Palamite system of *bodily* participation in the divine energies, and thus also in the divine nature. "Nature" is used here in the broader sense as the reality of God, including being and act. This understanding is, according to Schultze, unclear, in that it seems to suggest a way of perception that is different from intellectual or cognitive understanding. Rowan Williams sharpens the critique voiced by Schultze. Both fail to notice that the idea of participation also plays a role in the history of western theological thought.[18] Kallistos Ware attempts to answer the criticism as it finds expression in Williams, who declares his preference for a notion of an "intentional community" of love and will with God. Ware begins by arguing that the notion of "intentional community" is itself not without problems. Two opposite, and from Ware's point of view, problematic tendencies appear. The first is a nominalist tendency simply to deny any unmediated experience of God. The other is a neo-Platonic tendency to speak of union or communion with God in such a way that the difference between creator and creature is bridged, and the identity of the creature is simply submerged in the divine identity. Ware insists that we must hold in balance God's immanence and God's transcendence without confusing them. He allows a notion of intentional communion with God, but argues that this fails to do justice to the possibilities for relationship with God. If we intend to build a communion with God, this assumes the priority of grace, and God's grace already signifies rather more than intentionality. "If by 'grace' we mean the immediate presence of God to man's soul, then as soon as we begin to speak in terms of grace we have already passed beyond the 'intentional' to the 'entitative' or 'ontological.'"[19]

Participation is a difficult concept whose philosophical sources lie deep in Platonism. But this in itself is no reason to avoid the concept. Virtually every theological term is a loan-word from another context in life and thought, transformed and redefined for its new theological purpose. Palamism takes with utmost seriousness those New Testament texts that refer to participation in the divine nature as adopted children of God. In doing so, the biblical insight into our psychosomatic unity as human beings is also taken with full seriousness. In comparison, the western tendency to speak of

---

18. C. Fabro, "Participation," in *New Catholic Encyclopedia*, vol. 10 (New York, 1967); A. M. Allchin, *Participation in God: a Forgotten Strand in Anglican Tradition* (London, 1988).

19. K. Ware, "The Debate about Palamism," *ECR* 9 (1977): 60.

something less than full bodily participation (e.g., Williams's "intentional community") sounds disembodied and Platonic.

There remains a further issue, and that is the claim to the unmediated experience of God's grace. It is an axiom of contemporary western theology that revelation is of necessity always a mediated experience.[20] It seems to me that Palamite theology seeks to make two points in claiming an unmediated experience of grace. First, it is asserting the energies are in fact the mediators of God's essence, which itself is never encountered in an unmediated way. Secondly, it is saying that this experience of grace is not mediated or appropriated in a merely intellectual way—rather it is experienced bodily, and in a way that concerns the whole human person.

---

20. Though this axiom may not be as clear-cut as is often thought: see P. D. Molnar, "Can we know God directly? Rahner's Solution from Experience," *Theological Studies* 46 (1985): 228–61.

Chapter 7
DIFFERENT CONCERNS AND COMMON INTENTIONS IN THE TWO APPROACHES

Thus far I have considered the various criticisms that can be and in fact are made of the two positions. I suggest that each of the approaches is coherent, and that each reflects certain theological interests or concerns. These concerns arise out of the particular theological and cultural context of Byzantine Christianity on the one side and Latin Christianity on the other. Underlying the two approaches, while their real differences are not to be denied or minimized, it is possible in my opinion to uncover a deeper layer of common intention—ultimately the intention to take seriously and give expression to the biblical experience of God.

There are two traditional ways of speaking to God's being, either as identical with the activity of God (identity principle) or as differentiated from God's activity (doctrine of energies). The language used is not always precise. Sometimes being (or nature) is used within the doctrine of energies as a general term to cover superessentiality and activity together, sometimes equated specifically with superessentiality. But always a real distinction is posited between God's activity in relation to us and an inner, to us inaccessible side of God. In twentieth-century theology, Karl Barth and Karl Rahner can be taken as representatives of the western identity principle; Georges Florovsky and Vladimir Lossky as representatives of eastern doctrine of energies. Western writers who question the identity principle or contemporary eastern writers who do not accept the doctrine of energies, are the exceptions. A comparison of the identity principle and the doctrine of energies offers a way of access to the different approaches to the doctrine of the trinity, while seeking to avoid the better known path of the *filioque* debate.[1] It also suggests a way toward establishing a common ecumenical understanding of God's gracious relationship to the world. The results of this discussion can be summarized under three headings. First, the identity principle and the doctrine of energies represent two coherent though

---

1. Representatives of positions as different as those of G. Podskalsky and D. Ritschl are in agreement on this point: see D. Ritschl, "Warum wir Konzilien feier—Konstantinopel 381," *Theologische Zeitschrift* 38 (1982): 223f. and G. Podskalsky, *Theologie und Philosophie in Byzanz* (München, 1977), p. 15.

apparently mutually exclusive ways of thinking about the doctrine of God. Secondly, we can nevertheless bring these two ways of thinking into a fruitful dialogue and uncover a number of common intentions. Thirdly, the doctrine of energies offers a number of practical advantages when compared with a theology that allows no room for such a doctrine.

Two Coherent Ways of Thinking

In the foregoing chapters I have tried to answer the criticisms that can be made of each approach. Each approach uses the same (or very similar) terms, but quite differently. "Modes of existence," for example, distinguishes for Lossky between essence and energy,[2] while for Barth and Rahner respectively the very similar terms "modes of being" and "modes of subsistence" denote the trinitarian persons. The terms "nature" and "grace," again in eastern theology, refer to the essence and the energies respectively, while in western theology (especially scholastic theology) they refer to a distinction between the created natural order and a created supernatural realm. God's freedom, for Florovsky, refers to God's free decision to create a world and to enter into a relationship with this world; in other words, God's freedom *for* the created order. God's freedom, for Barth, means almost the opposite, namely the aseity of God, or God's freedom *from* the economy of salvation.

Much more important than these differences in the usage of terms is the differing ways of thinking about the trinity. The trinity is either a filioquist or a non-filioquist trinity. The starting point is either in the unity of God or the plurality of hypostases, the implicit model being either a unitary model or a plurality (or social) model of God's triunity. The trinity is thought of either in essentially functional terms (for example, God as creator, redeemer, and sanctifier), even if these terms at least in theory are qualified, or else the trinity is thought of in a way that places it unconditionally beyond any such functional or economic thinking. Behind these differences in approach we have the sense of a perhaps deeper split between two ways of thinking. As Kuhlmann[3] has argued, there is perhaps a difference between a more ontological interest and a primarily cognitive approach on the one hand, and a more personalistic interest and a primarily experiential approach on the other.

The two approaches seem to be mutually exclusive, and this impression is often reinforced when one or the other position is asserted polemically.[4]

---

2. V. N. Lossky, *The Vision of God* (Leighton Buzzard, 1963), p. 127.
3. J. Kuhlmann, *Die Taten des einfachen Gottes* (Würzburg, 1968), p. 25.
4. It is no accident, for example, that Wendebourg (*Geist oder Energie* [München,

The identity principle emphasizes the reliability or faithfulness of God, and tends to devalue mystical experience. Western skepticism about mysticism is not only a Protestant phenomenon. The western approach, with its history of scholastic and academic theology, tends to be more precise in its usage of terms, and western commentators often express an understandable sense of frustration at what they see as the "irrationality" of the Palamite approach. To the identity principle, realistic speech about deification seems arrogant. The doctrine of energies emphasizes the inaccessibility of God in Godself, but at the same time the possibility of an "unmediated" mystical experience of the divine glory. To the doctrine of energies, any claim to know God's essence thus appears either arrogant or misguided.

Both approaches are to be understood within their own cultural and theological contexts. The identity principle in Barth is a reaction to the romantic pantheism of the nineteenth century, and also to the Protestant liberalism that could make no sense of the doctrine of the trinity as a whole. In Rahner, the identity principle is a reaction to the textbook theology that tended to read the doctrine of the trinity as a given, having no practical or existential significance. The doctrine of energies was formulated originally, according to Meyendorff, as an answer to early nominalism. In this century it has been rediscovered as an answer to a western European culture that appears, from an Orthodox standpoint, to carry the stamp of neo-Platonism and nominalism. It is also worth remembering that the trinity doctrine made relevant by the identity principle, like the doctrine of energies, is a rediscovery of the twentieth century. This may explain to some extent why the two approaches have at times been so polemically asserted.

It has already been noted that some of the interests or concerns of one or the other approach can be upheld without the particular approach being developed fully. For example, the—for Florovsky—very important distinction between necessity and will requires no fully developed doctrine of energies. The—for Barth—central notion of God's faithfulness requires no absolute identity of God's inner triunity and economic activity. There is, in other words, room for dialogue.

Common Intention

The notion of common intention behind divergent doctrinal statements has been widely employed in recent ecumenical discussions.[5] The idea has

---

1980]), makes considerable use of the polemical anti-Latin texts of Orthodoxy.

5. K. Ware and C. Davey (eds), *Anglican-Orthodox Dialogue: The Moscow Statement* (London, 1977), p. 49, distinguishes between "the true intention of the dogmatic definition of a Council" and "the particular terminology in which it is expressed, which latter has less authority than the intention." Qv. M. Kinnamon, *Truth and Community*

been explored more systematically both by George Lindbeck and by Dietrich Ritschl in terms of a "grammar"[6] or a set of "implicit axioms".[7] Doctrinal statements are fashioned in certain contexts, and these contexts (which include the surrounding clusters of doctrines) tend to shape the actual formulation of a doctrinal statement so that it is stated in a way that is coherent within its context. A doctrine or collection of doctrines then functions like a language. Speakers of different languages (or different dialects of the same language—perhaps a better analogy in this case) have trouble understanding one another even though their intentions may be similar or identical. We need to look for what Lindbeck calls the "abiding doctrinal grammar" with its own particular rules beneath the varying theological vocabularies. My concern here is to uncover what common ground, what common *intentio fidei* there may be between the contemporary Eastern Orthodox and western positions, while remaining aware that these statements of common ground are themselves condemned *a priori* to being at best temporary and contextually valid pointers to a deeper reality.

In the case of the doctrinal differences under consideration, I suggest that we can take each position as an internally coherent or intra-systematically true teaching. This much can be demonstrated by exposing the inadequacy of attempts from each of the positions to prove the other incoherent. What I hope has now become clear is this: the basis on which each side tries to call the other in question has its own concerns and anxieties, which stand in contrast to the questions and concerns of the other tradition. In other words, I suggest that western theologians tend to criticize the doctrine of uncreated energies on the grounds that it does not make sense (and perhaps is not necessary) in the context of the western theological tradition and may even, from a western perspective, seem to endanger some of the basic "rules" or intentions of Christian faith. The same holds true in the reverse direction. I now turn to the more specific discussion of these common intentions.

The Doctrine of the Trinity

There is nothing behind the three hypostases whose activities are experienced in the history of salvation

---

(Grand Rapids/Geneva, 1988), p. 55, citing *Three Reports of the Forum on Bilateral Conversations* (Geneva, 1981).

6. G. Lindbeck, *The Nature of Doctrine: Religion and Theology in a Postliberal Age* (London, 1984), p. 113.

7. D. Ritschl, *The Logic of Theology* (London, 1986), pp. 108ff.

For the identity principle, this intention is very clear. God the trinity *is* the three hypostases as they reveal and communicate themselves in the economy of salvation. This assertion is to be understood in the context of the unity model of western theology, a model that comes to expression historically in the psychological analogy of the trinity. In the modern era this tendency to a unity model developed into the virtual unitarianism we can see, for example, in Kant and Schleiermacher. For this reason any doctrine of the trinity, if it is to be tenable, must be functional. That is, God must be *experienced* as trinitarian. It must be asserted, against any modalism, that there is no ultimate, hidden unity *behind* the three hypostases. The life of Jesus Christ must be explored *historically*—this because of the emphasis in the West since the Renaissance on the importance of historical veracity.

The intention behind the doctrine of energies is also to insist that the trinitarian activities of God are experienced in the economy of salvation, and that God is not different from what we experience. But here the context, and thus the concerns, are rather different from those in the West. Here a social or plurality model of the trinity is presupposed. The need, then, is to affirm the divine unity, or the common divine identity, of the three hypostases. In the East there is an awareness of the dangers inherent in a purely functional trinity. If we understand the Son and the Spirit on the basis of their functions (that is, their energies) then they might easily be taken *to be* energies of an unknown God. Then either the Son would be subordinated to the Father or the Spirit regarded as a mere power or dynamism of the Father and the Son. Thus it becomes very important to free the trinity from any suggestion of what Florovsky calls "economic motifs".

The concerns of the two approaches, or the problems of which the two approaches are particularly aware, are, because of these different theological contexts and presuppositions, themselves quite different. The intention of the two approaches, however, is the same. It is to assert a proper doctrine of the trinity. Western theology does this by insisting that God reveals Godself as a triunity of modes of being (Barth), or modes of subsistence or givenness (Rahner), and God in Godself corresponds to this self-revelation. Eastern theology also seeks to secure the doctrine of the trinity against any hidden deity that may perhaps be different from the trinity we know. It does this by locating the trinitarian superessentiality of God beyond our knowledge, and asserting that God is known in God's activities.

God is neither essence nor person, but community of persons

The identity principle in Barth and Rahner understands the trinitarian God as a self-revealing and self-communicating person. This notion of God as a person is subjected to criticism by Wenisch, Bantle, and others. But the concept of God as person must be understood as a reaction against the older notion of God as substance or essence. Barth and Rahner are trying to find a more personal way of speaking of God. More recent discussions of the trinity speak of a community of subjectivities (Jürgen Moltmann) or a plurality model (David Brown), thus seeking to speak personally of God but without falling into an individualistic notion of personhood. The doctrine of energies uses a concept of superessentiality, which is not simply to be equated with the term "God". Here God is not understood as essence or substance, but affirmed to be beyond such concepts. The term "person" is always reserved for the trinitarian hypostases. The trinity is a perichoretic community of persons or subjectivities. The perichoretic nature of this community is important, because it expresses the harmony of will or energy of the three trinitarian persons. Thus Staniloae speaks of an intersubjectivity, in which we can speak antinomically or paradoxically sometimes of one subject, at other times of three subjects. The personalism of the newer Palamite theology has not necessarily always been a feature of eastern theology. Rather it is a reaction against the Orthodox scholasticism of a theology influenced by western (especially Thomist) thought. The well-known text "God is love" (1 John 4:8) points to a communitarian Godhead. Systematically it is given expression by the notion of trinitarian perichoresis and the social analogy of the trinity. This way of thinking of God as community rather than a person or a substance is also to be found in recent western theology. We must not opt simply for a trinity of three subjectivities. Rather we should seek to retain the trinitarian antinomy in the way Staniloae suggests, or—to quote Fridhof Capra in a rather different context—"to emphasize the paradoxes rather than conceal them".[8]

The Doctrine of Creation

The idea of the world is pretemporal but not necessary

Barth's doctrine of creation includes a pretemporal "decree" on God's part to create a world. Barth does not discuss whether this decree or idea of a world is coeternal with God, but before the beginning of time the decree is not actualized. It remains potential. It stands in contrast to God, who is from eternity to eternity. The concept of God as pure actuality (*actus purus*) thus serves to distinguish God from the idea of a world. Its origin lies in Aristotle's distinction between potentiality (δύναμις) and actuality (ἐνέργεια). This distinction is less important in eastern theology which tends to identify δύναμις with ἐνέργεια. There is a pretemporal order of

---

8. F. Capra, *The Tao of Physics* (London, 1983), p. 56.

manifestation in western theology, and this is made explicit by the *filioque* clause. The economic missions correspond to the eternal trinitarian missions. Palamite theology distinguishes the ineffable inner-trinitarian origins of the Son and the Spirit on the one hand from the aeonic (that is, pretemporal) order of trinitarian manifestation on the other. In this order the second and third hypostases shine through one another mutually. The Spirit receives from the Son and the Son is hypostatically transfigured by the energies of the Spirit. This "shining through" is completely independent of any temporal mission of the Son or the Spirit.

The eastern approach, locating the idea of the world in aeonic eternity, emphasizes that not only the actual world but even the idea of a world lies in the realm of contingency. Here, the actuality of God refers to the realm of the activity (ἐνέργεια) or possession of God. God *has* the idea of a world, and this having is essentially different from the being of God, which remains always more than having. Being is emphatically not to be equated with having. God acts in the world initially insofar as the idea of a world is actualized; that is, the actual world comes into existence. Both approaches emphasize, in different ways, that God ever was and is, but that the world is the outworking of a free decision of God. In other words, it is the intention of both approaches to assert that the idea of a world is *pretemporal but contingent*.

The being of God is experienced by human beings in the activity of God

The incarnation of the Son plays a central role in the Christian experience of God. For the western tradition, the incarnation is to be experienced primarily in the biblical story of Jesus of Nazareth. Discipleship of Jesus involves a conformity of self to Christ (*imitatio Christi*). The eastern tradition tends to understand the incarnation and indeed the history of salvation as present in the liturgy; that is, in doxology. The presence of Christ is to be apprehended here, liturgically and doxologically, and especially in the living *Christusbild*, the holy person. Conformity to Christ takes place through ascetic praxis, though neither this nor the liturgy is constructed without reference to the biblical *Heilsgeschichte*. Discipleship is regarded less as *imitatio*, more as *participatio*. In both traditions, East and West, the presence of the living Christ is strongly emphasized, but in different ways. In Palamite thought, God is known through mystical experience—experience which is bodily rather than merely intellectual. This mystical experience is the possession not just of the individual believer, but of the whole church.[9] Western theology also bases our knowledge of God in

---

9. D. M. Allchin, "The Appeal to Experience in the Triads of St. Gregory Palamas," *TU*

the experience of the church—though this experience here is conveyed much more, especially for Protestantism, in the preaching of the church. In proclaiming the history of salvation the word of God is, according to Barth, either heard or not heard. The experience is more intellectual, less embodied or sensual.

Despite these differences of emphasis both approaches insist that our knowledge of God is a theological, not primarily an anthropological, matter. This is the point of the Palamite assertion of a *real* distinction within God, an assertion that is very frequently misunderstood in the West. The insistence that statements about God are theological, not anthropological, is also the major point of Barth's critique of the human "point of contact" with God. Even without going to the extreme position of the early Barth on this, even if some basis within humanity is allowed for the reception of God's self-communication—as it is allowed, for example, by Rahner—there is still the emphasis in the West, as in Palamite theology, that our access to God is dependent upon God alone. In both approaches, God is known experientially, through the experience of God's actions. Through these actions it is indeed the trinitarian God who is believed to be encountered.

Both approaches posit a primary ontological distinction between the creator and the creation

This axiom is very clear indeed in Barth's striving to rule out any natural point of contact between creator and creation. Barth criticizes Palamism for its panentheism, which he sees as a dangerous bridging of the primary ontological boundary, viz. between creator and creation. Florovsky, by contrast, detects here an "ontological dualism" separating creator and creation. The problem for him lies in a simple separation, because then the *idea* of a creation is identified with God in Godself. The idea of a creation becomes eternal and necessary, and this in turn suggests a necessary actualization of the world. Both Barth and Florovsky endeavor, in different ways, to avoid any such notion of the created order being rendered necessary, and thus coeternal with God. Barth is primarily aware of the secular idealist and romantic philosophies of the nineteenth century, and seeks to barricade that particular way to pantheism. Florovsky is primarily conscious of the older danger inherent in Origen's theology, and he sees its reemergence in the "German Idealism" of the nineteenth century. Both approaches intend an ontological distinction between creator and creation. For Barth, this intention is simply axiomatic. For Florovsky, the prior distinction between necessity and will is indispensible to a reliable doctrine

---

93 (1966): 326.

of creation. The tendency of Palamite authors to use Platonic terminology has been noted, but with the help of Louth's[10] criteria I have argued that that terminology is radically reinterpreted in Palamite theology.

The Doctrine of Grace

The creation is renewed through God's grace

Protestant theology affirms this in its traditional emphasis that justification is through God's grace alone (*sola gratia*). Human beings are, at least in the first instance, passive recipients. Grace is not to be bought. For Rahner, the human being is first of all an addressee, that is, the one to whom God communicates Godself. Although, here again, humanity is passive initially, there is no intention to diminish the final state of the justified human person. Human beings are adopted through grace as children of God, and thus as sisters and brothers of the eternal Son of the Father.

The doctrine of energies presents us quite explicitly with what Lossky calls "maximalism". Creatures are deified through God's energy, or grace. The ontological distinction is retained between the one who is Son of the Father by nature and those who—even in deification—are children of God by adoption. The Son is eternally God, one of the holy trinity, while deified human beings participate in the energies of God. There is thus a difference in emphasis between the two approaches, a difference that comes to expression in the differing terminologies used. Western theologians speak sometimes of the vision of the divine essence, or of intentional participation. They seldom speak of entitative participation in the life of God, for that would mean to become God in Godself. Eastern theologians speak of a vision of God's glory or the divine light, or of entitative participation in the divine energies. They refrain from speaking of a vision of the superessentiality or an entitative participation in it, for that would mean to become a hypostasis of the trinity. I think we can dismiss any claim on one side to be more "maximal" than the other. Both approaches in fact assert a maximal understanding of the new creation. For both, we are destined to become "like God" (1 John 3:3). In both approaches, the issue at stake is the transformation of creation into new creation through the operation of God's grace. Both approaches allow for a human response to that grace, and thus a form of co-operation with God.

The real indwelling of the Holy Spirit in the human being is emphasized both by the identity principle and by the doctrine of energies. In both

---

10. A. Louth, *The Origins of the Christian Mystical Tradition: From Plato to Denys* (Oxford, 1981), chap. 10.

approaches, the creature is made whole through God's grace. *Gratia perfecit naturam.* This grace, moreover, is never understood in isolation from the person of the Holy Spirit. Barth and Rahner emphasize that the Spirit is as a hypostasis given to the human person. "Grace is the Holy Spirit received" (Barth); "Christology and the doctrine of grace are, strictly speaking, doctrine of the Trinity" (Rahner[11]). Palamite theology understands grace as God's uncreated energy, that is, as that side of God that encounters and "shines through" the created order. This grace is mediated by the Holy Spirit. It is "inhypostatized" in the Spirit.[12] The essential hypostasis of the Spirit thus does not indwell the human person. But an energetic indwelling is no less a real indwelling than a hypostatic indwelling. Neither the eastern nor the western approach intends to minimize the status of our life in God or God's life in us. If eastern theology sometimes speaks of θέωσις, deification, it is always careful to retain, even with reference to eternity, the ontological distinction between the creator and the deified creatures.[13] The end purpose of the human being, for both approaches, is to become a child of God by adoption, neither more nor less. The doctrine of energies asserts a notion of reaching out (ἐπέκτασις) into the life of God, thus emphasizing that the deification effected by grace is never a perfected status in time, but is rather a process whereby the human subject is invited ever deeper into God's eternity.

Practical Advantages of a Doctrine of Energies

I have tried to set out the common intentions of the two approaches. It is important not to overlook the hermeneutical problem here. The *intention* of an author, let alone a whole school of theology, is seldom unambiguous. Each of the four theologians considered here writes in an ecumenical context—Florovsky and Lossky as Orthodox in America and France respectively, Barth as one of the pioneers of the ecumenical movement, Rahner as a Roman Catholic theologian who consciously seeks for common

---

11. K. Rahner, *The Trinity* (Tunbridge Wells, 1970), p. 120.

12. Y. Congar, *I Believe in the Holy Spirit* (New York/London, 1983), vol. 3, p. 63.

13. N. A. Nissiotis, *Die Theologie der Ostkirche im ökumenischen Dialog* (Stuttgart, 1968), pp. 50–51. Nissiotis is careful not to translate θέωσις with "deification," on the grounds that θέωσις is rather "that spiritual development which is effected in us by the Paraclete in the church, on the basis of salvation through Christ, and which leads us toward true and complete humanity. True humanity (*verus homo*) is to be found only in dynamic connection with the divine grace of Christ as the *verus Deus* (true God). The theology of the human being in the Holy Spirit, the θέωσις of the human being, forms a basis for the human being who is on the way to becoming what he/she is in the depth of his/her being, as this is revealed in Christ. This can be realized in any human being in whom the Holy Spirit draws towards his/her highest purpose: to be in Christ."

ground with the Orthodox. Each of the four writes from his own theological background and seeks, partially apologetically, partially polemically, to give expression to this theological background. Despite the difficulties of interpretation, I believe it is possible to uncover the commonality of intention indicated above.

At the beginning I raised the question as to what western theology can learn from the doctrine of energies. I hope I have established that the principle of the identity of the doctrines of the inner trinity and the economic trinity is no final criterion for the validity of trinitarian thinking. The *filioque* clause, usually taken as the major point of conflict between eastern and western models of trinitarian thinking, can itself be seen as a corollary of this fundamental principle of western theology. It is thus not satisfactory to discuss the *filioque* without reference to this deeper source of division. But neither is it satisfactory to stop at the divergence between the two approaches. If we see the underlying common intentions, this opens up the possibility, from a western standpoint, of exploring the advantages of the other approach. The doctrine of energies offers us another point of entry to reflection on the relationship of God to the world.

Both the identity principle and the doctrine of energies are possible interpretations of the doctrine of the trinity and the relationship of the trinitarian God to the world. Both interpretations offer coherent explanations of the relationship between God in Godself and God in relation to creation. The same intentions underlie both approaches. Both are attempts to speak of the experience of the grace of the trinitarian God. We cannot pass judgment on the truth of the underlying intentions. We can, however, point to some practical advantages of a doctrine of energies.

(a) *The doctrine of the trinity*. The identity principle endeavors to speak descriptively, in the nominative, about God's inner being. The doctrine of energies calls this procedure in question by asserting that we may only speak descriptively about the acts of God; about the inner being of God we may speak only ascriptively, in the vocative. "Of God's inner being, the 'immanent' trinity," says Dietrich Ritschl, "can one speak in the end only as worship, only doxologically".[14] This is not merely a reflection on human intellectual capacities. Rather, it concerns the way in which *God* deals with us and acts for us. The names and analogies we apply to God are in this way fundamentally conditional. If we use these names and analogies descriptively, let us be careful only to apply them to God in relation to us. This means that our speech *to* God is set free. We may use a variety of

---

14. D. Ritschl, *The Logic of Theology* (London, 1986), pp. 146–47.

anthropomorphisms (and other metaphors) in worship. At the same time the doctrine of energies insists that *every* name and *every* analogy must be, in the end, subjected to the radical demythologization[15] of the apophatic way. I believe this principle must also apply to the inner-trinitarian names of the three hypostases: Father, Son, and Holy Spirit.

(b) *The doctrine of creation.* Modern physics leads to death, mysticism to life—thus argues the central figure in a novel by Chaim Potok.[16] Perhaps we need not be quite so pessimistic, especially when we look at some of the integrative thinking of the new physics. But the point is that the analytical method of classical modern physics, resting on the Cartesian division between subject and object, observer and observed, did indeed divide and kill the natural order. Christianity in the West has for a long time now accommodated itself to this Cartesian worldview. The Platonic dualism of intellect and matter, subject and object, leads directly to the dualism that sets the all-powerful God over against the world, and the human "I" over against all that which is not "I". The doctrine of energies offers us an alternative view of God's presence in the world, arising out of the praxis of Christian prayer. God is no longer the all-powerful God, but first and foremost the one who holds things together, interacts with the creation and responds to its needs.[17] The world itself is to be viewed holistically and synthetically rather than mechanistically and analytically.

The doctrine of energies views the world as lying within God (in the womb of the one who holds all together), and as "transfused" with the divine energies. This necessarily involves a tendency to view the world holistically (καθόλου) rather than analytically, or according to the parts (καθ' ἕκαστον). Human beings are understood as persons in relationship, and reality as being in relation to God. Matter—the human body and the physical environment—is highly valued in such a theological system, without, however, the ontological distinction between the creator and the creation being lost. In our present time of ecological crisis, the significance of such a positive theological evaluation of the material world goes without saying. In the Australian context it suggests a way of giving positive value to Aboriginal spirituality, a spirituality in which the land itself holds a central place. The important thing, methodologically, is that the doctrine of energies opens up

---

15. G. Galitis ("Apophatismus als Prinzip der Schriftauslegung bei den griechischen Kirchenvätern," *EvTh* 40 [1980]: 25–40) draws a parallel between the apophatic method and demythologization.

16. C. Potok, *The Book of Lights* (London, 1981), see esp. pp. 290 ff.

17. Cf. similar recent trends in the theology of creation, e.g. M. Welker, "What is Creation? Rereading Genesis 1 and 2," in *Theology Today* 48 (1991): 56–71.

a view of created reality not merely as object to be analytically investigated and controlled, but as a reality that shares in our being, and through our transfiguring participation in God, can find its own transfiguration.

(c) *The doctrine of grace.* What we have here is the vision of a sort of penumbra of glory, or a field of energy[18] that surrounds the trinitarian Godhead. In this way the universe can be considered as lying within God's field of energy or "field of resonance"[19] while at the same time remaining distinct from and contingent upon God's superessentiality. Within this penumbra or energy-field, there is a resonating and a quickening of the natural, material universe, so that the material order is drawn into the experience—however we may understand "experience"—of God. The human being is conscious of being drawn into the life of God and can consciously choose for him- or herself to participate more or less fully in this life. This participation of the material world in the life of God involves matter (inanimate and animate) as well as conscious mind. The energies "shine through" the whole of the universe. Experience is not simply a matter of consciousness, but—as Charles Birch[20] has pointed out—occurs at all levels of the material universe, in the strictly inanimate as well as the animate. Consciousness is realized to the highest degree—at least, as far as we are aware, and bracketing out any discussion of angelic beings—in our own human species. Our consciousness of God may be thought of as consciousness of God's energies at work in and through the material universe, and a sense of the material universe as lying within the energy-field of God. The analogy here would be to an electromagnetic field that affects and reorients the molecules within it. We have to be clear here that this *is* an analogy. We are considering God's energy, "uncreated energy," not the energy that forms part of the universe and that stands in a particular mathematical relationship to mass.

The doctrine of energies emphasizes the essential inaccessibility of God, and at the same time the constant accessibility of God in God's energetic emanations. The Palamite teaching about grace always emphasizes the notion of reaching out (ἐπέκτασις) into the life of God, a growing relationship with God and an ever deeper pathway into the inexhaustible resources of God's grace. This means just the opposite of a disembodied quest for an abstract divinity. Rather it is a pilgrimage, which brings with it a practical, embodied, and even political *ascesis*. It is a pilgrimage of co-

---

18. M.Welker, *Gottes Geist: Theologie des Heiligen Geistes* (Neukirchen-Vluyn, 1992), pp. 224ff.
19. Ibid., p. 273.
20. C. Birch, *On Purpose* (Kensington, NSW, 1990), pp. 84 and 120f.

operation with the God of Israel to prepare the world for the reign of justice and peace. Deification here means a radicalized personhood whereby the individual self-consciousness is transcended, while at the same time human existence as bodily being is both respected and transfigured. This fulfilled personhood is realized in an ever deepening participation in the trinitarian life of God.

These briefly sketched advantages have not been fully explored, not even as yet by the Orthodox themselves. What I suggest is that a careful synthesis of eastern and western approaches to the relationship between God and the world may be able to offer these as the corollaries to an ecumenical doctrine of energies.

BIBLIOGRAPHY

Aagaard, A. M. "Christus wurde Mensch, um alles Menschliche zu überwinden." *StTh* 21 (1967): 164–81.

———. "Der Heilige Geist in der Welt." In H. Meyer et al., *Wiederentdeckung des Heiligen Geistes*. Frankfurt a.M.: Verlag Otto Lembeck/Verlag Josef Knecht, 1974.

———. "Die Erfahrung des Geistes." In O. A. Dilschneider (ed.), *Theologie des Geistes*. Gütersloh: Gerd Mohn, 1980, pp. 11–24.

———. *Helligånden sendt til Verden*. Aarhus: Forlaget Aros, 1973.

Abramowski, L. "Die dritte Arianerrede des Athanasius-Eusebianer und Arianer und das westliche Serdicense." *ZKG* 102 (1991): 389–413.

Aghiorgoussis, M. "Christian Existentialism of the Greek Fathers: Persons, Essence and Energies in God." *GrOrthThR* 23 (1978): 15–41.

Allchin, A. M. "The Appeal to Experience in the Triads of St. Gregory Palamas." *TU* 93 (1966): 323–28.

———. *Participation in God: A Forgotten Strand in Anglican Tradition*. London: Darton, Longman & Todd, 1988.

Anon. *The Way of a Pilgrim*. Trans. R. M. French. London: SPCK, 1972.

Aristotle. *Metaphysica*, Ed. W. Jaeger. Oxford: Clarendon Press, 1957.

Armstrong, A. H. "Plotinus." In *GMP*, pp. 193–268.

Bantle, F. X. "Person und Personbegriff in der Trinitätslehre Karl Rahners." *MThZ* 30 (1979): 11–24.

Barker, M. *The Great Angel: A Study of Israel's Second God*. London: SPCK, 1992.

Barrios, G. "Palamism Revisited." *StVladThQ* 19 (1975): 211–31.

Barth, K. *Die christliche Dogmatik im Entwurf: Die Lehre vom Worte Gottes*. Munich: Chr. Kaiser Verlag, 1927.

———. *Church Dogmatics*. Edinburgh: T. & T. Clark, 1936.

Baur, F. C. *Die christliche Lehre von der Dreieinigkeit und Menschwerdung Gottes in ihrer geschichtlichen Entwicklung*. Tübingen: Osiander Verlag, 1841 ff.

Beck, H.-G. *Kirche und theologische Literatur im Byzantinischen Reich*. Munich: C. H. Beck'sche Verlagsbuchhandlung, 1959.

Birch, C. *On Purpose*. Kensington, NSW: New South Wales University Press, 1990.

Blum, G. G. "Oikonomia und Theologie: Der Hintergrund einer konfessionellen Differenz zwischen östlichem und westlichem Christentum." *OstkirchSt* 33 (1984): 281–301.

Bobrinskoy, B. "The Filioque Yesterday and Today." In *IIe Concile: Les etudes theologiques de Chambesy, 2: La Signification et L'actualite du IIe Concile Oecumenique pour le mond chretien d'aujourd'hui.* Chambesy-Geneva: Editions du Centre Orthodoxe du Patriarchat Oecumenique, 1982, pp. 275–87.

Böhner, P., and Gilson, E. *Christliche Philosophie von ihren Anfängen bis Nikolaus von Cues.* Paderborn: Ferdinand Schöningh, 1954.

Boff, L. *Liberating Grace.* Maryknoll: Orbis, 1979.

Bolotov, V. V. "Thesen über das Filioque von einem russischen Theologen." *Revue Internationale de Théologie* (1898): 681–712.

Bonhoeffer, D. *Letters and Papers from Prison.* London: SCM, 1971.

Brady, V. *A Crucible of Prophets: Australians and the Question of God.* Sydney: Theological Explorations, 1981.

Brown, D. *The Divine Trinity.* London: Duckworth, 1985.

Capra, F. *The Tao of Physics.* London: Fontana, 1983.

Chrestou, P. (ed.). Παλαμᾶ Συγγράμματα. Thessaloniki, 1962, 3 vols. English translation of select passages by N. Gendle in *The Triads.* London: SPCK, 1983.

Clement, O. *Orient–occident–deux passeurs: Vladimir Lossky et Paul Evdokimov.* Geneva: Editions Labor et Fides, 1985.

Coffey, D. "The Palamite Doctrine of God: a New Perspective." *StVladThQ* 32 (1988): 329–58.

Congar, Y. *I Believe in the Holy Spirit.* New York: Seabury Press/London: Geoffrey Chapman, 1983, vol. 3.

Contos, L. C. "The Essence-Energies Structure of St. Gregory Palamas with a brief examination of its Patristic Foundations." *GrOrthThR* 12 (1967): 283–94.

Conzelmann, H. χάρις, in TDNT, vol. 9.

Einstein, A. *The Meaning of Relativity.* London: Science Paperbacks, 1967.

Elert, W. *Der Ausgang der altkirchlichen Christologie: Eine Untersuchung über Theodor von Pharan und seine Zeit als Einführung in die alte Dogmengeschichte.* Berlin: Lutherisches Verlagshaus, 1957.

Evdokimov, P. *Christus im russischen Denken.* Trier: Paulinus-Verlag, 1977.

Fabro, C. "Participation." In *New Catholic Encyclopedia.* New York: McGraw-Hill, 1967, vol. 10.

Florovsky, G. V. "Bogoslovskie otryvki." *Put'* 31 (1931): 3–29.

———. "The Christian Hellenism." *Orthodox Observer* 442 (1957): 9–10.

———. *Collected Works.* Belmont Mass.: Nordland Publishing Company, 1972ff.

    Vol. 1: Bible, Church, Tradition: An Eastern Orthodox View (1972);

    Vol. 2: Christianity and Culture (1974);

    Vol. 3: Creation and Redemption (1976);

Vol. 4: Aspects of Church History (1975).

———. "The Concept of Creation in Saint Athanasius." *TU* 81 (1962): 36–57.

———. "The Idea of Creation in Christian Philosophy." *ECQ* 8 (1949; Supplementary Issue: Nature and Grace): 53–77.

———. "Maximos und der Origenismus." In *Diskussionsbeiträge zum XI. Internationalen Byzantinisten Kongress.* München, 1958, pp. 37–40.

———. "Offenbarung, Philosophie und Theologie." *ZZ* 9 (1931): 463–80.

———. "Patristics and Modern Theology." In H. S. Alivisatos (ed.) *Procès-verbaux du Premier Congrès de Théologie Orthodoxe a Athènes.* Athens, 1939, pp. 238–42.

———. "Protivorecija Origenizma." *Put'* 18 (1929): 107–15.

———. "Spor o nemetskom idealisme." *Put'* 25 (1930): 51–80.

———. "The Work of the Holy Spirit in Revelation." *The Christian East* 13 (1932): 49–64.

Freyer, T. *Pneumatologie als Strukturprinzip der Dogmatik: Überlegungen im Anschluß an die Lehre von der "Geisttaufe" bei Karl Barth.* Paderborn: Ferdinand Schöningh, 1982.

Gadamer, H.-G. *Wahrheit und Methode: Grundzüge einer philosophischen Hermeneutik.* Tübingen: J. C. B. Mohr (Paul Siebeck), 1965.

Galitis, G. "Apophatismus als Prinzip der Schriftauslegung bei den griechischen Kirchenvätern." *EvTh* 40 (1980): 25–40.

Gerlitz, P. *Ausserchristliche Einflüsse auf die Entwicklung des christlichen Trinitätsdogmas: Zugleich ein religions- und dogmengeschichtlicher Versuch zur Erklärung der Herkunft der Homousie.* Leiden: E. J. Brill, 1963.

Gregorios, Paulos. *The Human Presence: an Orthodox view of nature.* Geneva: World Council of Churches, 1978.

Grondijs, L. H. "The Patristic Origins of Gregory Palamas' Doctrine of God." *TU* 80 (1962): 323–28.

Grundmann, W. δύναμαι. In TDNT, vol. 2.

Gunton, C. *The Promise of Trinitarian Theology.* Edinburgh: T. & T. Clark, 1991.

Habra, G. "The Sources of the Doctrine of Gregory Palamas on the Divine Energies." *ECQ* 12 (1957): 244–52, 294–303, 338–47.

Hadot, P. *Einleitung zu Christlicher Platonismus: Drei Theologischen Schriften des Marius Victorinus.* Ed. C. Andresen. Zürich: Artemis Verlag, 1967.

Hanson, R. C. "The Doctrine of the Trinity Achieved in 381." *ScotJTh* 36 (1983): 41–57.

Hauschild, W.-D. "Die Trinitätslehre des Konzils von Konstantinopel und die Situation der Kirche im 4. Jahrhunderts." *In IIe Concile: Les etudes theologiques de Chambesy, 2: La Signification et L'actualite du IIe Concile Oecumenique pour le mond chretien d'aujourd'hui.* Chambesy-Geneva: Editions du Centre Orthodoxe du Patriarchat Oecumenique, 1982.

Hegel, G. W. F. *Phänomenologie des Geistes* (1807), Ed. J. Hoffmeister. Hamburg: Felix Meiner, 1952.

———. *Vorlesungen über die Philosophie der Religion, 3. Teil: Die Absolute Religion* in *Sämtliche Werke.* Ed. G. Lasson. Leipzig: Felix Meiner, 1929, Bd. 14.

Heiler, F. *Die Ostkirchen.* Munich: Reinhardt, 1971.

Hendry, G. S. *The Holy Spirit in Christian Theology.* London: SCM, 1965.

Heron, A. "The Holy Spirit in Origen and Didymus the Blind: A Shift in Perspective From the Third to the Fourth Century." In A. M. Ritter (ed.), *Kerygma and Logos: Beiträge zu den geistesgeschichtlichen Beziehungen zwischen Antike und Christentum. Festgeschrift für Carl Andresen zum 70. Geburstag.* Göttingen: Vandenhoeck & Ruprecht, 1979, pp. 298–310.

Heschel, A. J. *The Prophets.* New York: Harper & Row, 1975, part 2.

Hochstaffl, J. *Negative Theologie: Ein Versuch zur Vermittlung des patristischen Begriffs.* Munich: Kösel-Verlag, 1976.

Hussey, M. E. "The Palamite Trinitarian Models." *SVTQ* 16 (1972): 83–89.

———. "The Persons-Energy Structure in the Theology of St. Gregory Palamas." *StVladThQ* 18 (1974): 22–43.

Ivánka, E. von. "Hellenisches im Hesychasmus: Das Antinomische der Energienlehre." In J. Fontaine and C. Kannengiesser (eds), *Epektasis: mélanges patristiques offerts au Cardinal Jean Danielou.* Beauchesne: 1972, pp. 491–500.

———. "Hesychasmus und Palamismus: Ihr gegenseitiges Verhältnis und ihre geistesgeschichtliche Bedeutung." *JÖBG* 2 (1952): 23–34.

———. "Palamismus und Vätertradition." In L. Beauduin (ed.), *1054–1954: L'Église et les eglises: neuf siècles de douloureuse séparation entre l'orient et l'occident.* Editions de Chevetogne, 1955, vol. 2.

———. *Plato Christianus: Übernahme und Umgestaltung des Platonismus durch die Väter.* Einsiedeln: Johannes Verlag, 1964.

———. "Zur hesychastischen Lichtvision." *Kairos* 13 (1971): 77–95.

Jammer, M. "Energy." In P. Edwards (ed.), *The Encyclopedia of Philosophy.* London: Collier-Macmillan, 1967, vol. 2, pp. 511–17.

John of Damascus. *Die Schriften des Johannes von Damaskos,* Vol. II, *Expositio Fidei* in B. Kotter (ed.), *Patristische Texte und Studien.* Berlin: Walter de Gruyter, 1973, vol. 12. English translation: *Exposition of the Orthodox Faith,* In *A Select Library of Nicene and Post-Nicene Fathers of the Christian Church.* London: James Parker, 1899, vol. 9.

Johnson, E. "The Incomprehensibility of God and the Image of God Male and Female." *Theological Studies* 45 (1984): 441–65.

Jüngel, E. "Das Verhältnis von ökonomischer und immanenter Trinität." *ZThK* 72 (1975): 353–64.

———. *God as the Mystery of the World.* Grand Rapids: Eerdmans, 1983.

Jugie, M. "Palamas, Gregoire." In *Dictionnaire de Theologie Catholique.* Paris: Libraire Letouzey et Ane, 1931.

Bibliography

———. *Theologia Dogmatica Christianorum Orientalium ab Ecclesia Catholica Dissidentium.* Paris: Sumptibus Letouzey et Ane, 1933.

Kasper, W. *The God of Jesus Christ.* New York: Crossroad,1991.

Kawerau, P. *Das Christentum des Ostens.* (Religionen der Menschheit, vol. 30). Stuttgart: Verlag W. Kohlhammer, 1972.

Kern, K. *Antropologija Sv. Grigorija Palamy.* Paris: YMCA Press, 1950.

———. "Duchovnye predki Svjatovo Grigorija Palamy." *Bogoslovskaja Mysl'* (Paris), 1942, pp. 102–31.

Kern, W. and Niemann, F.-J. *Theologische Erkenntnislehre.* Düsseldorf: Patmos Verlag, 1981.

Kinnamon, M. *Truth and Community: Diversity and its Limits in the Ecumenical Movement.* Grand Rapids: Eerdmans/Geneva: WCC, 1988.

Kittel, G. δόξα in *TDNT*, vol. 2.

Kretschmar, G. *Studien zur frühchristlichen Trinitätslehre: Beiträge zur Historischen Theologie.* Tübingen: J. C. B. Mohr (Paul Siebeck), 1956.

Kretschmer, W. "Theologie und Subjektives Erlebnis: Ein Beitrag zum Verständnis der palamitischen Mystik." *Greg Pa* 43 (1960): 37–50.

Krivocheine, B. "The Ascetic and Theological Teaching of Gregory Palamas." *ECQ* III (1938–39): 26–33, 71–84, 138–56, 193–214.

———. "Problema poznavaemosti Boga." *Messager* 61 (1968): 48–55.

———. "Simplicity of the Divine Nature and the Distinctions in God, according to St. Gregory of Nyssa." *StVladThQ* 21 (1977): 76–104.

Küry, U. "Die Bedeutung des Filioque-Streites für den Gottesbegriff der abendländischen und der morgenländischen Kirche." *IKZ* 33 (1943): 1–19.

Kuhlmann, J. *Die Taten des einfachen Gottes: Eine römisch-katholische Stellungnahme zum Palamismus.* Würzburg: Augustinus-Verlag, 1968.

La Cugna, C. M. *God for Us: the Trinity and Christian Life.* San Francisco: Harper, 1991.

Lampe, G. W. H. *God as Spirit: The Bampton Lectures, 1976.* Oxford: Clarendon Press, 1977.

Lampert, E. "The Orthodox Church's Teaching of Grace." *ECQ* 6 (1946): 248–58.

Langen, J. *Die Trinitarische Lehrdifferenz zwischen der abendländischen und der morgenländischen Kirche.* Bonn: Eduard Weber's Verlags-Buchhandlung (Rudolf Weber), 1876.

Lialine, C. "The Theological Teaching of Gregory Palamas on Divine Simplicity." *ECQ* 6 (1945–46): 266–87.

Lindbeck, G. *The Nature of Doctrine: Religion and Theology in a Postliberal Age.* SPCK: London, 1984.

Lison, J. "L'Energie des trois hypostases divines selon Gregoire Palamas." *Science et Esprit* 44/1 (1992): 67–77.

Lossky, N. O. *History of Russian Philosophy.* London: Allen & Unwin, 1952.

Lossky, V. N. *In the Image and Likeness of God.* New York: St. Vladimir's Seminary Press, 1974.

———. *The Mystical Theology of the Eastern Church.* New York: St. Vladimir's Seminary Press, 1976.

———. *Orthodox Theology: An Introduction.* New York: St. Vladimir's Seminary Press, 1978.

———. "The Personality and Thought of Patriarch Sergius." *Diakonia* 6 (1971): 163–71.

———. "The Problem of the Vision Face to Face and Byzantine Patristic Tradition." *GrOrthThR* 17 (1972): 231–54.

———. *The Vision of God.* Leighton Buzzard: Faith Press, 1963.

Louth, A. *Discerning the Mystery: An Essay on the Nature of Theology.* Oxford: Clarendon Press, 1983.

———. *The Origins of the Christian Mystical Tradition: From Plato to Denys.* Oxford: Clarendon Press, 1981.

McIntyre, J. "The Holy Spirit in Greek Patristic Thought." *ScotJTh* 7 (1954): 353–75.

Mackey, J. P. *The Christian Experience of God as Trinity.* London: SCM, 1983.

———. "The Holy Spirit: Relativising the Divergent Approaches of East and West." *Irish Theological Quarterly* 48 (1981): 256–67.

Maloney, G. A. *A History of Orthodox Theology since 1453.* Belmont Mass: Nordland Publishing Company, 1976.

———. *Inscape: God at the Heart of Matter.* Denville, N.J.: Dimension Books, 1978.

———. *A Theology of "Uncreated Energies."* Milwaukee: Marquette University Press, 1978.

Mantzaridis, G. I. *The Deification of Man: St. Gregory Palamas and the Orthodox Tradition.* Contemporary Greek Theologians, no. 2. New York: St. Vladimir's Seminary Press, 1984.

———. "Tradition and Renewal in the Theology of Saint Gregory Palamas." *ECR* 9 (1977): 1–18.

Mascall, E. L. *The Openness of Being: Natural Theology Today.* London: Darton, Longman & Todd, 1971.

Meeks, D. "Gott und die Ökonomie des Heiligen Geistes." *EvTh* 40 (1980): 40–58.

Meyendorff, J. *Byzantine Theology: Historical Trends and Doctrinal Themes.* New York: Fordham University Press, 1976.

———. *Christ in Eastern Christian Thought.* New York: St. Vladimir's Seminary Press, 1975.

———. "Creation in the History of Orthodox Theology." *StVladThQ* 27 (1983): 27–37.

———. "Doctrine of Grace in St. Gregory Palamas." *StVladSQ* 2 (1954): 17–26.

———. "The Holy Trinity in Palamite Theology." In *Trinitarian Theology East and West: St. Thomas Aquinas—St. Gregory Palamas*. Patriarch Athenagoras Lectures; Boston: Holy Cross Orthodox Press, 1979.

———. "Philosophy, Theology, Palamism and Secular Christianity." *StVladSQ* 10 (1966): 203–8.

———. *St. Gregory Palamas and Orthodox Spirituality*. New York: St. Vladimir's Seminary Press, 1974.

———. *A Study of Gregory Palamas*. Leighton Buzzard: Faith Press, 1974.

Moeller, C. and Philips, G. *The Theology of Grace and the Oecumenical Movement*. London: Mowbray & Co., 1961.

Molnar, P. D. "Can we know God directly? Rahner's Solution from Experience." *Theological Studies* 46 (1985): 228–61.

Moltmann, J. *The Crucified God: The Cross of Christ as the Foundation and Criticism of Christian Theology*. London: SCM, 1974.

———. "Die versöhnende Kraft der Dreieinigkeit im Leben der Kirche und der Gesellschaft." *Ökumenisches Forum* 6 (1983): 45–59.

———. *God in Creation: An Ecological Doctrine of Creation*. London: SCM, 1985.

———. *History and the Triune God: Contributions to Trinitarian Theology*. London: SCM, 1991.

———. *The Trinity and the Kingdom of God*. London: SCM, 1981.

Muck, O. *Philosophische Gotteslehre*. Düsseldorf: Patmos Verlag, 1983.

Musther, J. "Exploration into God: an Examination." In A. M. Allchin (ed.), *Orthodoxy and the Death of God: Essays in Contemporary Theology*. Studies Supplementary to Sobornost, no. 1, 1971, pp. 57–77.

Mühlen, H. *Der Heilige Geist als Person: Beitrag zur Frage nach der dem Heiligen Geiste eigentümlichen Funktion in der Trinität bei der Inkarnation und im Gnadenbund*. Münster: Aschendorffsche Verlagsbuchhandlung, 1963.

———. "Person und Appropriation. Zum Verständnis des Axioms: In Deo omnia sunt unum, ubi non obviat relationis oppositio." *MThZ* 16 (1965): 37–57.

Nissiotis, N. A. *Die Theologie der Ostkirche im Ökumensichen Dialog: Kirche und Welt in orthodoxer Sicht*. Stuttgart: Evangelisches Verlagswerk, 1968.

O'Donnell, J. J. *The Mystery of the Triune God*. London: Sheed & Ward, 1988.

O'Donoghue, N. D. "Creation and Participation." In R. W. A. McKinney (ed.), *Creation, Christ and Culture: Studies in Honour of T. F. Torrance*. Edinburgh: T. & T. Clark, 1976.

Osborn, E. *The Beginning of Christian Philosophy*. Cambridge: Cambridge University Press, 1981.

Owens, J. *The Doctrine of Being in the Aristotelian Metaphysics*. Toronto: Pontifical Institute of Mediaeval Studies, 1951.

Palamas, Gregory. *The One Hundred and Fifty Chapters*. Ed. R. E. Sinkewicz. Toronto: Pontifical Institute of Mediaeval Studies, 1988.

———. See Chrestou, P.

Pannenberg, W. "Der Gott der Geschichte: Der trinitarische Gott und die Wahrheit der Geschichte." *KuD* 23 (1977): 76–92.

———. "Die Subjektivität Gottes und die Trinitätslehre: Ein Beitrag zur Bezeichnung zwischen Karl Barth und der Philosophie Hegels." *KerDo* 23 (1977): 25–40.

———. "Person und Subjekt: Zur Überwindung des Subjektivismus im Menschenbild und im Gottesverständnis." *NZSysTh* 18 (1976): 133–48.

Patacsi, G. "Palamism before Palamas." *ECR* 9 (1977): 64–71.

Pelikan, J. *The Christian Tradition: A History of the Development of Doctrine.* Chicago: University of Chicago Press, 1971ff., vols. 1 and 2.

———. *Development of Christian Doctrine: Some Historical Prolegomena.* New Haven: Yale University Press, 1969.

Philipp, W. "Wesen und Eigenschaften Gottes als kontroverstheologisches Grundproblem." *ThLit* 85 (1960): cols. 223–26.

Podskalsky, G. "Die griechisch-byzantinische Theologie und ihre Methode. Aspekte und Perspektiven eines ökumenischen Problems." *ThPh* 58 (1983): 71–87.

———. *Theologie und Philosophie in Byzanz: der Streit um die theologische Methodik in der spätbyzantinischen Geistesgeschichte (14./15. Jh.), seine systematischen Grundlagen und seine historische Entwicklung.* Munich: C. H. Beck'sche Verlagsbuchhandlung, 1977.

———. "Zur Bedeutung des Methodenproblems für die byzantinische Theologie." *ZKathTh* 98 (1976): 385–99.

Prestige, G. L. *God in Patristic Thought.* London: SPCK, 1952.

Rahner, K. *The Trinity.* Tunbridge Wells: Burns & Oates, 1970.

———. *Foundations of Christian Faith: an Introduction to the Idea of Christianity.* London: Darton, Longman & Todd, 1978.

———. "Kleine Bemerkungen zum dogmatischen Traktat De Trinitate." In L. Lenhart (ed.), *Universitas: Dienst an Wahrheit und Leben.* Mainz: Matthias-Grünewald-Verlag, 1960, vol. 1.

———. *Theological Investigations.* London: Darton, Longman & Todd, 1961ff., vols. 1–21.

Ritschl, D. "Die Einheit mit Christus im Denken der griechischen Väter." In *Konzepte: Gesammelte Aufsätze, Band I: Patristische Studien.* Bern: Herbert Lang, 1976, pp. 78–101.

———. "Heiliger Geist." In *Taschenlexikon Religion und Theologie.* Göttingen: Vandenhoeck & Ruprecht, 1983.

———. *The Logic of Theology: A Brief Account of the Relationship between Basic Concepts in Theology.* London: SCM, 1986.

———. "Trinität." In *Ökumene Lexikon: Kirchen, Religionen, Bewegungen.* Frankfurt a.M.: Verlag Otto Lembeck/Verlag Josef Knecht, 1983, col. 1177–80.

———. "Warum wir Konzilien feier—Konstantinopel 381." *Theologische Zeitschrift* 38 (1982): 213–25.

Rodzianko, V. "'Filioque' in Patristic Thought." *TU* 64 (1957): 295–308.

Rosenthal, K. "Bemerkungen zur gegenwärtigen Behandlung der Trinitätslehre." *KerDo* 22 (1976): 132–48.

Romanides, J. S. "Notes on the Palamite Controversy and Related Topics." *GrOrthThR* 6 (1960–61): 186–205, and 9 (1963–64): 225–70.

Rougemont, D. de. *Passion and Society*. London: Faber, 1956.

Rousseau, D. *Ascetics, Authority and the Church in the Age of Jerome and Cassian*. Oxford: Oxford University Press, 1978.

Russo, G. "Rahner and Palamas: A Unity of Grace." *StVladThQ* 32 (1988): 157–80.

Schachten, W. "Das Verhältnis von 'immanenter' und 'ökonomischer' Trinität in der neueren Theologie." *FranzS* 61 (1979): 8–27.

Schaeder, H. "Das Glaubensbekenntnis des Gregor Palamas: Seine theologische und kirchenpolitische Bedeutung." *Theol (A)* 27 (1956): 283–94.

———. "Die Christianisierung der aristotelischen Logik in der byzantinischen Theologie repräsentiert durch Johannes von Damaskus und Gregor Palamas." *Theol (A)* 33 (1962): 1–21.

Schleiermacher, F. D. E. *Der christliche Glaube nach den Grundsätzen der evangelischen Kirche im Zusammenhange dargestellt*. Berlin, 1831. Ed. M. Redeker. Berlin: Walter de Gruyter, 1960.

Schlink, E. *Ökumenische Dogmatik: Grundzüge*. Göttingen: Vandenhoeck & Ruprecht, 1983.

Schmaus, M. *Die Psychologische Trinitätslehre des Heiligen Augustinus*. Münster: Aschendorffsche Verlagsbuchhandlung, 1967.

Schmemann, A. *The World as Sacrament*. London: Darton, Longman & Todd, 1966.

Schönborn, C. von. "Immanente und ökonomische Trinität: Zur Frage des Funktionsverlustes der Trinitätslehre in der östlichen und westlichen Theologie." *FreiburgZPhTh* 27 (1980): 247–64.

Schultze, B. *Das Gottesproblem in der Osttheologie*. Münster: Aschendorff, 1967.

———. "Die Bedeutung des Palamismus in der russischen Theologie der Gegenwart." *Scholastik* 26 (1951): 390–412.

———. "Die Pneumatologie des Symbols von Konstantinopel als abschliessende Formulierung der griechischen Theologie, 381–1981." *OrientChrPer* 47 (1981): 5–54.

———. "Grundfragen des theologischen Palamismus." *OstkirchSt* 24 (1975): 105–35.

———. "Hauptthemen der neueren russischen Theologie." In W. Nyssen, H.-J. Schulz, and P. Wiertz (eds), *Handbuch der Ostkirchenkunde*. Düsseldorf: Patmos Verlag, 1984, vol. 1, pp. 321–92.

———. "Zur Gotteserkenntnis in der griechischen Patristik." *Greg* 63 (1982): 525–58.

Schwöbel, C., and Gunton, C. (eds). *Persons, Divine and Human: King's College Essays in Theological Anthropology.* Edinburgh: T. & T. Clark, 1991.

Seeberg, R. *Zum dogmatischen Verständnis der Trinitätslehre.* Leipzig: A. Deichert'sche Verlagsbuchhandlung, 1908.

Sheldon-Williams, I. P. "The Greek Christian Platonist Tradition from the Cappadochians to Maximus and Eriugena." *GMP,* pp. 421–533.

Sherrard, P. *The Greek East and the Latin West: A Study in the Christian Tradition.* London: Oxford University Press, 1959.

Sopko, A. J. "'Palamism before Palamas' and the Theology of Gregory of Cyprus." *StVladThQ* 23 (1979): 139–47.

Stiernon, D. "Bulletin sur le Palamisme." *Revue des études byzantines* 30 (1972): 231–341.

Staniloae, D. "Der dreieinige Gott und die Einheit der Menschen." *EvTh* 41 (1981): 439–50.

———. "The Holy Spirit in the Theology and Life of the Orthodox Church." *Sobornost* 7 (1975): 4–21.

———. *Orthodoxe Dogmatik* (Ökumenische Theologie, Bd. 12). Zürich: Benziger Verlag/Gütersloh: Gerd Mohn, 1985.

———. *Theology and the Church.* New York: St. Vladimir's Seminary Press, 1980.

Stead, C. *Divine Substance.* Oxford: Clarendon Press, 1977.

Stickelberger, H. E. *Ipsa assumptione creatur: Orthodoxe Christologie und weltliche Existenz in der "Kirchlichen Dogmatik" Karl Barths.* Bern: Peter Lang, 1979.

Swete, H. B. *The Early History of the Doctrine of the Holy Spirit.* Cambridge: Deighton, Bell & Co, 1873.

———. *On the History of the Doctrine of the Procession of the Holy Spirit, from the Apostolic Age to the Death of Charlemagne.* Cambridge: Deighton, Bell & Co, 1876.

Theodorou, A. "Die Mystik in der Orthodoxen Ostkirche." In P. Bratsiotis (ed.), *Die Orthodoxe Kirche in Griechische Sicht.* Stuttgart: Evangelisches Verlagswerk, 1970, pp. 176–209.

Theoleptos of Philadelpheia. *The Monastic Discourses,* Ed. R. E. Sinkewicz. Toronto: Pontifical Institute of Mediaeval Studies, 1992.

Thomas Aquinas. *Summa Theologiae.* London: Eyre & Spottiswoode/New York: McGraw-Hill, 1964ff.

Thunberg, L. *Microcosm and Mediator: The Theological Anthropology of Maximus the Confessor.* Lund: Hakan Ohlssons Boktrycheri, 1965.

Torrance, T. F. *Theology in Reconciliation: Essays towards Evangelical and Catholic Unity in East and West.* London: Geoffrey Chapman, 1975.

———. "Towards an Ecumenical Consensus on the Trinity." *ThZ* 31 (1975): 337–50.

Trtik, Z. "Die Personbegriff im Dogmatischen Denken Karl Barths: Eine kritische Untersuchung." *NZSysTh* 5 (1963): 263–95.

---. "Die Trinität als ewiges Subjekt." *ThZ* 37 (1981): 35–44.

Ullmann, W. "Geist oder Energie: Buchbesprechung." *ThLit* 108 (1983): 607–10.

Vischer, L. (ed.). *Spirit of God, Spirit of Christ: Ecumenical Reflections on the Filioque Controversy.* London: SPCK/Geneva: WCC, 1981.

Walls, R. C. "St. Gregory Palamas." *ScotJTh* 21 (1968): 435–48.

Ware, K. and Davey, C. (eds). *Anglican-Orthodox Dialogue: The Moscow Statement Agreed by the Anglican-Orthodox Joint Doctrinal Commission, 1976,* with introductory and supporting material. London: SPCK, 1977.

Ware, K. "The Debate about Palamism." *ECR* 9 (1977): 45–63.

---. "God Hidden and Revealed: The Apophatic Way and the Essence-Energies Distinction." *ECR* 7 (1975): 125–36.

Watson, G. "The Filioque—Opportunity for Debate?" *ScotJTh* 41 (1988): 313–30.

Weizsäcker, C. F. von. *Die Einheit der Natur.* Munich: Carl Hanser Verlag, 1972.

Welker, M. *Gottes Geist: Theologie des Heiligen Geistes.* Neukirchen-Vluyn: Neukirchener Verlag, 1992.

Welker, M. "What is Creation? Rereading Genesis 1 and 2." *Theology Today* 48 (1991): 56–71.

Wendebourg, D. "From the Cappadocian Fathers to Gregory Palamas: the Defeat of Trinitarian Theology." *TU* xvii/1 (1982): 194–97.

---. *Geist oder Energie: Zur Frage der innergöttlichen Verankerung des christlichen Lebens in der byzantinischen Theologie.* Munich: Chr. Kaiser Verlag, 1980.

Wenisch, B. "Zur Theologie Karl Rahners." *MThZ* 28 (1977): 383–97.

Williams, R. D. "The Philosophical Structures of Palamism." *ECR* 9 (1977): 27–44.

---. *The Theology of Vladimir Nikolaievich Lossky: An Exposition and Critique.* Oxford: unpublished dissertation, 1975.

Wolfson, H. A. *The Philosophy of the Church Fathers, Vol. 1: Faith, Trinity, Incarnation.* Cambridge, Mass.: Harvard University Press, 1970.

Yannaras, C. *De l'absence et de l'inconnaissance de Dieu d'après les ecrits aréopagitiques et Martin Heidegger.* Paris: Editions de Cerf, 1971.

---. "The Distinction between Essence and Energies and its Importance for Theology." *StVladThQ* 19 (1975): 232–245.

---. *The Freedom of Morality.* New York: St. Vladimir's Seminary Press, 1984.

---. "Orthodoxy and the West." *ECR* 3(1971): 286–300.

---. *Person und Eros: Eine Gegenüberstellung der Ontologie der griechischen Kirchenväter und der Existenzphilosophie des Westens.* Göttingen: Vandenhoeck & Ruprecht, 1982.

Zimany, R. D. "The Divine Energies in Orthodox Theology." *Diakonia* 11 (1976): 281–85.

———. "Grace, Deification and Sanctification: East-West." *Diakonia* 12 (1977): 121–44.

Zizioulas, J. D. *Being as Communion: Studies in Personhood and the Church.* New York: St. Vladimir's Seminary Press, 1985.

INDEX OF NAMES

Aagaard, A. M., 4f., 14, 74, 96
Abramowski, L., ix, 36
Aldenhoven, 87, 106
Allchin, A. M., 118, 127
Aristotle, 8ff., 11f., 26
Arius, 62, 89
Armstrong, A. H., 10
Athanasius, 14, 36, 43ff., 60, 104f.
Augustine, 11ff., 25, 33, 47, 49, 59, 62, 85, 104
Bakunin, M., 99
Bantle, F. X., 82ff., 125
Barker, M., 25
Barlaam, 19, 51
Barrois, G., 3
Barth, K., 27–31, passim
Baur, F. C., 22, 24
Beck, H.-G., 16
Birch, C., 133
Boff, L., 97, 109
Bolotov, V. V., 101
Bonhoeffer, D., 22
Brady, V., 22
Brown, D., 22, 78, 83, 126
Brunner, E., 56
Bulgakov, S., 47
Capra, F., 109f., 126
Chrestou, P. K., 16
Clement of Alexandria, 65
Clement, O., 83
Coffey, D., 89, 108
Congar, Y., 84, 101f., 130
Contos, L. C., 16
Davey, C., 6, 8, 123
Descartes, R., 109

Didymus the Blind, 53
Donne, J., 7
Einstein, A., 109
Elert, W., 80
Evdokimov, P., 45
Fabro, C., 118
Florovsky, G., 34–46, passim
Freyer, T., 14, 74
Gadamer, H.-G., 108
Galitis, G., 132
Gendle, N., 2f., 16
Gerlitz, P., 12
Gollwitzer, H., 7
Gregorios, P., 106
Gregory of Cyprus, 101
Gregory of Nyssa, 1, 18
Gregory Palamas, passim
Grondijs, L. H., 16
Gunton, C., 6, 83
Habra, G., 16
Halleux, P. de, 4
Hegel, G. W. F., 24f., 32, 85
Heidegger, M., 86
Hendry, G., 74
Heron, A., 53
Heschel, A., 7, 97, 99, 110, 116
Irenaeus, 39, 53
Ivánka, E. von, 10, 15
John Chrysostom, 27
John of Damascus, 1f., 15, 18f., 21, 62
Johnson, E., 62
Joseph Bryennios, 100f.
Jugie, M., 6
Jüngel, E., 22, 88
Kant, I., 23, 105, 125

147

Kasper, W., 22
Kern, K., 15, 18, 73
Kern, W., 68, 74
Khomiakov, A. S., 45
Kinnamon, M., 5f., 123
Kretschmar, G., 25, 39
Krivoshein, B., 3, 16
Kuhlmann, J., 70ff., 90, 122
LaCugna, C. M., 22f., 73, 76, 87
Langen, J., 24
Lindbeck, G., 124
Lossky, V. N., 46–54, passim
Louth, A., 10, 12, 89, 108, 129
Mackey, J. P., 6, 12
Maloney, G., 4f., 20, 116f.
Marius Victorinus, 12, 21
Markus, R. A., 12
Maximus the Confessor, 1, 17f.
Meyendorff, J., 2f., 8, 11, 16, 19, 72f., 85ff., 97, 115, 123
Molnar, P. D., 119
Moltmann, J., ix, xiii f., 7, 22, 79, 83, 85, 87, 109, 111, 114f., 117, 126
Mühlen, H., 25
Nicephorus Gregoras, 95
Niemann, F.-J., 68, 74
Nissiotis, N. A., 59, 74, 130
O'Donnell, J. J., 22f.
Origen, 14ff., 36f., 42, 53, 61f., 104, 128
Ostwald, W., 109
Owens, J., 10
Palamas—see Gregory Palamas.
Pannenberg, W., 24
Patasci, G., 16
Petavius (Petau), D., 52
Philo, 15
Photius, 76
Plato, 8f., 92
Plotinus, 10f., 12, 17, 25
Podskalsky, G., 92, 121
Polanus, 27

Porphyry, 12, 18
Potok, C., 132
Pseudo-Dionysius, 19, 53f.
Radovic, A., 101
Rahner, K., 31–34, passim
Ritschl, D., ix, 4ff., 7, 21, 104, 121, 124, 131
Rodzianko, V., 48
Romanides, J. S., 19, 97
Rosenstock-Huessy, E., 7
Rosenthal, K., 24
Rougemont, D. De, 109
Russo, G., 108
Schachten, W., 24
Schaeder, H., 9, 15f., 18f.
Schleiermacher, F., 3, 22, 125
Schmaus, M., 11ff., 17
Schmemann, A., 107
Schultze, B., 88, 90f., 99, 118
Schwöbel, C., 83
Seeberg, R., 24
Sheldon-Williams, I. P., 15, 17
Sopko, A. J., 16
Staniloae, D., xiv, 17, 70, 74, 77, 80, 87, 100, 102f., 105f., 116f., 126
Suzuki, D., 108
Swete, H. B., 24
Tertullian, 25
Thomas Aquinas, 14, 33, 49, 52, 69f., 90, 105
Toland, J., 23
Ullmann, W., 6, 8
Vischer, L., xiii, 4, 87, 106
Walter, R. von, 25
Ware, K., 6, 8, 87ff., 101, 118, 123
Watson, G., 60
Weizsäcker, C. F. von, 108
Welker, M., 132f.
Wendebourg, D., 5f., 8, 22, 75ff., 94, 114, 122f.
Wenisch, B., 69f., 125

Williams, R. D., ix, 8f., 15, 88–92, 118f.
Wolfson, H. A., 15f.
Yannaras, C., 12, 86f., 99, 106
Zeller, E., 10
Zizioulas, J., 38